Disciplines in Art Education: Contexts of Understanding
General Series Editor, Ralph A. Smith

Art Education

Giorgione, *The Tempest*, ca. 1503, Academy, Venice.

ART EDUCATION:
A CRITICAL NECESSITY

*Albert William Levi and
Ralph A. Smith*

UNIVERSITY OF ILLINOIS PRESS
Urbana and Chicago

Illini Books edition, 1991

© 1991 by the the Board of Trustees of the University of Illinois

Manufactured in the United States of America

P 5 4 3 2

This volume and the others in the series Disciplines in Art Education: Contexts of Understanding are made possible by a grant from the Getty Center for Education in the Arts. The J. Paul Getty Trust retains all publishing rights to the individual essays in the series. The views expressed in the volumes are those of the authors and not necessarily those of the J. Paul Getty Trust.

Library of Congress Cataloging-in-Publication Data

Levi, Albert William, 1911–
    Art education: a critical necessity/Albert William Levi
and Ralph A. Smith.
        p. cm. — (Disciplines in art education)
    Includes bibliographical references (p.   ) and index.
    ISBN 0-252-06185-3 (pb)
    1. Art—Study and teaching—United States. I. Smith,
Ralph Alexander. II. Title. III. Series.
N105.L48   1991
707'.073—dc20

                                            90–26637
                                                 CIP

To A. W. L.
In Memoriam

Contents

General Series Preface

Since the early 1980s, the Getty Center for Education in the Arts, which is an operating entity of the J. Paul Getty Trust, has been committed to improving the quality of aesthetic learning in our nation's schools and museums. According to the organizing idea of the center's educational policy, teaching about the visual arts can be rendered more effective through the incorporation of concepts and activities from a number of interrelated disciplines, namely, artistic creation, art history, art criticism, and aesthetics.

The resultant discipline-based approach to art education does not, however, mandate that these four disciplines be taught separately; rather, the disciplines are to provide justifications, subject matter, and methods, as well as exemplify attitudes, that are relevant to the cultivation of percipience in matters of art. They offer different analytical contexts to aid our understanding and aesthetic enjoyment, contexts such as the making of unique objects of visual interest (artistic creation), the apprehension of art under the aspects of time, tradition, and style (art history), the reasoned judgment of artistic merit (art criticism), and the critical analysis of basic aesthetic concepts and puzzling issues (aesthetics). Discipline-based art education thus assumes that an ability to engage works of art intelligently requires not only our having attempted to produce artworks and gained some awareness of the mysteries and difficulties of artistic creation in the process, but also our having acquired familiarity with art's history, its principles of judgment, and its conundrums. All are prerequisite to building a sense of art in the young, which is the overarching objective of aesthetic learning.

Although no consensus exists on precisely how the various components of aesthetic learning should be orchestrated in order to accomplish the goals of discipline-based art education, progress toward these objectives will require that those charged with designing art education programs bring an adequate understanding of the four disciplines to bear on their work. It is toward generating such needed understanding that a five-volume series was conceived as part of the Getty Center's publication program. To narrow the distance separating the

disciplines from classroom teaching, each book following the introductory volume will be coauthored by a scholar or practitioner in one
of the disciplines (an artist, an art historian, an art critic, and a philosopher of art) and an educational specialist with interest or special
competence in a given art discipline. The introductory volume provides
a philosophical rationale for the idea of discipline-based art education.
It is hoped that the series, which is intended primarily for art teachers
in elementary and secondary education, for those who prepare these
teachers, and for museum educators, will make a significant contribution to the literature of art education.

Ralph A. Smith
General Series Editor

Preface

Art Education: A Critical Necessity presents a systematic rationale for discipline-based art education that features a humanities-based interpretation of teaching and learning in the visual arts. Coauthored by a philosopher of culture and the humanities and a theorist of aesthetic education with a special interest in the definition of cultural and educational relations, this volume represents the kind of collaboration that is central to the idea of discipline-based art education—the fusion of scholarship with considerations of creativity and practical educational activities.

The late Albert William Levi achieved prominence in the field of philosophy when he was awarded the first Phi Beta Kappa Ralph Waldo Emerson Prize for his *Philosophy and the Modern World* (1959), a monumental work that elaborated the ruling philosophical ideas underlying contemporary Western civilization. In observing the ways in which life in Western nations today is suffused with the traditional ideas and spirit of Western thinking, Levi was led to conclude that the diversity and divisions of modern Western society reflect more the Hellenistic phase of Western history than they do great moments of cultural synthesis, for example, the secular millennium of the Athenian city-state or the religious unity of medieval Europe from the tenth century to the fourteenth century. In other words, he recognized that pluralism is a pervasive feature of modern existence.

Several of Levi's later themes are discernible in this earlier work. One theme, set forth in his *Philosophy as Social Expression* (1974), asserts that social factors strongly influence the cultural and intellectual life of a society and therefore condition the shaping of personal identity. Another theme stresses a concept of knowledge that distinguishes between the aims and purposes of the scientific chain of meaning and the humanistic complex. This concept was formulated chiefly in his *Literature, Philosophy, and the Imagination* (1962). Levi's keen awareness of the interweaving of politics and culture and of the tendency of artists and writers alternately to advance and withdraw in a dialectic of political involvement and disengagement inspired his impressive *Humanism and Politics* (1969).

Ever distrustful of the abstract, Levi, as his tenure as rector of the experimental Black Mountain College attests, was also sensitive to the practical problems of curriculum and teaching. Commenting later on this attempt to create an interdisciplinary community of artists, writers, and performers in the hills of North Carolina, Levi remarked that while it taught him much about the necessity for freedom of expression, it also persuaded him of the need for authority and discipline in efforts to cultivate the artistic imagination.

But it was Levi's redefinition of the traditional humanities in his *The Humanities Today* (1970) that prompted his invitation to be a coauthor of this volume. A strong believer in cultural continuity, Levi synthesizes the medieval conception of the humanities as liberal arts or ways of understanding and the Renaissance conception of the humanities as subject matters or fields of study. The traditional liberal arts of the trivium and the quadrivium became for Levi the arts of communication, the arts of continuity, and the arts of criticism. Though these arts are phrased in procedural terms as ways of doing and understanding things, they are associated with such substantive subjects as languages and literatures (the arts of communication), history (the arts of continuity), and philosophy (the arts of criticism). What is distinctively humanistic about them is that they answer to basic human needs: the need to communicate with others and share experience, the need to find a place in the stream of time and be reminded of things worth remembering, and the need to be reasonable in deliberations about matters of importance.

Where does artistic creativity fit into this picture? This question is handled with a simple emendation of Levi's original interpretation. If, with appropriate qualification, art may be regarded as a language and its utterances as artistic or dramatic statements, then the complete act of artistic creation can be said to consist of an artist who through the language of art makes artistic statements that are presented to others. The character or meaning of such artistic statements, however, is almost never obvious or simple and hence works of art often require description, analysis, and interpretation. These are typically provided by art historians and art critics, or historian-critics as the case may be, who by disclosing the nature of a given artistic statement in effect complete the act of artistic communication initiated by the artist. Discussions of artworks further generate a number of perplexing problems and puzzles the clarification of which typically falls to philosophers of art or aestheticians. Accordingly, we may say that a well-developed understanding and enjoyment of art presupposes some familiarity with the arts of creation (the making of artworks), the arts of communication (works of art as artistic statements), the arts of continuity (the under-standing of artworks in historical context), and the arts of criticism (criticism that interprets artistic statements as well as philosophically analyzes aesthetic concepts).

The arts of creation, communication, continuity, and criticism (a quartet of modes of understanding) and the disciplines of artistic creation, art history, art criticism, and aesthetics (a quartet of subject matters), though not precisely coordinate with one another, are closely enough associated to suggest that discipline-based art education can be justified in terms of the humanities and the distinctive human values they serve. If we understand discipline-based art education as a challenge to conceptualize and philosophize, then the interpretation presented here represents a response to this challenge; it locates visual arts instruction in the realm of the humanities and recommends teaching art as a humanity.

Levi's redefinition of the humanities for today's world provides the philosophical framework for justifying discipline-based art education. My task as coauthor was to translate a humanities-based conception of this approach into a curriculum plan for teaching and learning. Since, however, Levi had completed only three chapters prior to his death, my responsibility was expanded. In addition to chapters 7 and 8, I am also responsible for chapters 4, 5, and 6 on art history, art criticism, and philosophy of art, though some of the material that Levi had intended to use in the volume is interspersed at various points in the text.

Levi's introductory remarks on art history in chapter 4 (he had completed only two typed pages) stressed the role of tradition in gaining a sense of art's history. Amplifying some observations made by T. S. Eliot in his influential essay "Tradition and the Individual Talent," Levi emphasized that gaining an awareness of art history is difficult and must proceed in a manner that conveys a sense of both the pastness of art and its relevance for the present. I have retained the accent on tradition and stressed the importance of studying art under the aspects of time, tradition, and style. In the process, three meanings of art history are set out: art history as the chronology or genealogy of art, as a discussion of discrete studies of various kinds, and as a self-reflective discipline. The chapters on art criticism and aesthetics center on three functions of criticism—the refinement of perception, the reasoned assessment of artistic value, and the improvement of the atmosphere in which we think about and experience art, and, in addition, philosophical analysis of four important aesthetic concepts—representation, expression, aesthetic experience, and critical evaluation.

The final two chapters reflect Levi's interpretation of the humanities for purposes of art education. This interpretation also expresses my belief that a well-developed sense of art, which I take to be the overarching aim of art education, builds first of all on a feel for the sensuousness and tractability (or intractability) of artistic materials and the ways they can be melded into formal and expressive designs. Without some creative experience one is unlikely to gain an appreciation of the immediate sensuous qualities of artworks or the strengths and subtleties of their formal relations. Furthermore, without practice in the sustained contemplation of an artwork's elements there can be no consciousness of the fact that works of art at their best repay the attention paid to them, which is to say, there can be no appreciation of the quality of experience they are capable of affording. Without a sense of art's history there can be no realization that the greatest art reflects not only the expression of a particular artist and time but also the traces of a creative dialogue with the past, a dialogue that is crucial in assessing the magnitude of individual artistic achievement. And, finally, without the capacity to think critically about art and the numerous issues and controversies to which it can give rise, there is little possibility of achieving independence of thought in matters of art and culture—little hope, that is, of seeing contemporary controversies in proper perspective. To be sure, there is no way of predicting the overall effects that the possession of a well-developed sense of art by the large majority of the population might have on the quality of individual and social life. What *is* apparent are some of the undesirable consequences of the lack of such a sense—a badly scarred human habitat, the corruption of high art, a mass art of low quality, and a deluge of pornography.

The question thus becomes how to build a significant sense of art gradually over the elementary and secondary school years. Once the magnitude of this task has been appreciated and the outcomes and methods of art education are clearly in mind—failing which aesthetic learning will lack direction or a reason for being—it becomes possible to think rationally about curriculum design, teaching and learning, and assessment. Chapters 7 and 8 assume the burden of this assignment. I believe that the attainment of a sense of art that embraces the values of the humanities and evolves in consonance with principles of human development marks the culmination of aesthetic learning. This learning would extend from kindergarten through high school in a program of nonspecialist general education, access to which is a basic right of all individuals in a democratic society.

A sense of art congruent with the interpretation of art education just presented can be developed in five phases of aesthetic learning. These phases consist of simple exposure and familiarization and training in aesthetic perception in the early years, and then the development of a sense of art history, exemplar appreciation, and critical thinking in the later years. The underlying assumption is that aesthetic learning should be cumulative and progressive. One phase leads into another, which in turn provides a foundation for the next phase. Ideally nothing important is left behind but is carried forward in fashioning an ever more comprehensive and systematic map of aesthetic awareness by which to guide engagements with works of art.

A variety of labels can be applied to a curriculum designed to cultivate this sense of art. Elsewhere I have referred to it as an excellence and as an art world curriculum; here I call it a percipience curriculum, though I retain the commitment to excellence and the notion of an art world. I adopt an image of the curriculum as itinerary and an image of learning as preparation for traversing the art world with tact and sensitivity in order to help maintain concentration on relevant activities and goals. No matter what the label or image, however, the important outcome is percipience, where "percipience" implies a capacity for mature and discerning awareness in matters of art and culture.

But after all is said and done, is art education really a critical necessity? That it is so is made evident through a humanities-based interpretation of art education. The humanities, after all, satisfy a vital human hunger, a hunger for personal meaning and identity in a meaningless universe. Teaching art as a humanity affords the sort of humanistic insight and experience found nowhere else in what the great German philosopher Ernst Cassirer called the circle of humanity—certainly not in the sciences, where the constraints of inquiry drain away all sense of human purpose in favor of highly abstract considerations. Art education is a critical necessity, then, because art is: art answers the need for human drama and purposiveness, and it completes the circle of human potentiality and fulfillment.

Ralph A. Smith

Acknowledgments

I am grateful first of all to Leilani Lattin Duke, the director of the Getty Center for Education in the Arts, for her support of the idea of a series of volumes that would be devoted to providing a systematic rationale for discipline-based art education and scholarly discussions of artistic creation, art history, art criticism, and aesthetics and their relevance to the teaching of art. Further thanks are due Stephen M. Dobbs and Phillip C. Dunn, former program officers of the Getty Center, who provided valuable counsel and guidance during the initial stages of the publication project.

I am further indebted to a number of readers who read either the entire manuscript or individual chapters and whose comments and observations helped to improve the tone and substance of the volume. Readers of the chapter on art history were Anthony Janson, Danielle Rice, Stephen Addiss, and Mary Erickson; on art criticism, Theodore Wolff, George Geahigan, and Terry Barrett; on aesthetics, Donald Crawford, H. Gene Blocker, and Michael J. Parsons; and on artistic creation, Maurice Brown and Diana Korzenik. An acknowledgment of these readers does not, of course, imply their endorsement of the volume's interpretations, the responsibility for which is solely that of the authors.

A special debt of appreciation goes to Mrs. Ute Levi. Without her understanding and cooperation at a time of great personal loss the completion of this volume would have been seriously delayed. I am grateful not only for her warmth and friendship but also for her permission to search her late husband's library in St. Louis for references that were not provided for the first three chapters of the volume, most of which I was fortunate to locate and verify. The immeasurable respect and affection felt for my coauthor is recorded on the dedication page of this volume. I would be remiss if I did not further mention Penelope McKeon of the City Arts College of Sydney, Australia, who provided invaluable research assistance during the writing of the volume and whose knowledge of art history kept me abreast of recent art-historical thinking.

Finally, I want to thank Clarence J. Karier, head of the Department of Educational Policy Studies at the University of Illinois, and Richard Wentworth, the director of the University of Illinois Press, for their continuing support of the arts and aesthetic education. C. M. Smith, as usual, contributed her excellent editorial judgment and editing skills. I would also like to thank Selena Douglass for her expert typing, and Elizabeth Bower for numerous improvements of the text.

Ralph A. Smith

The following have kindly provided permission to reproduce the photographs used in this volume (shorter citations are used in the text):

Frontispiece. Giorgione, *The Tempest.* About 1503. Canvas. 31¼″ × 28¾″. Galleria dell' Accademia, Venice. Alinari/Art Resource, N.Y.

Henri Matisse, *Still Life on a Green Buffet.* 1928. Canvas. 32½″ × 39⅜″. National Museum of Modern Art, Georges Pompidou Center. Giraudon/ Art Resource, N.Y.. Copyright 1990 Succession H. Matisse/ARS, N.Y.

Giorgione, *The Trial of Moses.* About 1500. Panel. 35″ × 28″. Uffizi Gallery, Florence. Giraudon/Art Resource, N.Y.

Giorgione, *The Tempest.* About 1503. Canvas. 31¼″ × 28¾″. Galleria dell' Accademia, Venice. Alinari/Art Resource, N.Y.

Giorgione, *Castelfranco Madonna.* About 1505. Panel. 78¾″ × 59⅞″. S. Liberale, Castelfranco, Veneto. Alinari/Art Resource.

Giorgione, *Three Philosophers.* About 1506. Canvas. 47⅞″ × 55¾″. Kunsthistorisches Museum, Vienna. Alinari/Art Resource, N.Y.

Johannes Vermeer, *Woman Holding a Balance (Woman Weighing Pearls).* About 1662–1665. Canvas. 16¾″ × 15″. National Gallery of Art, Washington, D.C. Widener Collection, 1942.

Diego Velázquez, *The Tapestry Weavers.* About 1645–48. Canvas. 7′2⅞″ × 9′2½″. Prado, Madrid. Giraudon/Art Resource, N.Y.

Pablo Picasso, *Guernica.* 1937. Oil on canvas. 11′6″ × 25′8″. Prado, Madrid. Giraudon/Art Resource. Copyright 1990 ARS, N.Y./Spadem.

Cimabue, *Madonna and Child Enthroned with Angels.* About 1285–90. Panel 12′7½″ × 7′4″. Uffizi, Florence. Giraudon/Art Resource, N.Y.

Giotto, *Madonna Enthroned.* About 1310. Panel. 128³⁄₁₆″ × 80⅜″. Uffizi, Florence. Giraudon/Art Resource.

Paul Cézanne, *The Cardplayers.* 1890–92. Canvas. 17¾″ × 22½″. Museum d'Orsay, Paris. Giraudon/Art Resource, N.Y.

Jasper Johns, *Target with Four Faces.* 1955. Encaustic on newspaper over canvas. 26″ × 26″. Surmounted by four tinted plaster faces in wooden boxes with hinged front. Box, closed, 33¾″ × 26³⁄₁₂″. Overall dimensions with box open, 33⅝" × 26" × 3". Museum of Modern Art, New York. Gift of Mr. and Mrs. Robert C. Scull. Copyright 1990 Jasper Johns/VAGA New York.

Willem de Kooning, *Asheville*. 1949. Oil on illustration board. 25½" × 32". The Phillips Collection, Washington, D.C. Copyright 1990 Willem de Kooning/VAGA New York.

James Stirling and Michael Wilford, *Neue Staatsgallerie*. 1977–84. Stuttgart, Germany. Photograph: copyright 1986, Richard Bryant/Arcaid.

Art Education

1

The Arts in the United States Today

Man is taught to admire beautiful things, not by books but by social
example, and by living in a society of good taste.
—Lin Yutang

In late spring of 1988 the National Endowment for the Arts released
the results of a study on arts education that had been two years in the
making, titled *Toward Civilization: A Report on Arts Education*. Its assessment of our present state was deeply pessimistic. "The problem
is," the report states, "*basic arts education does not exist in the United
States today.*"[1] On the other hand, like the quotation of authorities from
some medieval *summa*, it appended citations of favorable remarks about
the arts made by our first three presidents, George Washington, John
Adams, and Thomas Jefferson, and commented pointedly that we
should resolve "that our schools should teach our children the same
respect and appreciation for the arts and humanities that the Founders
had" (pp. 13–14). The report was long on the statement of aims and
principles, but short on sociological analysis and historical explanation.
Above all, it did not bridge the gap between the artistic sophistication
of the Founding Fathers and the lamentable state of arts education
today. This discrepancy cries out for consideration and explanation.

By this comment I do not mean to minimize the importance of the
report or to denigrate its very useful statement of the four purposes
of arts education: to give our young people a sense of civilization, to
foster creativity, to teach effective communication, and to provide tools
for the critical assessment of what one reads, sees, and hears (pp. 14–
19). The report summarized these aims in its major recommendation
toward a future arts curriculum: "Arts education should provide all
students with a sense of the arts in civilization, of creativity in the
artistic process, of the vocabularies of artistic communication, and of
the critical elements necessary to making informed choices about the
products of the arts" (p. 35). I shall return to an examination of these
aims and purposes in the next chapter, but now I want to consider

briefly the reasons that the Founding Fathers appreciated the arts and the two epochs in our history that have so disastrously reversed their evaluation.

The mythology of the American Revolution as created by the later epoch of Jacksonian democracy has served to exaggerate the differences between Englishmen living in the motherland under the Georges and the revolutionary heroes of colonial Boston, Philadelphia, and New York. But the fact is that both shared the same constellation of values of the eighteenth-century Enlightenment gentleman. George Washington, John Adams, and Thomas Jefferson were as much men of Continental culture and enlightenment as Lord Chesterfield, Horace Walpole, the Earl of Shaftesbury, and David Hume. When George Washington in a letter of 1781 wrote, "The arts and sciences essential to the prosperity of the state and to the ornament and happiness of human life have a primary claim to the encouragement of every lover of his country and mankind," it was no enigma and no fluke. And Thomas Jefferson wrote in a 1785 letter to James Madison: "You see I am an enthusiast on the subject of the arts. But it is an enthusiasm of which I am not ashamed, as its object is to improve the taste of my countrymen, to increase their reputation, to reconcile to them the respect of the world, and procure them its praise" (p. 128). Washington and Adams, Jefferson and Madison were all members of an eighteenth-century intellectual and cultural elite. George Washington and Thomas Jefferson both lived the lives of the English landed aristocracy, and Mount Vernon and Monticello (each maintained by an army of black slaves) were as sumptuous and elegant as the English landed estates of Lord Chesterfield and the Earl of Shaftesbury.

The Enlightenment culture of our revolutionary patriots is, of course, a chief reason for their sustained enthusiasm for the arts, but equally important is the advanced town culture within which they lived out their lives. Eighteenth-century Boston and Philadelphia, no less than eighteenth-century London and Edinburgh, were centers of elegance, dignity, and culture. Patrician colonial America was a society in which the arts flourished. There were great architects who created our enduring public monuments, like Charles Bulfinch's Massachusetts State House (1795–98), Faneuil Hall (1742), and the Old South Meeting House (1729) in Boston and Philadelphia's noble Independence Hall (1732). As for domestic architecture, there were the stately Georgian town houses of Boston's Beacon Hill, Philadelphia's original Rittenhouse Square, and Washington Square in New York. Painting flourished, and with John Singleton Copley (1738–1815) in Boston, Charles Willson Peale (1741–1827) in Philadelphia, and Gilbert Charles Stuart

(1755–1828) in both these cities, Colonial America produced a school of portrait painters in no way inferior to the great British school of Raeburn, Gainsborough, Romney, and Sir Joshua Reynolds. No less did the minor arts flower: many were the splendid examples of furniture made by the finest American cabinetmakers of Boston, Baltimore, and Philadelphia—exquisite and imposing Chippendale highboys in mahogany made in Philadelphia, lowboys and tables of Virginia walnut made in Baltimore, block-front desks from Newport, Rhode Island, and a multitude of Hepplewhite and Sheraton chairs made in all four cities. And Paul Revere, known by every schoolchild for his dramatic midnight ride, was in fact one of the most renowned silversmiths of the century.

There seems little doubt that the flourishing of the arts in colonial America was associated with two phenomena—the dominance of the aristocratic point of view and the culture of cities. Because of our later history the first is difficult to admit. In this respect some similarity exists between colonial Boston and Philadelphia, on the one hand, and Periclean Athens, on the other—that is to say, a society nominally "democratic" but in fact ruled by an aristocratic principle. It is sometimes forgotten how consistently conservative and even "elitist" the Founding Fathers really were. This is to be expected since their intellectual sources were chiefly English rather than French—John Locke rather than Jean-Jacques Rousseau. Perhaps only Jefferson was deeply influenced by the French point of view, but here too it was more a matter of philosophy than of genuine life-style. His devotion to "the rights of man" and "the people" was always taken with a grain of salt. Men like Madison and Hamilton, and particularly John Adams, were always deeply conservative. There is a story, probably apocryphal, about a conversation between Thomas Jefferson and John Adams in which the former was urging the rights of "the people," whereupon Adams replied with indignation and considerable heat, "Your 'people,' Sir, your 'people' is a Great Beast!" (It could have come directly out of Hobbes's *Leviathan*.)

The association of culture with the urban environment seems more acceptable. Goethe was always complaining about the "provincialism" of the small rural German principalities. Thomas Mann called urban dwelling a *geistige Lebensform*—a spiritual form of life. And Oswald Spengler insisted that the urban environment is the indispensable crucible of art and culture. The cultural history of the West appears to confirm it. Aeschylus seems impossible without Periclean Athens, Virgil without Augustan Rome, Dante without late medieval Florence,

Shakespeare without Elizabethan London, Molière without seven-teenth-century Paris, Mozart without Baroque Vienna, Hannah Arendt, Simone de Beauvoir, and Iris Murdoch without cosmopolitan New York, Paris, and London.

The point that high culture is often associated with urban life is important because the second epoch of American culture, what might be called the "ruralization" of America—a movement of people from the established cities of the Atlantic seaboard first to the Middle West and from there to the Far West—was an age that put high culture on the defensive. During this period two movements cooperated to bring the arts into disrepute: the opening of the frontier and the movement west, and the high tide of Jacksonian democracy, with its populist creed of "the common man." Out of the combination of these two elements arose two prejudices that have afflicted the practice and the appreci-ation of the arts even up to the present day. The first is the belief that concern with the arts is "elitist." The second is the belief that concern with the arts is somehow "unmasculine."

Neither of these two prejudices has merit, and they can be effectively defused by the simplest of semantic and historical considerations. First the prejudice of "elitism." Here we have a word that is pejorative in itself. But transform this word into the phrase "that which is concerned with excellence," and the negative association completely vanishes. Ralph A. Smith has written a valuable book, *Excellence in Art Education,* and his fourth chapter, "The Question of Elitism," bears directly on our topic: "Is it elitist," he asks, "to stress excellence in art and art education? . . . Is it consistent with democratic values to recognize and reward excellent performance? . . . That it is necessary to raise such questions . . . attests to the pervasiveness and intensity of the conviction that excellence and democratic values are somehow incompatible."[2] His persuasive solution to the question is the concept of unconditional access—"open" as distinct from "closed" elites. "We are," he says, "first of all justified in condemning *closed elites* which permit membership solely on the basis of a person's wealth, class, or social standing; these are elites of unearned privilege. But not all elites are like this. There are *open elites* of demonstrated merit which control admission by in-sisting on adherence to professional standards. No advanced society can exist without such elites, and even less advanced societies depend on them" (p. 69).

The point is well taken, and it is interesting to compare this position with that of John Adams, second president of the United States, who, as we have seen, was far from a populist and an egalitarian. In a sincere and passionately felt but unguarded moment, he expressed his theory of government—his hope that in the new federal republic rule should be "by the rich, the well-born, and the able." This, of course, combines both "open" and "closed" elites, the first admissible, the second clearly incompatible with what are now perceived to be true democratic values. Rule by the rich means plutocracy. Rule by the "well-born" means aristocracy. Only rule by the "able" means that meritocracy which is the true ideal of excellence in a genuine democracy.

The term "unmasculine" is much like the term "elitist." It is clearly pejorative on the face of it, but this sense too fades in the process of semantic transformation. If for the term "unmasculine" we substitute the phrase "perceptive, sensitive, able to be emotionally moved," an entirely new atmosphere is created, and we become aware of how powerful outmoded concepts of gender have remained despite modern advances in humanistic psychology and the enormous influence of the great insights of the contemporary women's movement. For we have learned that temperamental differences between the sexes are not absolute, that men possess "feminine" characteristics as women possess "masculine," and that the older stereotypes attributing certain fixed personality traits like strength, courage, endurance, and aggressiveness to men and certain others like softness, sensitivity, and emotionality to women, however widespread they remain, still express a crude distortion of psychological and moral reality.

Of course, this problem of stereotyping extends very far back, even to the classical age in Western culture. In the great funeral oration that Thucydides attributes to Pericles in his *History of the Peloponnesian War*, he has Pericles say of the Athenians: "We cultivate refinement without extravagance and knowledge without effeminacy." In this statement, if one reads between the lines, one can perhaps sense a defense of Athenian philosophy and aesthetic sensitivity against the cruder and more militaristic "masculinity" of the Spartans.

Edith Hamilton in her fine book *The Greek Way* tells a story that bears directly on this point.

Once upon a time—the exact date cannot be given but it was not far from 450 B.C.—an Athenian fleet cast anchor near an island in the Aegean as the sun was setting. Athens was making herself mistress of the sea and the attack on the island was to be begun the next morning. That evening the commander-in-chief, no less a one, the story goes, than Pericles himself, sent an invitation to his second in command to sup with him on the flag-ship. So there you may see them sitting on the ship's high poop, a canopy over their heads to keep off the dew. One of the attendants is a beautiful boy and as he fills the cups Pericles bethinks him of the poets and quotes a line about the "purple light" upon a fair young cheek. The younger general is critical: it had never seemed to him that the color-adjective was well chosen. He preferred another poet's use of rosy to describe the bloom of youth. Pericles on his side objects: that very poet elsewhere used purple in the same way when speaking of the radiance of young loveliness. So the conversation went on, each man capping the other's quotation with one as apt. The entire talk at the supper table turned on delicate and fanciful points of literary criticism. But nonetheless, when the battle began the next morning, these same men, fighting fiercely and directing wisely, carried the attack on the island.[3]

All we now need is Edith Hamilton's comment on this tale.

The little story, however apocryphal, gives a picture true to life of what the Athenians of the great age of Athens were like. Two cultivated gentlemen are shown to us, of a great fastidiousness, the poets their familiar companions, able the evening before the battle to absorb themselves in the lesser niceties of literary criticism, but with all this, mighty men of action, soldiers, sailors, generals, statesmen, any age would be hard put to excel. The combination is rarely found in the annals of history. It is to be completely civilized without having lost in the process anything of value.[4]

This little story, and Edith Hamilton's comment upon it, should already be sufficient evidence even to the prejudiced that there is no incompatibility between the most sturdy masculinity and the most sensitive aesthetic perception.

That society in the age of Jacksonian democracy and frontier westward expansion thought that there might be such an incompatibility is evidence of great crudeness and ignorance and lack of cultivation in this epoch of our national history. If there was a democracy native to the frontier, it was a rough and often shoddy collection of "backwoods" democrats, "coonskin apostles of liberty and equality," with no familiarity whatsoever with the arts or their current development in England or the continent of Europe. What could Daniel Boone (1734–1820) know of the fabulous narrative painting of the great French master Jacques Louis David (1748–1845), his contemporary? Or what could Davy Crockett (1786–1836) know of the miraculous landscapes of the English painter John Constable (1776–1837), his exact contemporary also? And when the movement went even further from the Middle to the Far West, what could be the attitude toward art and culture of the rancher, the cowboy, and the prospector for gold? In this second period of our national history, there is nothing of the cultivated aristocracy or urbanity of the first. How the mighty have fallen! How the arts have become irrelevant! How high culture has vanished from the face of the Western earth! It should now be clear that the aesthetic tragedy of America's westward expansion consists in the infinite distance that separates the social climate of the dust-blown western town and its rowdy saloon culture from the admirable elegance and taste of eighteenth-century Boston, Philadelphia, and New York.

The third epoch in the evolution of American society (which many would say we are still in) probably begins just after the Civil War. It is marked by the coming of the Industrial Revolution, which enthroned the commercial spirit among the American people and the profit motive as our major value. During this time economic considerations have become paramount and the acquisition of wealth and the commodities it can buy our major preoccupation. Needless to say, this has been far from an unmixed blessing for culture, the humanities, and the arts. Its fruits are to be seen in the society of today, in our system of higher education where the young seek less cultivation for a lifetime through the humanities and the arts than opportunities in the business world and access to the benefits of superior wealth. More and more in the modern world, esteem comes to us not for what we are or for what we do, but for what we have.

The middle years of the nineteenth century marked at once the closing of the western frontier and the greatest period of our industrial expansion. It was an age of opportunity, and its whole tendency and preoccupation was to promote the acquisition of wealth. The appeal was powerful, and it has laid the whole world under its spell. As R. H. Tawney has said:

> The secret of its triumph is obvious. It is an invitation to men to use the power with which they have been endowed by nature or society, by skill or energy or relentless egotism or mere good fortune, without inquiring whether there is any principle by which their exercise should be limited. . . . It . . . concentrates attention upon the right of those who posses or can acquire power to make the fullest use of it for their own self-advancement. . . . [It] offers unlimited scope for the acquisition of riches, and therefore gives free play to one of the most powerful of human instincts. To the strong it promises unfettered freedom for the exercise of their strength: to the weak the hope that they too one day may be strong. . . . Under the impulse of such ideas men do not become religious or wise or artistic. . . . But they become powerful and rich.[5]

What is at stake here is a crucial conflict of values. What counts in an acquisitive society like our own are "prosperity" and "security"; what counts much less are moral and spiritual values, education for wisdom, and, of course, aesthetic perception and artistic taste. It is my contention that the entire problem of the subordination of aesthetic claims and the sorry plight of arts education in the United States today must be placed in the context of the three historical epochs I have sketched above. What concerns our politicians today are such items as per-capita income, our international trade balance, the size of our gross national product, and our rate of unemployment. And what they seem to have totally forgotten is our per-capita education in the arts, the balance in our system of education, the size and quality of our gross national artistic product, and the rate of our cultural literacy.

This is obvious from the flavor of our current political debate. In fact our politicians are almost hysterically obsessed with the issues of "economic growth" and "national defense." But who among them is concerned with encouraging of our "cultural growth" and the measures that are needed for the production of a cultivated society worth defending?

In what has come before, I have tried to account for what the National Endowment for the Arts report on arts education made explicit—the enthusiasm for art of the Founding Fathers contrasted with the lamentable state of arts education today. In doing so I have outlined the two subsequent epochs of our national history. The first one saw the confluence of Jacksonian democracy with the opening of the western frontier, with its attendant submergence of the arts and the aesthetic impulse under frontier crudity and nonreliance upon any but the most thoughtless and insensitive of masculine capabilities. The next epoch saw the coming of the Industrial Revolution, the transformation of America into a commercial and acquisitive society where those qualities that make persons appreciative of art are infinitely less important than those qualities that make them successful in the accumulation of wealth. In both cases the eclipse of the arts and the nonvaluation of arts education are functions of their social context. The fortunes of art and arts education are dependent upon the general system of values prevalent at any one time. Jacques Barzun has said, "The wedded life of art and society is the union we call by the single name of culture."[6] But the converse is also true. The divorce of art and society is the catastrophe that we call by the two words "cultural barbarism." Aesthetic tragedy sets in where the perception has been lost that art is a crucial ingredient in the general welfare. It is now perhaps important to examine this relationship between art and the general welfare in greater detail.

Our judgment of the level of civilization of any specific Western nation may well hinge upon the propositions it takes for granted. That today in the United States one is forced to ask, "Does art promote the general welfare? What, after all, does culture contribute to the common good or general enlightenment?" indicates an aesthetic skepticism endemic to a narrowly pragmatic or commercial age, where the cash nexus reigns supreme and even the arts themselves have become corrupted by the values of mechanical efficiency and private profit. Le Corbusier believed that a city street is a machine for traffic to pass through as efficiently as possible. Other urban architects are under the quaint delusion that a housing project is a home. And serious books are now written with such titles as *Art as Investment* to aid those whose collections perform the same role as portfolios of blue-chip stocks and bonds.

In other ages it was profoundly different. Cosimo de' Medici, Sigismondo Malatesta, and Federigo da Montefeltro were also great collectors, and in some cases great businessmen, but they would have been scornful and contemptuous of a collector's passion guided by the principles of investment and tax deduction. The streets of the agora in Athens permitted rapid passage when necessary, but Alcibiades used them to meet and greet his friends, and Socrates lingered in them talking ethics and politics with Sophists and young aristocrats as if they were a private club. And when Bess, Countess of Shaftesbury, commissioned Hardwick Hall in Derbyshire at about the same time that Shakespeare was writing his first plays, it took three years to build and, however symmetrical the plan and Italian the detail, it was meant to service the exigencies of her life and had no other purpose.

I do not mean that the contrast has always been so black and white. Sometimes, as under the Protestant bourgeoisie of the Netherlands, the picture was more mixed. But even there the plastic arts began as a necessity of civilized life. In Antwerp in 1560, with only 169 bakers and 78 butchers, there were said to have been over 300 masters busy in painting and the graphic arts, proving that a fine landscape or portrait seemed no less a necessary food for the soul than bread and meat were for the body. No philosopher, aesthetician, or educator of the Dutch seventeenth century would have bothered to ask the question, "Does art promote the general welfare?" The answer would have been only too obvious.

It is obvious to me, too; and, if the programs of the National Endowment for the Arts are any evidence, I think it is also slowly becoming obvious in the United States generally. I shall not therefore present arguments to *prove* that art promotes the general welfare; rather, I shall attempt to indicate the way in which I think this promotion can best be accomplished and in so doing indirectly show why the issue is of the clearest relevance to a program of discipline-based art education in our schools.

In this task I shall use the terms "art" and "the general welfare" in restricted senses. A broad meaning of aesthetic welfare would include all acts of private enjoyment, appreciation, and enlightenment.[7] For example, in seventeenth-century Holland there was an enormous private market for paintings. Terborch and Metsu worked for the very wealthy, de Hooch and Nicolaes Maes for the poorer class. But a passion to own and continually view works of art was universal; they were sold like gloves and fans at the Rotterdam fair and in the end managed to appear on the walls of even the most modest houses. Here art could be said to work for the general welfare, but distributively rather than collectively, in the service of private rather than public acts of appreciation. This is not the sense of the general welfare that I will have in mind, nor the art I wish to focus on in this context.

Likewise, it has always been possible to judge the intentions of artists and the consequences of their work sociologically—that is, according to the Marxist criterion of whether art serves to underwrite or to undermine the society within which it originates. The sculptures of Verrocchio and Donatello, commissioned for Florence, expressed acceptance of Florentine society's needs and values. Giovanni Bellini, as official state painter in Venice, and his contemporary Carpaccio painted solemn processions and happy festivals to express the awe and respect they felt for their beloved republic. But in a much later age Daumier's prints knew the rottenness of establishment "justice," George Grosz hated the smug sensualism of capitalist decadence, and Ben Shahn busied himself with urban poverty with all the irony of a man profoundly distrustful of a commercial society and its cruel standard of distributive justice. In our own time Herbert Marcuse, always subtle and imaginative (if profoundly wrongheaded) in his treatment of the arts, interprets literature, painting, and all expressions of "high culture" as if they were by nature "oppositional"—that is to say, an imaginative bastion against the status quo, containing important transcending elements that stand over against and "refute" the given social reality.

But this is also not the kind of art with which I wish to deal in showing how art promotes the general welfare. For, with respect to the United States today, the private sector of the general welfare and the critical function of art are less relevant than an art socially accepted and directed toward the promotion of public life, which is the kind I wish to discuss.

The mutual dependence of politics and culture is an old story. When Leonardo Bruni wrote his famous *Laudatio* ("Panegyric to the City of

Florence") in 1404, he was elegiac not only of the city's liberal constitution, but also of its aesthetic order and proportions: "For just as
harpstrings are attuned to each other so that, when they are twanged,
a single harmony arises from all the different tones . . . just so this
farsighted city has so adapted all her parts to each other that from
them results a harmony of the total structure of the republic." And
this great humanist goes on to say that "nothing in this state is ill-
proportioned; nothing improper, nothing incongruous, nothing left
vague; everything occupies its proper place which is not only clearly
defined but also in the right relation to all others."[8] With such classic
principles of harmony and proportion applied at once to the physical
structure of the city and to its legal constitution, it is not difficult to
see here the inspiration for Jacob Burckhardt's contention that every
major city-state of the Italian Renaissance was essentially a "work of
art."[9]

The idea that politics and culture are mutually dependent was also
congenial to the Founding Fathers of the American republic—to Adams
and Madison, and above all to Jefferson, whose idea of the separation
and cooperation of the orders of classical Greek architecture was probably not unlike his ideas of the separation and cooperation of powers
in the new Constitution. But this analogy between politics and aesthetics must seem infinitely less credible to the contemporary inhab-
itants of Birmingham, Newark, or Detroit, where ruined countryside
and sprawling commercial ugliness constrict the spirit and suggest
rather the unhappy relationship between economic lawlessness and
physical decay. True, we can point to pockets of urban beauty in some
of our great cities, but as Kenneth Clark has remarked in his book
Civilisation (1969),[10] it is their heroic materialism that impresses us
more than anything else. And urban planning is not well ingrained in
our civic ethos, a fact Jane Jacobs pointed out in her book *The Death
and Life of American Cities* (1961).[11]

Here is a contrast that invites our contemplation of the Renaissance
alternative, for the acknowledged and crucial intimacy between art and
the general welfare gives to the cities of the Italian Renaissance an
exemplary character still striking even to the modern tourist. Consider
the case of Florence. Today the busy modern city of Florence surges
with endless traffic. To the visitor, the cathedral with its baptistry and
bell tower, the old city hall, the Bargello, the Or San Michele, and the
churches—Santa Maria Novella, Santa Croce, and the others—with
their vast interior treasures, seem like some museum of fabulous won-
ders that has survived out of a dead past. But the past in its own day
was anything but dead: it was the product of order and plan, of artistic

competitions and outright commissions, all in the service of a single noble idea, civic humanism, to which a varied and heterogeneous collection of groups and individuals contributed. And the young people who grew up in this environment were "taught to admire beautiful things, not by books but by social example, and by living in a society of good taste."

Already in the first great period of urban development (1280–1350) the pattern of civic planning was set. In the late thirteenth century the wealthy merchant guild of cloth processors assumed the expenses for the maintenance and improvement of the baptistry of the cathedral, faced its outer walls with marble, and a few decades later commissioned the design and construction of its three magnificent bronze doors. At the same time the cathedral itself was enlarged and decorated through funds raised by an automatic levy on every city expenditure and by a small head tax on every male citizen, although in the early fourteenth century the funding and construction were given into the hands of the wool manufacturers—the richest guild in the city.

Meanwhile, other edifices came into being at prodigious cost. The Dominicans laid the foundations of Santa Maria Novella; not to be outdone, the Franciscans began Santa Croce. Arnolfo di Cambio, architect of the cathedral, also designed the new town hall. Giotto was put in charge of the design and construction of the new bell tower. And Orcagna was instructed to design for the site of the old grainmarket the most beautiful shrine possible to house the great altarpiece that Bernardo Daddi had just been commissioned to paint. All this took place early—a full century before Brunelleschi created the dome of the cathedral, the Foundling Hospital, and the church and sacristy of San Lorenzo; Michelozzo, the Convent of San Marco and the Medici palace; and Donatello, the great marble sculptures for the exterior niches of Or San Michele.

What is important is the continuity of the effort and the spirit in which civic patronage is carried out. For the new burgher mentality—despite that class's commercial interests—also represented aspirations growing out of civic pride and ambition: a sense of community founded upon the recognition that art is essential to the general welfare and that a polity growing daily in wealth and power should express this fact visibly through outer garments devised to be the noblest imaginative products of its greatest architects, sculptors, and painters. And, if one finds here much of the mentality of the *nouveaux arrivés*—of citizens who wish their city not only to *be* the first in the world, but also to *appear* as such—today's observer of Giotto's tower and the sculptures in the Bargello finds this sentiment easy to forgive.

Admittedly, there is little expression here of the ideals of equality and true democracy. Florence experienced the constant economic crises of uncontrolled capitalism; during most of the Renaissance the city was run by a clique of very rich merchants and bankers led by the Medici family. Morally, these men had little to recommend them. Politically, their motive was self-interest, and they continually used their power to siphon the city's riches into their own pockets. Yet these early rulers had one saving grace: they had been born into a tradition of civic patronage. Their ancestors had endowed churches, monasteries, and charitable foundations. The sense of sin that still hung over the practice of usury seemed to demand restitution, yet even those rich merchants and bankers clearly deficient in their sense of sin still felt the need to express gratitude for their good fortune through civic donations and endowments. If it seems unacceptable to some to find any redeeming value in the lives of these Renaissance rulers, we must acknowledge the fact that they did commit themselves to the ideal of civic humanism, an idea inherited from the classical humanism of antiquity. What is more, we have the evidence of the works themselves, which stand today as vivid and unquestionable sources of aesthetic value. We also do well to remind ourselves of Hannah Arendt's words in her profound philosophical study, *The Human Condition* (1958).[12] Works of art, she said, gloriously transcend their original connections with religion, magic, and myth—and, we may add, politics and commerce.

A century later the generous habits of civic philanthropy were securely buttressed by the theories and attitudes of classical humanism. Those in the governing circles of Florence became convinced that their city was the true heir of republican Rome. The great oligarchs, in their leisure from conducting diplomacy and collecting taxes, read Plato and above all Cicero, and they began to feel as never before that the good life was possible only if a man devoted himself to civic virtue. Civic humanism thus became the true presupposition of the doctrine that art is essential to the promotion of the general welfare. It was true then, and if art is ever in our time to be reestablished as an ingredient in the general welfare, civic humanism will once more have to come into its own.

During the half-century of Medician power, Florence dominated the intellectual and artistic life of the Italian Renaissance. Cosimo de' Medici poured out a fortune on buildings, sculptures, and paintings for the public good—so much so that his grandson Lorenzo the Magnificent, astounded by the staggering sums spent by his grandfather, found it cheaper simply to patronize philosophers. However, he did not completely turn his back on the traditions of his family; Florentine civic life continued to prosper

Nevertheless, when the full two centuries of Florentine greatness are considered, it is impossible to attribute them to the munificence of a single family. In fact, what is enormously impressive is the extent to which the city's benefactors are heterogeneous in name and composition: the great noble families like the Medici, Strozzi, and Rucellai; the great monastic orders of the church; and the enormously wealthy and powerful craft guilds like the cloth processors, goldsmiths, wool manufacturers, and leather workers. This is heartening to remember in a mixed economy like our own, where government agencies and private philanthropists, giant corporations and mammoth unions could turn their attention to the physical and aesthetic rehabilitation of America—if only the ideology were available and the civic attitudes revivified.

But there is one more thing to remember in considering the case of Florence. The slow formation of a humanistic culture, which renewed the foundations of knowledge by recreating the classic past and which, in so doing, at once interpreted anew man's place in nature and his importance as a creature of history and tradition, made Florence the first to view and to publicize the activities of city life as the heart of an organized society. No longer a mere association of trading and commercial interests, the city itself, in its meaning and historical accretions, became a product of reason and fine art. In the new elite that assumed control over the political and cultural life of the city there was a special place for those whose imagination of the city combined the requirements of reason and beauty. The most cultivated and influential artists—and those closest to the centers of political power—were the architects. But they were architects whose elaborate designs were for the revision of the older city layout by the creation of new urban vistas and wide regular squares, for the addition of new sections to the city and the construction of structures whose masses were meant to monitor the development of the future homes and public edifices of the evolving urban center. It is no accident that treatises on architecture in the fifteenth and sixteenth centuries were full of ideal cities and that many of the proposed vistas are suggestive of stage designs. The architectural drawings of Leon Battista Alberti in the mid-1400s and of Andrea Palladio one hundred years later show that the specific problems of individual buildings had become subordinate to the global aspects of the city plan.

The organic interconnection between the fine arts that this development entails is obvious. Paintings and sculptures become part of the idea of the building and integral to its meaning and valuational expression, just as these same buildings become the jewels in the total setting that constitutes the urban plan. The very metaphor of "jewel" is appropriate, since the orientation from the tradition of civic humanism brings to the fore for the first time the importance of "the historical monument" and causes the architect/city planner to design in full awareness of the importance of the city's "cultural resources." From this perspective the shape and meaning of the city should depend not on its modes of production or commercial advantages, but on its great historical monuments. Thus, however much the architectural planners of Florence played with the geometrical forms of the "ideal city," their actual work was based less on logic than on history.

It is the essence of a monument that it is a building or edifice that symbolizes and expresses historical and ideological values of moral and spiritual importance to the community. When architects or city planners are themselves cultured individuals, they sense instinctively that what makes a city valuable from a historical or traditional point of view is its fortunate accumulation of cultural assets—universities, libraries, collections of antiquities, great churches with their works of art, monuments to wars and heroes, noble theaters, academies of music and fine art—which are at once a valuable heritage and a source of civic pride. In this perspective the arts contribute to the general welfare even in the humble and inglorious corners of civic life, as, for example, its charitable and remedial aspects. When Brunelleschi is asked to give artistic form to an orphanage (Ospedale degl' Innocenti) and Rembrandt to paint one of his noblest canvases for the public poorhouse in Amsterdam, this expresses an attitude that our Department of Health and Human Services, our Department of Education, and our state boards of education and housing would do well to follow.

It may seem that I have dwelt too long and self-indulgently on the aesthetic history of Renaissance Florence. But my purpose has been twofold: in the first place, to show what is aesthetically possible within a highly cultivated society and thus to provide a shining counterexample to the aesthetic torpor of our current situation in the United States with its paranoid concentration on political domination and acquisitive success; and in the second place, it is to focus attention, indirectly, upon the philosophy of civic humanism, which was Florence's glory. As I see it, civic humanism offers the only possibility of our own restoration to the golden age of our Founding Fathers. I have long been convinced that the future of the arts and the humanities, both as lived and as taught, is bound up with a renaissance of civic pride that should trigger the rehabilitation of our cities and the elimination of the worst of their ugliness and degradation.

History thus seems to show that cultural achievement and social living flourish best in the organic community of manageable size: Periclean Athens, Medician Florence, the Venetian Republic of the fourteenth and fifteenth centuries, Baroque Vienna under Maria Theresa, where painting, sculpture, architecture, music, and drama, as well as reading and good conversation, flowered within an environment of social cohesion and civic concern. Urban life has always been the fountainhead of culture, and the contemporary metropolitan crisis, with its erosion of public safety, flight to the suburbs, and the physical decay of the central city, bodes ill for the humanist as well as for the human future. Not until the urban environment is once again manageable in size, walkable, proud of its monuments and open spaces, and the locus of a revived civic and cultural concern will America's aesthetic future be secure.

I began this chapter with the paradox suggested in the National Endowment for the Arts report *Toward Civilization*—the gap between the high culture of our eighteenth-century Founding Fathers and the wretched state of arts education today. And I have taken as my first task the historical and sociological explanation of this paradox in the two epochs—both less than hospitable to the arts—that have intervened. And since the considerations here are largely political and economic—that is to say, *public*—I have provided a public counterexample, Renaissance Florence, a culture that assumed, without the requirement of proof or argument, the necessary coincidence of art and the general welfare and thus, unconsciously, embodied a dream of permanent aesthetic possibility. In such a culture, formal arts education was hardly needed; it would, in fact, have been redundant. For the youth who grew up in Renaissance Florence or Venice or Padua or Siena, every public building or monument, every church, as well as the domestic architecture on every street corner, provided a lesson in arts education. In our own age of neglect and artistic impoverishment, by contrast, such an education becomes an absolute necessity.

2

The Arts and the
Human Person

Art is not a plaything, but a necessity, and its essence, form, is not a decorative adjustment, but a cup into which life can be poured and lifted to the lips and tasted.

—Rebecca West

The major topic this book addresses is, of course, discipline-based art education, that is to say, the contribution that creative work in the visual arts, art history, art criticism, and aesthetics makes to the educational process and the school curriculum. But education is always an instrument, a means, a procedure, and that which it serves is a subject, a content, a human value, or a way of life. Thus it is obvious that the raison d'être of art education is simply *art*—the intuition of the artist and its embodiment in a particular material. And this is why all the problems of contemporary art education are ultimately dependent upon the nature and status of art. To secure the instrument we examine the activity and the product, and that is precisely why we begin with two chapters, the first having exhibited art as a public utility, and this, the second, declaring art to be a personal and a private necessity.

This latter stance is slightly different from and, I think, much more crucial than that taken by the National Endowment for the Arts in its report *Toward Civilization*. The four purposes the book sets for arts education—to provide a sense of civilization, foster creativity, teach effective communication, and supply tools for the critical assessment of what one reads, sees, and hears—except perhaps for the second, all seem to have an "instrumental" rather than an "intrinsic" character. They seem, that is, to endow the self with capacities or capabilities whose exercise leads outward instead of constituting internal resources of illumination, wisdom, and growth. Is it asking too much of art to accomplish the latter?

I do not think so. Of course it is certainly true that a good deal of inflated, exaggerated, and hyperbolic talk about art came out of the nineteenth century. Some great foolishness about the transcendent character of the aesthetic was perpetrated by Nietzsche in the introduction to his early work, *The Birth of Tragedy*, where he claimed that "art . . . constitutes the essential metaphysical activity of man," that "existence could be justified only in aesthetic terms," and that "art is the highest human task, the true metaphysical activity" of this life.[1] But quite apart from this extreme philosophical exaggeration, there has always been an enduring tradition in the West that relates art and arts education to some of the most important concerns of the human person. I believe we have two theories of art and arts education here rather than one. The first I should call *constitutive*. The second I should call *revelatory* or redemptive. Both are important, and I shall proceed to take them up in order.

The constitutive theory of art and arts education in the modern world begins with the important series of letters, *The Aesthetic Education of Man*, by Friedrich von Schiller and continues in the theories of his contemporary disciple, Sir Herbert Read. The amazing aspect of Schiller's theory is that it takes its origin in the political century of the great democratic revolutions.

On July 13, 1793, two years before the publication of *The Aesthetic Education of Man*, Schiller addressed a letter to the Duke of Augustenburg in which he said, "Freedom, political and civil, remains ever and always the holiest of all possessions, the worthiest goal of striving, the great rallying point of all culture; but this glorious structure can only be raised upon the firm basis of an ennobled character: and before a citizen can be given a constitution, one must see that the citizen be himself soundly constituted."[2] This quotation says it all: the highest of all values is freedom, political and civil. But its achievement is dependent upon the personality and character structure of a society's citizens. And the crucial resultant question is, What is requisite in order that these individuals should be "soundly constituted"? Schiller's amazing solution directs us to the field of art and arts education, and this is why he devoted the whole of *The Aesthetic Education of Man* to a specific answer to this question.[3]

Schiller was, of course, a poet and and a writer of romantic plays, but the age in which he lived was intensely political. It was the time of the French Revolution and the American Revolution and of considerable political ferment in Central Europe. Thus his most famous plays (like *Don Carlos, Maria Stuart, Wallenstein*, and *Wilhelm Tell*) were obsessed by the concept of political freedom.

Given Schiller's preference for freedom and the duties of citizenship in a free society and his insistence that the citizen be soundly constituted, just one further step needs to be taken—to outline the process whereby this sound constitution can be achieved. And, miraculously enough, this process, Schiller maintains, is one of *aesthetic education.* At first he seems to have his reservations. "Is it not," he asks, "untimely to be casting around for a code of laws for the aesthetic world at a moment when the affairs of the moral offer interest of so much more urgent concern, and when the spirit of philosophical inquiry is being expressly challenged by present circumstances to concern itself with the most perfect of all the works to be achieved by the art of man: the construction of true political freedom?" But he answers decisively. "Art is a daughter of Freedom, and takes her orders from the necessity inherent in minds, not from the exigencies of matter." And he adds, "If man is ever to solve that problem of politics in practice, he will have to approach it through the problem of the aesthetic, because it is only through Beauty that man makes his way to Freedom" (pp. 7, 9). This is a slightly puzzling statement, and we must try to determine what Schiller means by it.

The answer lies in the valuational progression that leads from the state of nature to the state of civil society, from the realm of mere force to the rule of law. The production of the moral personality is the stage that lies in between, and this stage is itself accomplished through the educational potential of the fine arts. "All improvement in the political sphere is to proceed from the ennobling of character—but how under the influence of a barbarous constitution is character ever to become ennobled? To this end we should, presumably, have to seek out some instrument not provided by the State, and to open up living springs which, whatever the political corruption, will remain clear and pure. . . . This instrument is Fine Art; such living springs are opened up in its immortal exemplars" (p. 55).

Schiller has an idealistic, even a romantic faith in the ultimate saving grace of Beauty. Only this, he thinks, will save us from the coarseness and perversity of the age. For he has a feeling, almost Athenian, that a cultivated aesthetic taste is practically an indispensable condition of all dignity of conduct. How could the citizens of the Periclean age not act with nobility and decorum, surrounded as they were by the beauties of the Parthenon, the Erechtheum, and the public monuments of Praxiteles and Polygnotus?

Schiller is determined to follow that transcendental road where "Beauty would have to be shown to be a necessary condition of Human Being." And he is able to do this by an analogy, much appealed to in Greek culture, that served to relate "the beautiful" *(to kalon)* and "the good" *(to agathon).* The analogy, probably Pythagorean in origin, found the essence of both in certain principles derived from mathematics—the principles of proportion, balance, harmony, and organic unity—and it was held that they were equally applicable in the judgment of a work of art and the judgment of human character. It was in fact held that an excellently developed character was itself a work of art. How could it be otherwise since both represented a participation in *form?* Form means not merely shape, but structure, balance, symmetry, harmony, and integrity—at once the essence of the work of art and the properly constituted human self. And I believe that this is precisely what Rebecca West meant in the epigraph quoted at the beginning of this chapter. Art becomes a necessity by virtue of its vital forms, which afford a unique taste of life itself.

This idea is probably also the unconscious presuppposition to which Schiller appeals in *The Aesthetic Education of Man,* and it is what makes possible the transition from the aesthetic to the moral condition. It is aesthetic culture that leads to moral nobility, and moral nobility that is the precondition of a truly free society. "Though it may be his needs which drive man into society," says Schiller, "and reason which implants within him the principles of social behavior, beauty alone can confer on him a social character. Taste alone brings harmony into society, because it fosters harmony in the individual" (p. 215). Only the communication of the Beautiful unites the citizens of a free commonwealth because it relates to what is common to them all.

In the publication of his "Credo," Sir Herbert Read has brought Schiller's message up to date and has projected it into the modern world. "The moral regeneration of mankind," he says, "can be accomplished only by moral education, and until moral education is given priority over all other forms of education, I see no hope for the world. I have already indicated what I mean by moral education—*not* education by moral precept, but education by moral practice, which in effect means education by aesthetic discipline."[4] Schiller, as we have just seen, believed that aesthetic culture would lead to moral nobility. Read underwrites the same perception by defining aesthetic culture as "the grace we can instill by means of music, poetry and the plastic arts," which he calls "not a superficial acquirement, but the key to all knowledge and all noble behavior" (p. 25). Here, too, as in Schiller, aesthetic culture leads to moral development, which is itself a precondition for the existence of a free society. For society can function harmoniously only if the individuals composing it are integrated persons, that is to say, people whose growth to maturity has been nourished by prolonged confrontation with the fine arts. "We must," says Read, "give priority in our education to all forms of aesthetic activity, for in

the course of making beautiful things there will take place a crystal-
lization of the emotions into patterns that are the moulds of virtue"
(p. 143).

In Schiller's and Herbert Read's emphasis on aesthetic education
we have theories that do not separate but rather join art, ethics, and
politics, where the appreciation and practice of the arts are themselves
instrumental to the formation of an admirable character, to the maintenance of participatory democracy, and to the institution of the just
society. But, of course, the notion that art has a constitutive and a
formative influence on the human person is as old as Plato's treatment
of poetry and music in the *Republic*. And, becoming particularly influential with Schiller and Winckelmann in the German eighteenth century, it also has its advocates in the modern world. Herbert Read is
not its only modern representative. Even so down-to-earth a philosopher as John Dewey has in his *Art as Experience* recognized the role
of organic unification that art plays both in our experience of the external world and in the harmonious integration of our personality structure. "Just as it is the office of art to be unifying, to break through
conventional distinctions to the underlying common elements of the
experienced world, while developing individuality as the manner of
seeing and expressing these elements, so it is the office of art in the
individual person, to compose differences, to do away with isolations
and conflicts among the elements of our being, to utilize oppositions
among them to build a richer personality."[5] In short, from Plato to
Dewey, throughout the course of Western civilization, the constitutive
theory of art and arts education has played a commanding role.

The revelatory theory has, I think, done no less. It might perhaps
even be possible to call the constitutive theory "classical" while calling
the revelatory theory essentially "romantic." Hegel, who, along with
Kant and Schopenhauer, is one of the great aestheticians of the modern
world, has, in his *Philosophy of Fine Art*,[6] given us an example of revelatory theory in action in his account of painting. He says that only
by laboring over the content made available to it in the Christian Romantic era have painters discovered how best to use its characteristic
means and modes of expression. Entering the spiritual depths of consciousness of the Romantic art form, painters are able to bring within
the sphere of their art a wealth of things that lie beyond the reach of
sculpture. The entire religious sphere, visions of heaven and hell, the
history of Christ, the disciples and saints, the world of nature around
us, and our human life itself, down to its most fleeting situations—all
this, and more, insofar as it lives in the spiritual depths of the heart,
can find its place in painting. Whatever lives in the heart is present to

our consciousness in a wholly subjective way, of course, even when its specific content is grasped as something essentially objective. This focus of aesthetic consciousness through the depths of the heart is indeed what most clearly distinguishes painting. The presupposition of such expression has to be that the soul has worked its way through the depths of its own inner life, that it has overcome much, suffered much, experienced the worst sort of grief and pain, while yet maintaining the integrity to withdraw, finally, out of that soul-shattering experience back into itself. In short, through the agency of religious painting there is a possible approach to wisdom.

The claim here is extremely ambitious, but that quality is true of any aesthetic philosophy that takes the arts seriously. For both constitutive and revelatory theory, art is not a plaything, is not a decorative adjustment, but a necessity. And while the constitutive theory views the arts as crucial formative elements in the making of the human person, the revelatory theory sees the arts as instruments of illumination by which the human individual achieves wisdom.

This matter of "wisdom" is somewhat tricky because the term is so ambiguous there is always a suspicion that one is using it emotionally, perhaps even vaporously. I should like to attempt clarification by distinguishing three aspects or dimensions of wisdom. Wisdom as actual, as exhibited in the life, say, of Socrates or Jesus, of Seneca or Marcus Aurelius, is one thing only: an organic whole that does not readily lend itself to decomposition. But from another point of view wisdom is a little like the Christian Godhead: three and one at once. The trinity of wisdom to which I wish to direct attention is (1) wisdom in the cognition of reality, (2) wisdom in the setting of goals, and (3) wisdom in the appraisal of life. Only the first and last are, I think, amenable to the services of the arts. Goal setting is moral and practical and active, and, generally speaking, we do not use art for this purpose. But the other two dimensions are crucially relevant. Art has much to teach us about both the cognition of reality and the appraisal of life, and in both these areas its revelatory capabilities come powerfully into play.

But before I indicate more specifically how this is the case, I would like to turn to two famous proponents of the revelatory theory. The first is Rebecca West, focusing on her early book of criticism, *The Strange Necessity* (1928), and the second is Kenneth Clark, concentrating on his 1954 Romanes Lecture, reprinted in his *Moments of Vision* (1981).

Rebecca West's meditation upon the incalculable power of art was triggered by accident during a visit to Paris, where she was reading James Joyce's *Ulysses* at the same time that she was making visits to the Louvre. She describes herself as transfixed by a painting of Ingres and as having come to realize that the monologue of Molly Bloom that ends Joyce's novel achieves a unified beauty exactly comparable in its effect on her to Ingres's harem scene in the *Turkish Bath*. She reflects that the painter "had the innocence of the eye that all the rest of the world has lost long ago, so that he looks on flesh as Adam might have looked on Eve before lust rose in him, and lets its values be manifest in their purity."[7] Both the soliloquy of Molly Bloom and the monumental Ingres nude draw out in her the same powerful aesthetic emotion. What, she asks herself, is the necessity that is served by the contemplation of these two? "What is the meaning of this mystery of mysteries? Why does art matter? And why does it matter so much? What is this strange necessity" (p. 58)? And this musing leads her to the recognition of a similar functioning of all the arts, the powerful emotions to which they lead, and the exaltation of the self that they bring forth.

> When Michelangelo carved the waking woman on the Medici tomb he was recording the behavior of a certain mass at a certain instant which was a complete event in itself. When Shakespeare wrote the sonnet beginning "Let me not to the marriage of true minds Admit impediments," he was recording a certain event of a much more complicated kind (largely owing to the much more untidy position it occupies in regard to time) which offers the intellect just the job it can do in its need for clarification. When Beethoven wrote the Quartet in C sharp minor he recorded an event of still greater complication that was precipitated as the result of a series of experiences of the simple kind that are the subject of the plastic arts and those of the not so simple kind that are the subject of literature: in fact, he recorded what happens after a thing has happened, what life amounts to after it has been lived. *It seems to be true that all the arts are on a perfect equality regarding this necessity to collect information of one sort or another about the universe.* (emphasis added, p. 121)

Here West herself recognizes that "cognition of reality" is a prime purpose of the arts. And now her description of that overwhelming emotional response to the greatest, the most completely achieved of the fine arts:

> But . . . what about this? This blazing jewel that I have at the bottom of my pocket, this crystalline concentration of glory, this deep and serene and intense emotion that I feel before the greatest works of art? You know what Roger Fry means when he says somewhere, "This is just how I felt when I first saw Michael Angelo's frescoes in the Sistine Chapel." I got it myself most powerfully from 'King Lear.' It overflows the confines of the mind and becomes an important physical event. The

blood leaves the hands, the feet, the limbs, and flows back to the heart, which for the time seems to have become an immensely high temple whose pillars are several sorts of illumination, returning to the numb flesh diluted with some substance swifter and lighter and more electric than itself. Unlike that other pleasure one feels at less climactic contacts with art it does not call to any action other than complete experience of it. Rather one rests in its lap. Now, what in the world is this emotion? What is the bearing of supremely great works of art on my life which makes me feel so glad? (p. 195)

And finally the analysis and explanation of the intense emotion, which is the consequence of an exquisite aesthetic confrontation:

An analogy strikes me. Is it possible that the intense exaltation which comes to our knowledge of the greatest works of art and the milder pleasure that comes of our more everyday dealings with art, are phases of the same emotion, as passion and gentle affection are phases of love between a man and a woman? Is this exaltation the orgasm, as it were, of the artistic instinct, stimulated to its height by a work of art which through its analysis and synthesis of some experience enormously important to humanity (though not necessarily demonstrable as such by the use of the intellect) creates a proportionately powerful excitatory complex, which, in other words, halts in front of some experience which if left in a crude state would probably make one feel that life was too difficult and transform it into something that helps one to go on living? I believe that is the explanation. It is the feeling of realized potency, of might perpetuating itself. (pp. 196–97)

I have perhaps quoted more extensively from *Strange Necessity* than I should, but Rebecca West is an eloquent, talented, perceptive, and dramatic writer, and she has here expressed the revelatory theory of art with an exemplary vividness only seldom to be met with. Kenneth Clark, on the other hand, is an art historian and critic, perhaps less dramatic in expression but no less himself committed to the revelatory theory. These episodes of revelatory experience he calls "moments of vision."

At the most elementary level, for Clark a "moment of vision" is always a moment of intensified physical perception, but it is not due to a mere extension of our sensory equipment, as when sight is made more powerful by the use of binoculars or a magnifying glass. It is rather a mysterious potency in the object at which we are gazing that detaches itself from the usual sensory matrix in which it is embedded, suddenly to become "intensely clear and important to us." Heightened perception is often to be found in many aspects of great works of art, lighting up dull corners with inexplicable clarity, like the incredible blue heaven of Giovanni Bellini's *St. Francis in Ecstasy*, the melodramatic glass in Velasquez's *The Water Carrier of Seville*, the pink awning in van Gogh's *La Maison de Vincent à Arles*, and "the little patch of yellow wall" in Vermeer's great *View of Delft*, around which in *À la Recherche du Temps Perdu* Marcel Proust constructs the entire episode of the death of Bergotte.

However, in his Romanes Lecture Kenneth Clark singles out two painters in particular—van Gogh, whom he characterizes as "the nineteenth-century painter who saw common things with most intensity,"[8] and Giorgione, of whose great painting *The Tempest* in the Accademia in Venice he says, "Here we reach the point when our moments of vision are scarcely distinguishable from the imaginative faculty in general" (p. 8).

Clark connects the moment of vision with at least three other concepts: possession, self-discovery, and incandescence. "Possession: here is a word which in most of its varying senses, seems to throw some light on our problem. In a moment of vision we possess, and we are possessed" (p. 10). "Self-discovery, self-identification: here, it seems to me, is the chief reason for the compulsive, all-absorbing nature of moments of vision" (p. 11). "These flashes, which seemed at first to be no more than short—though mysteriously important—accidents in a work of art, turn out to be like sparks shot up from the molten center of the imagination" (p. 17).

Having given an exposition of the revelatory theory as it appears in the work of two of its proponents, Rebecca West and Kenneth Clark, I now wish to return to the plastic arts as producers of wisdom, that is to say, as vehicles for the cognition of reality and the appraisal of life. I think the phrase "cognition of reality" is not entirely satisfactory here since it can equally imply factual knowledge of the same kind as science gives, and this meaning makes Rebecca West's statement "that all the arts are on a perfect equality regarding this necessity to collect information of one sort or another about the universe" somewhat misleading. The phrase "to collect information about the universe" is a little too prosaic, a little too objective, a little too unemotional and uninvolved to indicate West's meaning clearly. What must be understood here is not a restricted, but a spacious sense of reality that perhaps comes less from "cognition of" than from "communion with" reality. What is required here is something intimate and participative; something closer to Bergsonian "intuition" than Cartesian analysis. And this difference is clearly inherent in the distinction between the initial capabilities of the visual and the linguistic arts.

It is, of course, true, as Rebecca West intimates, that to a philosophic question each of the various arts gives its unique answer. Thus if we would ask, What does it really mean to be old in mind, in body, and in spirit? we could turn for an answer equally to the old men of Rembrandt and the old men of Shakespeare, for each of these artists presents a formulatable and essential truth. A passionate search for the Platonic essence of old age might lead us to music, to literature, or to painting: to the poignant resignation in Brahms's late Clarinet Quintet and the final movement of Beethoven's last Piano Sonata, to *King Lear* and the last *Essays* of Montaigne, or, finally, to the self-portraits of the aged Rembrandt, Leonardo da Vinci's self-image created in extreme old age, or Albrecht Dürer's *St. Jerome in His Study* or his portrait of his aged mother.

It has often been observed that there is a certain cultural blindness to old age in the West, compared, say, with China, where in art, literature, and social custom the elderly are portrayed as objects of dignity and respect with a mental slant of shrewd realism and an emotional disposition of assured serenity. Yet unprejudiced examination of portraits of the elderly by the great masters of painting in the West overwhelmingly shows that they reveal this same constellation of values and thereby visually codify a crucial philosophic insight; and this, in fact, is precisely what is meant by defining art as a special "cognition of reality"—in this case a profound reaching for the truth of our humanity.

Worth noting at this point is St. Augustine's division of the total universe into three parts: "nature," or the level of things below man; the things on the level of man; and, finally, the things on the level above man, as God and His son, the angels, the incarnation, and the divine narrative. This division is a useful first introduction to the areas of painterly subject matter: nature, both landscape and still life (what the French call *nature morte*, literally "dead nature"); man, both portraiture and figure painting (including the nude, which is almost an obsession in painting in the West, although shunned and in rather bad repute in Chinese culture); and, lastly, the entire spectrum of religious painting in the Christian tradition.

It is, of course, obvious that painting is a medium that utilizes visual images—images as sensory patterns—and this fact makes it particularly easy to assimilate it to the revelatory theory, in fact to define painting as revelatory imagery. From this point of view its domain includes those images that reveal living nature or landscape, images that reveal dead nature (still life or more ordinary objects), images that reveal human nature in its physical or psychological or spiritual aspects, or, finally, images that reveal the supernatural realm of the divine nature. Many of these can produce profound delight, more than superficial knowledge, and, on occasion, haunting inspiration.

The spectrum of visual images in painting is as vast as human experience itself, and while it may originate in the domain of the senses, it can also aspire to the highest reaches of religious spirituality. In its original impulse it may be an essay in, or an exploration of, human sensuality. Rebecca West says frankly: "There is here a passion which is the root of our love for beauty, and therefore of our effort for art; the passion for beautiful substances." And Santayana, perhaps with Dewey, our greatest American aesthetician, confirms her insight: "Sensuous beauty is not the greatest or most important element of effect, but it is the most primitive and fundamental, and the most universal. . . . However subordinate the beauty may be which a garment, a building, or a poem derives from its sensuous material, yet the presence of this sensuous material is indispensable. . . . The Parthenon not in marble, the king's crown not of gold, and the stars not of fire, would be feeble and prosaic things."[9] The kings and queens must have their brocade, the great ladies their ermine, their satin, and their pearls. And so we have that feeling for the gorgeousness and the sumptuousness of materials that makes the white satin dresses of Terborch's domestic scenes almost a trademark (like that constantly reappearing white porcelain pitcher with the small, round, black metal top in so many of the paintings of Vermeer), and the same feeling is to be found constantly in royal or baronial portraits such as Holbein's of Jane Seymour in Vienna, Clouet's of Francis I, and Van Dyck's of Charles I in the Louvre, Vittore Ghislandi's of Count Giovanni Battista Vailetti in the Accademia in Venice, and even in the domestic scene of Vermeer's *Maid Presenting a Letter to Her Mistress* in the Frick Collection in New York.

At practically the other end of the spectrum are the great pictures of religious commemoration and adoration—like those of Giotto, Fra Angelico, and Giovanni Bellini. The dramatic potential of the painted image of holiness may be infinitely greater than that of the written text or the spoken sermon. Sometimes a picture of the Crucifixion or the Madonna and Child may have implications for both. Fra Angelico, for example, was himself a man of saintly habits, a learned friar, and a painter capable of expressing great spirituality. He dreamt of an exhilarating revival of faith, of a triumphant return to the fountainheads of Christian thought, and his was a crusade that relied upon art as one of the most potent tools of persuasion. There is absolutely no doubt about the devotional purpose of his paintings: for him religious contemplation precedes the act of painting and implies prayer, since the act of painting itself disseminates just that compassion which prayer entreats. There is also in Angelico a highly poetic, definitely Franciscan feeling for nature. He clearly felt that the beauties of natural creation were tangible proof of God's infinite goodness, and therefore even in those paintings dealing with the central drama of Christian faith (like the fabulous *Descent from the Cross* in the Museum of San Marco in Florence) there is a meticulously painted background of natural landscape.

Angelico rounds out his central theological dramas with brilliant landscape views in impeccable perspective. As he was among the first to solve the problems of recession and distance in religious paintings and landscape, the natural content here has itself a devotional role—to cushion the most crushing moments of the divine tragedy, to soothe the afflicted gaze and restore to it a mood of tranquil meditation. The landscape portion of the picture forms almost an ironic counterpoint, a sermon of bitter regret at the cruel ingratitude of men who martyred their own Savior, sent by that same God who devised and created the beauties of nature in the first place. Thus Angelico painted as a preacher preaches, and, as in the sermons of St. Francis that preceded his own, a supernatural message is woven into the naturalistic tapestry to produce what is to come to superb fruition in the Madonnas of Giovanni Bellini, another apostle of what can only be described as "a religious naturalism."

The great paintings of religious inspiration provide the metaphors and the paradigms for the penitential way of life. The greatest exemplars of the Holy Mother and Child—like those of Bernardo Daddi in the Or San Michele in Florence or of Giovanni Bellini in the Accademia in Venice or of Raphael's *Madonna in the Fields* in the Kunsthistorisches Museum in Vienna—project just those images of gentle mother love, innocence, and hidden destiny that the first act of the Christian drama requires, just as Fra Angelico's *Descent from the Cross*, to which we have already referred, as well as Giovanni Bellini's magnificent *Lament over the Dead Christ* in Venice, distill the bitterness of its final denouement. And for the quintessential image of the Savior himself, nothing can quite compare with the handsome, masculine, yet inexpressibly gentle and compassionate portrayal in the two great paintings of Cima da Conegliano in Venice: the first *The Incredulity of St. Thomas* in the Accademia, the second *The Coronation of the Virgin* in the Church of St. John and St. Paul. In the concern for the transcendent—St. Augustine's "level above man"—the art of painting provides just those revelatory images which serve to transfigure the human person.

When St. Augustine divided the entire cosmos into the three realms of Nature, Man, and God, his probable intention was to keep them separate and distinct. But, as we have seen, in Fra Angelico the central dramas of Christianity, placed within a setting of landscape background, provide almost a scholastic comment on the interpenetration of nature and the divine. This meditation is carried on and taken even further by Giovanni Bellini and Alvise Vivarini in fifteenth-century Venice. Bellini, one of the most prolific painters of Madonnas in the whole of Italy, played the game both ways. His two great paintings hang side by side in the Accademia, the one of a young and simple mother with her lusty baby, the other a pietà where the mother has grown old and tragic and now holds in her arms the crucified body of her son. Both scenes are set in full open air, in rich, architecture-encrusted landscapes, showing that God incarnated as man is rationally placed in man's own natural environment. On the other hand, two other Bellini Madonnas, the one in the sacristy of the Frari, the other, the magnificent *Virgin Enthroned with Saints* hanging on a side wall of San Zaccaria, both show the holy family indoors, in each case enclosed in the privacy of an identical semicircular niche. And, as if to unite these two diverse conceptions in an even more subtle commentary, the wonderful *Madonna and Child* of Alvise Vivarini, hanging in an obscure back corner of St. Giovanni in Bragora, presents the mother and child inside, while through two large arched windows, one on each side of the Madonna, a peaceful, tranquil landscape is to be seen.

There is, I think, a certain irony in the fact that what we know as the independent form of landscape painting first makes its appearance as backdrop in the religious painting of the fifteenth century. For here the interest in nature is derivative, not as a sphere loved and interesting in itself, but rather as indirect evidence of God's infinite goodness and power. The Renaissance brings a marked change in this perspective. Architects, painters, philosophers, and poets turn to nature as an object to be loved for its own sake, and within a scant two hundred years, in the seventeenth century, with Poussin and Claude in France and the great school of van Ruisdael, Hobbema, and van Goyen in Holland, landscape painting has become perhaps the most admired and the most characteristic artistic form.

In the case of religious painting, as we have seen most particularly in the instance of Fra Angelico, there is a deep affective relationship between artist and subject matter. This is no less true in the case of landscape painting, where the religious awe and reverence of the painter are transferred bodily from the area of the divine to the area of nature. An American tradition running back to the early nineteenth century gives this perception clear literary expression. Already in 1836 in his first essay, *Nature*, Emerson lists all those advantages that our senses owe to nature and emphasizes the multiple ways that the simple perception of natural forms, in being delightful, services the love of beauty. And ten years later Thoreau testifies to a relationship with nature which is vivid in its immediacy. "For many years," he says in *Walden*, "I was self-appointed inspector of snow storms and rain storms and did my duty faithfully. . . . They give me a new sense of the variety and capacity of that nature which is our common dwelling."[10] And later, in *A Writer's Journal*: "I will take another walk to the Cliff, another row on the river, another skate on the meadow, be out in the first snow, and associate with the winter birds. Here I am at home. In the bare and bleached crust of the earth I recognize my friend."[11] But if for Thoreau Nature in her intimacy is "my friend" or "our common dwelling," his familiarity never breeds contempt. For his constant imagery is one of adoration and awe. Nature for him is "holy and heroic." She is one who "preserves her innocence like a beautiful child." She is "full of genius, full of the divinity."

Thoreau's sense of the divinity of nature is combined with a corresponding awareness of the divinity of artists in their privileged access to the infinite realm of the imagination, and thus harmony is established between the actual qualitative gradations of nature and the answering potency of artistic sensibility. The implication is not that the feeling tone of landscape hangs upon the accidents of the artist's perspective and temperament, but upon the pristine ability to empathize through love. In exactly the same year in which Thoreau was writing *Walden*, an editorial appeared in an early American art journal, *The Crayon*, that insisted upon the affective identification of art and nature, the product of human making and its infinite source: "Let it be remembered that the subject of the picture, the material object or objects from which it is constructed, are the essential parts of it. If you have no love for them, you can have no genuine feeling for the picture which represents them. . . . We love Nature and Beauty—we admire the artist who renders them in his works. . . . The man to whom nature, in her inanimate forms, has been a delight all his early life, will love a landscape and be better capable of feeling the merits of it than any city-bred artist, and so through the categories of men and things. They are only capable of being just critics of art who have first learned to love the things that Art deals with."[12]

This cry from the middle of nineteenth-century America has a certain pathos, for in founding genuine feeling for the representing work of art upon the love of, and tenderness for, the natural object—the landscape that is represented—the customary rupture between formal accomplishment and the intrinsic lure of the natural subject matter is nullified. The love of landscape painting then becomes a function of the love of landscape itself, and the implication tends to be that such identifications of feeling are possible only within the ambiance of a concept of nature that has domesticated the infinite properties of natural space into the emotional specificity of that "lived space" which constitutes our home.

Something of this same feeling characterizes the great English landscape painter John Constable, for in his youth he had roamed the fields of his native East Anglia, bathed in the river Stour, and slept in the shadow of haystacks. Afterwards he wrote, "These scenes made me a painter (and I am grateful)."[13] Anyone who has had the great fortune to observe the staunch placidity of his *Trees near Hampstead Church* of 1821 or the beautiful autumn rootedness of the *Salisbury Cathedral from the Meadows* of 1831 cannot but be moved by these secure evidences that the long and arduous struggle with natural appearances had been sustained by an unwavering love for the objects with which landscape art deals.

Constable's dedication had, of course, its analogue and its inspiration in the great Dutch landscape painters of the seventeenth century. Here, too, a quiet but passionate love of the flatlands and the huge luminous sky, the dynamic cloud formations and the mysterious light playing on foliage and water alike, indicated a sense of possession and commitment. Hercules Seghers, Jacob van Ruisdael, Jan van Goyen, and Meindert Hobbema devoted their loving attention to the world of nature with the same meticulousness, cleanliness, and sense of order that Vermeer and de Hooch devoted to the Dutch interior, rich in stained glass and parchment, oriental rugs, gems, satins and brocade, fruitwood musical instruments, and checkerboard-marbled floors. In Seghers there is a romantic feeling, in van Ruisdael an elemental solitude, in van Goyen a rich autumnal glow, and in Hobbema a sedate grandeur that nonetheless reveals a nature vibrantly alive, yet balanced in an equilibrium soliciting not so much our contemplation as our entrance. For the quiet but implicit love of native land gives to Dutch landscape expression a participative urge that is overwhelming.

A great Chinese theoretician of landscape of the Sung period, himself a renowned landscape painter, is said to have remarked that there are four kinds of landscape paintings: those that can be contemplated; those in which one can travel; those through which one may ramble; and those in which one may dwell. The landscapes of Poussin and Claude, of Corot and perhaps of Cézanne yield themselves to our contemplation, but the paintings of van Ruisdael, Hobbema, and van Goyen present a natural universe suggestive of habitation and exploration. Van Goyen's leafy groves are a terrain through which one may ramble; van Ruisdael's placid water mills are mute pavilions in which we may dwell; and the rutted wagon paths leading from Hobbema's immediate foregrounds deep into his picture space are familiar entrances upon which one can easily travel.

When landscape painters stake out a piece of the chaotic streaming and infinite extent of the immediately given world, give it unity, and form it, they arbitrarily introduce some sense of "center" and "boundaries," of which the picture frame is the obvious instrument. And to everything within this frame or window they impart a certain formal integrity, which constitutes the "mood" of the landscape. It is an epistemologist's holiday to determine whether this mood lies in the object or only in the observer, but formally considered, it seems probable that the mood of the landscape and its intended unity are only one and the same thing considered from two different angles. The expressive quality or "physiognomy" of landscape, vibrating along such axes as cheerful/serious, heroic/monotonous, excited/melancholy, reassuring/menacing, beautiful/sublime, sentimental/picturesque, is a fact of observation that cannot be denied. Hobbema's great *The Avenue: Middelharnis* of 1689 is a serenely beautiful and reassuring invitation to enter into the presence of nature with confidence and delight. But Soutine's mad and contorted *Windy Day, Auxerre* of 1939, which has an almost identical subject matter, displays nature as menacing and frenzied, and the figures it contains cower and rush to escape, as Hobbema's figures walk calmly and confidently in the glowing light.

Such comparisons cast a new light upon the critical importance of landscape mood, and they exhibit the painterly a priori. Constable's famous statement "When I sit down to make a sketch from nature, the first thing I try to do is to forget that I have ever seen a picture" and Courbet's equally memorable "The museums should be closed for twenty years, so that today's painters may begin to see with their own eyes" are equally beside the point, for neither establishes Ruskin's dogma of "the innocent eye." For landscape it is not the tyranny of artistic tradition but the love of nature or its hatred that counts, not the chains of the history of art but the thirst for natural space or its contrary that controls the landscape enterprise.

Michelangelo the sculptor and Ingres the draftsman both despised landscape, while Degas failed to see in landscape a single object worthy of his effort. And in fact the Impressionist moment is the last in the West in which painters turn to unvarnished nature with a sense of liberation and release. For it is the last possible moment—the late nineteenth-century moonlight or twilight zone of urban culture—when nature still represented a brief episode of inspiration and vital health.

Religious art deals with the transcendent. Landscape art celebrates nature. How is it with art devoted exclusively to the human person? The chief art form here is certainly portraiture, and it is to this that I should like to turn briefly. Artists know the human face in a very special way and with a kind of aesthetic certitude. Skeptical as they may be of physiognomic means for determining character, it has been an enduring study of artists to examine how the facial configuration of the individual sitter reflects the spirit or the personality or the soul. For ancient thinkers the eyes were the gateway of the soul, and Renaissance and seventeenth-century painters felt that they could capture the inner qualities, and thus focus on the spiritual life, of their subjects through examining the eyes' fleeting expressions. Of course, the human visage is a twofold instrument. It can serve as a mask to protect and hide the mind's nakedness as well as a mirror of expressiveness to reveal its inmost nature. Through the ages artists, and portrait painters in particular, have mastered those mysterious intuitions that have permitted them to reveal, by an insistent and devoted attention to the face, the mind and the character that lie behind.

The great portrait painters like Titian, Clouet, Holbein, Dürer, Rembrandt, Velázquez, Frans Hals, Gainsborough, Sir Joshua Reynolds, Goya, and Ingres, masters of character all, reveal us to ourselves. They service our cognition of human life just as much as Shakespeare, Montaigne, and Tolstoy did, and they provide us with an appraisal of our human existence exactly as profound as that of Socrates, Erasmus, and Pascal.

Of course, portraiture has had a checkered career throughout the course of Western civilization. We have some portrait busts from Ancient Greece many more from Imperial Rome, but for a thousand years, from the decline of the Roman Empire to the very end of the Middle Ages, there was no interest whatsoever in portraiture as a realistic likeness of a specific individual. That interest revived only in the fifteenth century with the emergence of Renaissance Humanism and the rise to power of national royalty and a powerful and prosperous merchant and banking class in the city states of Italy and northern Europe. Something significantly new begins in the period from Raphael and Titian to Bronzino and Philippe de Champaigne, and we have not only tributes to local rulers like Clouet's to Francis I and Vasari's and Verrocchio's to Lorenzo the Magnificent, but the massive output of Hans Holbein in the sixteenth century, whose portraits of Erasmus and Sir

Thomas More, of Henry VIII and his personal physician John Chambers, and of Jane Seymour and Thomas Cromwell serve as the very paradigms of our historical memory. Anyone who views the greatest exemplars of this genre, like Raphael's portrait of Baldassare Castiglione in the Louvre, Holbein's of Sir Thomas More in the Frick Collection, or Ingres's of the influential newspaper owner Louis François Bertin, also in the Louvre, must realize the enormous contribution to our knowledge of human character made by portraiture in the course of our Western tradition.

In what has come before, in my canvassing of the possibilities painting presents in its response to the areas of the holy, the natural, and the human, I have pretended that the various expressions are all characterized by a certain lucidity, what the medievals called *claritas*, and that the perfection of the work is due to a total absence of tentativeness or ambiguity, for example, that of Fra Angelico, Jacob van Ruisdael, or Hans Holbein. This is perhaps true for most works of fine art, but not for all. Some few express a certain tension, almost a palpable nervousness, because the creator, the artist, becomes suddenly conscious of the impossibility of finding out the exact truth about humanity, and this seems to call into question even the possibility of finding a stable foundation for artistic endeavor itself.

One great painter in whom this tension and this nervousness are palpable is Giorgione (1476–1510), the Venetian pupil of Giovanni Bellini whom Vasari ranked with Leonardo da Vinci as one of the founders of modern painting. I know from long and sustained acquaintance three of Giorgione's paintings, *The Concert in Open Air* in the Louvre, *The Three Philosophers* in the Kunsthistorisches Museum in Vienna, and *The Tempest* in the Accademia in Venice. Each is a magnificent painting, wonderfully and dramatically painted, but in none of the three have I ever been certain of what exactly was the painting's subject or Giorgione's ultimate intention in painting it.

The most magnificent and the most enigmatic of the three is *The Tempest*, and I should like to dwell for a moment on its singularity. In general it can be said that a profound work of art has a complex nature. It is almost as if the artist is forced into creation by a need to resolve some important conflict, to determine where the truth lies among divergent possibilities on a vital issue or issues. The work, therefore, is often a painting surface on which are superimposed what seem to be several incompatible views about the subject. This is clearly true of *The Tempest*.

At the bottom right is a mostly nude young woman nursing a child. It could be Venus, for the naked flesh is voluptuous. Yet the image suggests that of a Madonna and Child, so often presented in the painting of that time and place. Is the figure sacred or profane? Madonna or Venus? Or perhaps both at once? At the bottom left is a richly but rather casually dressed young man holding a staff. Is he yeoman or noble? Is he a page, a courtier, or a shepherd? Or perhaps all three at once? There is something meditative, peaceful, and tranquil in the foreground of Giorgione's painting; something dark, stormy, and menacing in the background. What then is the painting's real mood? Hopeful? Melancholy? Or both at once? The chief setting of the painting is pastoral: grass, sky, water, and somber, dark foliage. Yet architectural forms and city shapes haunt the background, as in so many of the works of Carpaccio and Bellini. What rules here, the sense of wild countryside or urban civility? Or both at once? And finally, what predominates, what we are left with, is a feeling of great wonder, great mystery. We are troubled by the enormous margin of ambiguity, the tremendous area of the problematic. Into what genre has this painting been cast? Is it basically a metaphor? An allegory? An anecdote? A fairy tale? Or all four at once?

We ask these troubling questions of Giorgione and his genius. But he does not answer us. He is silent. And it may even be that for the greatest artists what is most important, what they have expressed with the greatest intensity—that perception which their nature finds the truest—can never be completely obvious from the narrative form that they have imposed upon it.

3

The Creation of Art

What I am after, above all, is expression. Sometimes it has been conceded that I have a certain technical ability but that, my ambition being limited, I am unable to proceed beyond a purely visual satisfaction such as can be procured from the mere sight of a picture. But the purpose of a painter must not be conceived as separate from his pictorial means, and these pictorial means must be the more complete the deeper is his thought. I am unable to distinguish between the feeling I have for life and my way of expressing it.

—Henri Matisse

Art is inescapably pluralistic. It thrives on diversity and knows nothing of contradiction: all its opposite truths are equally true.

—Jacques Barzun

The creation of art is ultimately a mysterious thing. We all know that art is the skillful and imaginative creation of objects that interpret experience and, in so doing, produce a definite aesthetic response. John Dewey, for whom works of art function best when they "idealize qualities found in common experience,"[1] thus defines art as an act of expression and the artist as one with the power to clarify an initially turbid emotion into such an expressive act through both a capacity of individual vision and technical skill. Therefore he says: "What most of us lack in order to be artists is not the inceptive emotion, nor yet merely technical skill in execution. It is the capacity to work a vague idea and emotion over in terms of some definite medium."[2] Of course, it is just this "capacity" that is an awesome and mysterious thing.

Obviously an intelligent appreciation of the creative activity of any individual artist must proceed from many sources: psychological insight, biographical data, attention to historical situation and social context, knowledge of the philosophical and aesthetic premises of the time. But when all this is laboriously assembled, there remains something hopelessly recalcitrant about the creative act itself.

Of course we know a great deal about the procedures and the predilections of individual painters. Consider the obvious matter of chromatic preference. Van Gogh loved yellow, Rembrandt loved brown, El

Greco loved alizerin crimson. Chardin painted in the darker "shades," Bonnard in the lighter "tints," Fra Angelico in "tones" of purest blue, red, and purple. Monet, like Bonnard, worked in tints, especially lavender, turquoise, and powder blue, whereas Mondrian, with his black lines, would have only the unmixed primaries red, yellow, blue, and green.

Or consider the vocabulary of line: the clarity of Raphael, Holbein, and Ingres compared with the cloudiness of Rembrandt and the Impressionists, or, in our own time, the hard edges of Albers and Noland compared with the smudginess of de Kooning or the careless drips and blots of Jackson Pollock. Or the actual calligraphy of the brush strokes: the rough and virile ones of Frans Hals or van Gogh compared with the smooth and suave ones of Manet and Van Dyck, or the somewhat fussy dots of the Impressionists and Seurat. How did Cézanne get from the guttural speech of his early thick impasto to the whispers of those thin washes (almost like watercolors) of the very late paintings? Isn't some brushwork bold or nervous, careless or deliberate, slashing or exact? Or consider the matter of characteristic mood: the violent gesturing of Michelangelo and van Gogh, the good humor of Frans Hals, the angry and violent Soutine, the gloomy Munch, and the sullen Vlaminck; the serenity and sweetness of Raphael and Cima da Conegliano, the quiet peacefulness of Vermeer and de Hooch and Terborch.

Finally we turn to content. What do the painters talk about? What are the subjects of their conversations? The answer might be mostly religion and God, as with Giotto, Fra Angelico, and Giovanni Bellini; or important people, as with Clouet, Holbein, and Van Dyck; or fine clothes, interior decoration, and beautiful domestic objects, as with Terborch, Vermeer, and de Hooch. Or the subject may be the countryside: for example, that of East Anglia by Constable, of Aix-en-Provence by Cézanne, of Arles by van Gogh, or of Delft, Leyden, and the Hague by van Ruisdael, Hobbema, and van Goyen. Or it might be the city: Paris by Utrillo or Pissarro, Venice by Canaletto or Francisco Guardi, or Dresden and Vienna by Bernardo Bellotto. Or perhaps it might be beautiful nude women, as with Boucher, Ingres, Modigliani, and Titian as he grew old; or, as in the case of Rembrandt throughout his life, it might be old men, rabbis, solid citizens, or even the artists themselves.

Unfortunately, these insights into the creative characteristics of individual artists are not enough, and what we need is something more comprehensive, some more generalized statements that provide an account of the painterly imagination. These, I think, we possess in abundance. The function of painters, we may say, is the production of images saturated with feeling—images that are immensely sensitive to the reverberations of our emotional life. And the condition of this production is the subjective ability of artists to feel and enjoy the whole world as lived experience (what the German philosopher Wilhelm Dilthey called *erlebtes Erlebnis*). The creative work of artists always depends on the intensity of their lived experience. This, I think, is exactly what Matisse means when he says, "I am unable to distinguish between the feeling I have for life and my way of expressing it." In the same way, a satisfaction in perceiving what is presented belongs to the reception of every work of art, and the function of art is then, basically, one of awakening, strengthening, and preserving the sense of life in us—in whetting the appetite of our perception, in helping us to see. This has been wonderfully stated by the philosopher Henri Bergson in a little-known essay of his, "The Perception of Change," in which he says that for hundreds of years "there have been men whose function has been precisely to see and to make us see what we do not naturally perceive. They are the artists." And he goes on:

> What is the aim of art if not to show us, in nature and in the mind, outside of us and within us, things which do not explicitly strike our senses and our consciousness? The poet and the novelist who express a mood certainly do not create it out of nothing; they would not be understood by us if we did not observe within ourselves, up to a certain point, what they say about others. As they speak, shades of emotion and thought appear to us which might long since have been brought out in us but which remained invisible; just like the photographic image which has not yet been plunged into the bath where it will be revealed. The poet is this revealing agent. But nowhere is the function of the artist shown as clearly as in that art which gives the most important place to imitation, I mean painting. The great painters are men who possess a certain vision of things which has or will become the vision of all men.[3]

And, almost as if he had read this passage from Bergson, Germain Bazin, at one time curator-in-chief at the Louvre, in his valuable monograph *French Impressionist Paintings in the Louvre*, speaks as follows of Monet, the great Impressionist: "For a century painters had been tentatively looking for something which Monet was the first to find . . . the art of seeing. Other artists always looked through a screen of antecedent art forms: Corot through Poussin and Claude, Theodore Rousseau through Ruisdael and Hobbema. To see properly is the hardest thing. It requires genius. Most people see by way of their parents, their masters, or the social milieu in which they live. Sometimes on a youthful morning the scales fall from their eyes and the world appears, but only for a second, and then for the rest of their lives they only look through that sombre curtain of images to the conditioned universe behind. Only painters and poets really see."[4]

Thus far we have considered some generalizations, casually and unsystematically arrived at, about artistic creativity: that true artists produce images saturated with feeling; that all artists' creative work always depends upon the intensity of their lived experience; that the effect of creativity upon the viewers of art is to augment their powers of perception, finally to enable them to see. Fortunately there are also more rational, more empirical, more systematic ways of approaching this topic, and the first step in this direction is to recognize that there are two quite distinct aspects of creation, one of which, I think, could be called creation as *act*, the other creation as *message*. For information about the first we may turn to the philosophic tradition in the West, which, since the days of Plato and Aristotle, has been much concerned with this aesthetic problem. And for evidence about the second we may turn to the artists themselves, among whom there is enormous concern with, and disagreement about, the aims, ideals, methods, and mechanics of their own creativity.

The Act of Artistic Creation

Sometime around 1928, Henri Matisse arranged on an old green chest in his studio a platter, a crumpled tablecloth, a blue-and-white pitcher, a fruit knife, a glass two-thirds full of water, and five ripe peaches, and set to work. The result is a lovely and serene work entitled *Still Life with Green Buffet*, in which the luna green of the buffet, the sky blue of the wall behind, the white of the platter and the pitcher, and the light blue of the tablecloth form a rich color harmony against which stand out the five rosy peaches, four on the white platter, one to the side of the light blue tablecloth. The painting first passed into the hands of a private collector but now is in the Museum of Modern Art in Paris, where it has been a favorite of the many who visit that institution.

As Henri Matisse sits in his studio before the green chest and the five peaches and other objects he has arranged upon the chest with his blank canvas on the easel and his colors before him, what does he do? Of course he dips his brushes in the pigments and transfers these pigments to the canvas, and slowly that previously white surface becomes a colored surface that begins to resemble (but with some distortion and not in the least photographically) the arranged objects on the green chest. It is clear that he has begun with "an idea," and that

Henri Matisse, *Still Life on a Green Buffet*, 1928, National Museum of Modern Art, Paris.

idea has something to do with that green chest and that platter and those five peaches and the way he has arranged them. He plans to make a statement about those peaches and their relation to the pitcher and to the blue tablecloth, and that statement is about objects in space. But he also plans to make a statement about the blue of the wall and its relation to the blue of the tablecloth and the relation of these two blues to the white of the platter and the green of the chest and the relation of all this to the pink-orange of the peaches. Naturally, those two statements are to be made not with words but with pigment upon canvas. Thus, to the idea implicit in the arrangement of his subject must be added the materials—blank linen canvas stretched tight on a wooden frame, pigments, oil, and brushes made of pig bristles or horsehair.

Now, one tradition, which is as old as Aristotle, describes the creative process in these terms. It is an imposition of form upon matter, it is to begin with an idea and to express it in a medium. To the blank potentiality of the canvas Matisse gives an actuality of color and shapes that expresses his idea, and this process is equally true of the sculptor imposing form upon the unworked block of marble, the writer imposing form upon the possibilities of written language, the composer imposing structure upon the language of musical sound, or the filmmaker creating film form.

Naturally, the work of art has been pondered, thought about, brooded over before being made. Matisse found five peaches more to the purpose than three or six. Perhaps he spent some time in the arrangement of the subject to be painted, and surely he searched for the colors that would provide the proper contrast and the proper harmony. For the work was not to be a mere copy (and so no "imitation") of the objects he chose; it was to be a presentation of these objects in the light of his own imagination of their natures and ideal properties. All along, the emergence of the painting was controlled by the direction pointed to by his "idea."

The theory of artistic creation we are sketching recognizes that art as the imposition of form upon matter also requires technique, that is, great skill and mastery on the part of the artist. But although the artist must know how to use brushes upon the canvas or chisel upon the stone in order to produce a great and successful work, the "art" lies less in the skill than in the "idea" that the artist wishes to realize. Technical skill is in fact not the art at all, but the condition that removes the impediment of clumsiness, which might prevent the work of art from coming into being. True art lies in the mind and imagination of the artist. It is the artist's idea.

This view of artistic creation (which for convenience can be called the Aristotelian theory) is very intellectual. It makes the particular virtue of artists reside in their intellect, and it suggests that, since their control of their media is in the service of their intellectual vision, to lose that control is to condemn their art to mere sensuality and confusion. Of course, artists have feeling, and they must love what they are doing, but their love is a love of order, and the sort of order that they impose upon matter is the expression of a kind of artistic knowledge.

It is precisely this view of artistic creation that Plato denies. For him artists do not have knowledge, they have inspiration. When Matisse sits down before his easel and starts to feverishly paint the still life, which an unerring instinct has caused him to arrange in an instant, his mind is a blank, and it is his feelings that rush over him and into his work. He feels the reality of his pitcher and his peaches as if they were living things. They appeal to him with the immediacy of a child's appeal to its mother, and in his work he conveys to others, as a "medium" would, the way in which these objects "cry out." Sometimes he works smoothly and without error. On these days he has the sense that it is not he but some higher power that is guiding his hand, as if a creative force from outside were working through him and using him for its own inscrutable ends. On other days, the hand is clumsy, nothing seems to work, he throws down the brush with disgust, the green buffet seems ugly, and even the peaches, now over a week old, are unappetizing and slightly rotting fruit.

This is the modern version of Plato's theory of art as inspiration. Matisse creates because he is inspired and possessed. In making his work of art he is the loadstone or magnetic source of a feeling that, like a contagion, spreads later to the spectators of the work of art. And since this theory of "creation through emotion" is in opposition to the Aristotelian doctrine of an imposition of an idea upon matter, there is another consequence, too. It is that if you ask Matisse what he has been doing, or trying to do, he will be inarticulate. He will not really know. Or at any rate, he will only be able to point to what he has done and permit the art object to speak for itself. When Socrates asks Ion, the reciter of Homer, about his craft and about that very poet Homer, whom he interprets, Ion shows his intellectual weakness; he can make no critical judgments. And probably if Socrates would have been able to ask Homer himself, no answer, no aesthetic theory, would have been forthcoming.

Some years ago Sidney Janis produced a book of reproductions of paintings, *Abstract and Surrealist Art in America*. He asked the artists to explain their pictures, what they meant, what they thought they had been doing, and what their idea had been. One of the pictures was Georgia O'Keeffe's *White Barn, Canada*, a painting of a long, clean, rectangular barn with two large doors and a full, sloping roof. It was as serene and quiet a painting as Matisse's *Still Life with Green Buffet* and presented its object with the same candor and straightforwardness. Many of the artists spoke of their pictures pretentiously, complicatedly, and glibly. But O'Keeffe's comment about hers was as stark and unadorned as the painting itself. "*White Barn, Canada* is nothing but a simple statement about a simple thing. I can say nothing about it in words that I have not said with paint."[5] Aristotle would have been disappointed with O'Keeffe's answer. But Plato would have been satisfied, for it would have confirmed him in his belief that creation is not intellectual but inspired and that artists cannot really know whence their inspiration comes.

Artistic objects are the product of the encounter between artists and their materials, and, whether one thinks of works of art in an Aristotelian way, as the imposition of form upon matter, or Platonically, as the expression of emotion through inspiration, the artists' relation to them ceases when they are created and sent out into the world. The act of artistic creation ends with the work of art. And with the work of art the act of artistic enjoyment begins. Yet the two phases of the artistic process are not as separate as one might think, and if I here consider the latter, it is less for its own sake than for the inferential light it throws on the act of creation: I mean the role of structure and organization as itself a part of the creative idea.

When as visitors to the Museum of Modern Art in Paris we stand before Matisse's *Still Life with Green Buffet,* we are in the presence of a second encounter, this time between the spectator and the work of art. What is the nature of that encounter? And what is the effect upon the spectators? The very title that we have given to this encounter provides the first clue. It is an act of artistic enjoyment.

To say that the spectators "enjoy" the work is to say that the work gives pleasure, but it is not the same kind of pleasure as that which attaches to the satisfaction of the needs of the body. If Matisse's half-filled glass of water suddenly makes the spectators thirsty or if the five peaches make the viewers long to bite into their juicy flesh, then, whatever their enjoyment, it is not artistic enjoyment. For the pleasure that the peaches guarantee to the observers is a pleasure of the eyes and of the mind, a pleasure in roundness and solidity and in the contrast of orange-pink with blue and green, and the effect of this pleasure is not to arouse desire but to induce a certain calm and quietness in the observers.

There is obviously an important sensuous element in artistic enjoyment; for how else explain the appeal of forms and the lure of color? But it is a sensuous element abstracted and enjoyed for its own sake and not one that leads to anything beyond itself or to a bodily act. Thus, to the pleasure that initially defines the act of artistic enjoyment, we must now add two other characteristics: first, that it is a contemplative experience and, second, that it is an an experience that points to nothing beyond itself, in short, that it is not a means to an end, that it is self-justifying. Such an experience is not come by easily. It makes heavy demands on spectators. They cannot take it lightly, finish it quickly, or give it only surface attention. To say that the act of artistic enjoyment is by nature pleasurable, contemplative, and self-justifying implies something about the quality of the attention that makes it possible.

The demands the work of art makes on the spectator are, although different in kind, hardly less than those it has made on its creator. For

artistic appreciation and enjoyment require that the spectator both submit to the object and cooperate with it. This cooperation is intuitive.
It means that the viewer (in the language of Bergson) does not so much
"walk around" in the work of art as try to "enter into it." Knowledge
on this level does not come without effort. It is like our acquaintance
with persons, which begins superficially and may pass on to deep
knowledge and even to love. The achievement of real artistic enjoyment requires time, and it probably requires us to return to the object
again and again. But suppose that this condition is fulfilled and that
the spectator of *Still Life with Green Buffet* has an experience both
pleasurable and contemplative. In what does the pleasure consist? And
just what is it that is contemplated?

The Aristotelian theory of creation has an answer to both questions.
For if the act of creation is the imposition of form upon matter and if
the work of art is the expression or revelation of the artist's "idea,"
then the spectator's pleasure must be an intellectual pleasure derived
from recognizing the form that the artist has imposed upon the work
and from the spectator's contemplation of the "idea" revealed in it.

Attention to the formal structure of *Still Life with Green Buffet* shows
it to be both complicated in design and extremely skillful in execution.
The line formed by the front edge of the top of the buffet cuts the
picture almost in two, with all the crucial objects—platter, peaches,
pitcher, glass, and knife—placed on top of the buffet along the upper
half. Yet two devices unify the two disparate horizontal segments of
the picture plane. On the far left is a lavender vertical stretch of wood
or wall running the entire length of the picture, and to the right of it
the blue-checkered tablecloth both sits on the surface of the buffet and
hangs over its edge far down into the bottom half of the picture.

But most remarkable of all is the way Matisse has given the objects
on the buffet a perfect and almost symmetrical "Z" formation, the
tablecloth being the downward vertical on the left, the platter and its
extension in the knife forming a downward diagonal thrust from upper
left to lower right, and the pitcher and glass forming an upper thrust
on the far right, completing the nearly perfect "Z" figure. We know
almost intuitively that the diagonal platter containing the four peaches,
placed almost in the exact center of the upper horizontal of the picture,
is the focus of Matisse's loving attention, his idea; but even if we did
not, one other painterly persuasion would have forced our attention
to this fact. The slightly open doors of the buffet are separated by a
broad vertical jet-black line, and this line is like an arrow forcing our
gaze immediately to the platter of peaches just above it. Matisse, the
wise and sophisticated master of painterly structure, has manipulated

our perceptual responses like the magician he is. Content is important, but it is form and structure that give a subject its unity and its life. There is nothing more difficult to achieve than a notable still life, for the objects are "dead," and all too often they confront one another in mute incongruity. It is to Matisse's great skill with structure that the success of this work is due; he has made of his miscellaneous items not a collection but a "family" of objects. And it is the appreciation of this formal element that provides the true artistic enjoyment. Thus, even from the standpoint of aesthetic reception we gain further appreciative insight into the creative process of the artist.

The two chief philosophic accounts of artistic creation that the Greeks provided, the Aristotelian concept of the imposition of form upon matter as having a distinctly intellectual source and the Platonic doctrine of inspiration under the force and direction of emotion, have both appeared in the rationalizations and the practices of Western artists, but not as equal influences. The Aristotelian view has, I think, become the established doctrine, with the Platonic position reemerging only at selected moments during the nineteenth and twentieth centuries. In fact the doctrine of artistic creativity as the imposition of form upon matter might be termed the "classic" position, while art as inspiration remains the contention of incurable romantics.

Jacques Maritain, whose *Art and Scholasticism* is perhaps the best exposition of the Aristotelian view we have, states it persuasively. "The work of art has been thought before being made, it has been kneaded and prepared, formed, brooded over, ripened in a mind before passing into matter. And in matter it will always retain the color and savor of the spirit. Its *formal* element, what constitutes it in its species and makes it what it is, is its being ruled by the intellect. If this formal element diminishes ever so little, to the same extent the reality of art vanishes. The *work to be made* is only the matter of art, its form is *undeviating reason.*"[6]

This may seem like a fanatically intellectualist approach to art, but its underlying rationale is a principle equally applicable to painting, to sculpture, to the theater, and to film, namely, that rehearsal precedes performance, and its Platonic opposite is a warrant of artistic improvisation: its motto is pure spontaneity is all. This formulation of the classic Aristotelian stance has the merit of giving us even greater insight into the act of painterly creation, for it establishes the role of drawing as the intermediate step between the first appearance of form as an act within the mind and the final production of the actually painted work of art. Western painters from the early Renaissance have made "drawings," "cartoons," or "sketches" of the prospective finished products they have in mind, and these sketches can be endlessly amended and reworked as a kind of artist's experimental laboratory for the ultimate design of the painting. These sketches or series of sketches may not only possess aesthetic merit in themselves but may also provide invaluable evidence to the aesthetic psychologist or art historian of the process of creation in the individual case. Thus we have Carpaccio's great sketches for *The Triumph of St. George* and *The Funeral of St. Jerome,* both in the Scuola di San Giorgio degli Schiavoni in Venice, Raphael's for *The Marriage of the Virgin* in the Brera in Milan, and Veronese's for *The Marriage at Cana* in the Uffizi in Florence. The production and use of sketches was standard practice for indoor creation—for what can rightfully be termed "studio art"—and this procedure lasted from the early Renaissance in Sienna and Florence and Venice well into the nineteenth century when the school of French Impressionism was born.

Impressionism marked the first great intrusion of the Platonic theory of artistic creation into Western art history, not because the Impressionists had read Plato or were conscious Platonists, but simply because they were romantic devotees of nature in the tradition of Rousseau and Wordsworth, passionate lovers of natural landscape who deserted their studios for vast and lengthy excursions into the countryside, where they could paint on the spot—*en plein air*—so as to catch every shadow cast by moving clouds, every glint and sparkle of the brilliant sun. Here Nature herself changes and improvises at every moment; artists must adjust their own spontaneity to match that of Nature. Perhaps the truest representation or "mirror" of nature becomes less instantaneous than "serial," like Monet's three great series *Haystacks in Normandy, Mornings on the Seine,* or *The Façade of Rouen Cathedral.*

Drawing and sketching become superfluous and redundant when one brings one's easel, brushes, and canvas to the sites themselves, and this the Impressionists characteristically do. Monet haunts the English Channel, where he reproduces *Etretat, The Harbor of Le Havre, The Hôtel at Trouville, The Jetty at Honfleur,* and *The Beach at Saint-Addresse.* Cézanne spent his entire later life painting in the vicinity of his native Aix-en-Provence, so that some of us know the Jas de Bouffan, Gardanne, the Château Noir, the mill at Pontoise, the Château Thollonet, the quarry Bibémus, and the Mont St. Victoire better than we know the topography of our own neighborhood.

One thing in all this has not yet been remarked: the devotion, the infinite dedication, and the overwhelming satisfaction that come to the artist through the creative activity itself. Maritain knew these despite the extreme intellectualism of the theory of creation he espouses: "The sphere of Making is the sphere of Art, in the most universal sense of this word. . . . This work is everything for Art; there is for Art but one law—the exigencies and the good of the work. Hence the tyrannical and absorbing power of Art, and also its astonishing power of soothing; it delivers one from the human; it establishes the *artifex*—artist or artisan—in a world apart, closed, limited, absolute, in which he puts the energy and intelligence of his manhood at the service of a thing which he makes. This is true of all art; the ennui of living and willing ceases at the door of every workshop."[7]

It also ceases, as any Impressionist painter would tell us, on the road or on the slope or in the fields in hot pursuit of natural "truth." Van Gogh, as well as Monet and Cézanne, had things to tell us about the French countryside around Arles and Auvers-sur-Oise and Saint-Rémy. There is one particularly wonderful landscape in the Van Gogh Museum in Amsterdam, *View of Arles with Irises in the Foreground,* a massive statement in chromatic layers: the city with a sky of thick blue-green impasto in the background, then a row of trees with bright green trunks, then a massive layer of bright yellow buttercups, and finally at the bottom a magnificent row of luna green and dark blue irises. The chromatic splendor of the scene was so overwhelming that van Gogh wrote to his brother Theo with a descriptive tone at once of adoration and wonderment. "The town is surrounded by immense meadows all abloom with countless buttercups—a sea of yellow—in the foreground these meadows are divided by a ditch full of violet irises. They were mowing the grass while I was painting, so it is only a study and not the finished picture that I had intended to do. But what a subject, hein! That sea of yellow with a band of violet irises, and in the background that coquettish little town of the pretty women!"[8]

I have been considering the rebirth of the Platonic theory of artistic creation in the procedures of the greatest painters of the nineteenth century: Monet, Cézanne, and van Gogh. But I have tried to make it clear that their commitment was not ideological but rather a logical consequence of their romantic attachment to nature, their abandonment of the studio for the countryside in the search for that immediacy of perception that made sketching superfluous and permitted the most intimate contact with light, weather, color, and the continuous fluctuation of natural appearances.

But this in turn has been followed in our own time by an espousal of the Platonic theory that is intensely ideological: I take as one example the articulated expression of the aesthetic philosophy of the school of Abstract Expressionism, of which Willem de Kooning, Jackson Pollock,

and Franz Kline were perhaps the most eminent members. This articulated expression was classically formulated by Harold Rosenberg in
a now-famous article published in the December 1952 issue of *Art
News* entitled "The American Action Painters."

> At a certain moment the canvas began to appear to one American painter
> after another as an arena in which to act—rather than as a space in which
> to reproduce, re-design, analyze, or "express" an object, actual or imag-
> ined. What was to go on the canvas was not a picture but an event....
> The painter no longer approached his easel with an image in his mind;
> he went up to it with material in his hand to do something to that other
> piece of material in front of him. The image would be the result of this
> encounter.... To the painter ... [what comes out] *must* be a surprise.
> In this mood there is no point to an act if you already know what it
> contains.... "B—— is not modern," one of the leaders of this mode said
> to me. "He works from sketches. That makes him Renaissance." Here
> the principle, and the difference from the old painting, is made into a
> formula. A sketch is the preliminary form of an image the *mind* is trying
> to grasp. To work from sketches arouses the suspicion that the artist still
> regards the canvas as a place where the mind records its contents—rather
> than itself the "mind" through which the painter thinks by changing a
> surface with paint.[9]

The whole idea here is that painting as "the imposition of form upon
matter" has been supplanted by the histrionic concept of "gesturing
with materials." This, as many critics immediately saw, is to turn
"painting" into "theater."

According to this philosophy of "painting as encounter," painters
do not know in advance what they are about to produce. They approach
the blank canvas and begin indiscriminately to slap on the pigment
until, to their vast surprise, forms and a structure begin to make themselves manifest and, finally and miraculously, a painting emerges—
innocent, dramatic, and unpremeditated—from this encounter. De
Kooning, for example, initially confronts his canvas with a certain sim-
ple-minded Dutch perplexity before things explosively begin to happen. Jackson Pollock nails his canvas to the floor and watches anxiously
for omens among the streaks and blots and puddles as he continues
to drip and pour. Franz Kline attacks with violence, imposing his slashing, Chinese-calligraphic, coal-black strokes, not crampedly with the
wrist as the Impressionists did when they gently affixed their color
dots, but athletically, exuberantly, with the whole arm, like some
swashbuckling d'Artagnan of the paintbrush. In each of these three
cases, our Abstract Expressionist artists do not move discreetly with
the paint so much as they seem to swagger with it.

The Message of Artistic Creation

In the previous section I have tried to consider the creation of art with a few concrete instances as well as in the light of philosophic theory—namely, the Aristotelian theory of the imposition of form upon matter and the Platonic theory of emotional inspiration—the two that have dominated the thinking and the practices of artists in the West. But now I should like to turn to something much more ideological and problematic: that is, the concepts artists themselves have about the aims, ideals, methods, and mechanics of their own creativity. Here we are in the realm of complete pluralism, disagreement, and confusion, which can only be dealt with through such a principle of tolerance as the one Jacques Barzun expressed in the second epigraph heading this chapter: "Art is inescapably pluralistic. It thrives on diversity and knows nothing of contradiction: all its opposite truths are equally true."[10] The enormous quantity and diversity of the material here makes any exhaustive treatment impossible, but I wish to concentrate on a very small number of selected areas to indicate just a few other dimensions of the problem of creation in the art of painting.

About twenty-five or thirty years ago Josef Albers embarked upon an obsessive series of paintings that he somewhat misleadingly titled *Homage to the Square*. The title was misleading because Albers was not really interested in the square as a structural masterpiece. He had chosen it as a neutral and easily repeatable figure to support the experiments in color contrasts and color harmonies that were indeed the vital object of his concern. He should have titled his series of paintings *Homage to the Colors within the Square*.

The point is not of crucial importance, for the entrance of the square into modern art as a matter of ideological concern had already occurred just before and during the First World War. Malevich's "Suprematist" paintings, which feature the square, originated in 1913. And already in 1917 Theo van Doesburg and Piet Mondrian, joint editors of the art magazine *De Stijl*, were intensely propagandizing the centrality of the square as a structural element for painting. Van Doesburg proclaimed histrionically that "the quadrangle is the token of a new humanity. The square is to us what the cross was to the early Christians."[11] It is difficult to believe that there ever existed such foolish fanaticism among painters. Mondrian is of the same school, but somewhat more intelligible and more moderate. His attack on the forms of nature is at least better argued. "The new plastic idea cannot, therefore take the form of a natural or concrete representation, although the latter does always indicate the universal to a degree, or at least conceals it within. This new plastic idea will ignore the particulars of appearance, that is to say, natural form and color. On the contrary, it should find its expression in the abstraction of form and color, that is to say, in the straight line and the clearly defined primary color."[12]

Van Doesburg's espousal of the square, as Mondrian's of the straight line, already foreshadows the modern artist's dilemma of the conflicting claims on painterly commitment made by abstraction as opposed to representation, a conflict already partly mirrored in the more philosophical quarrel between the organic and the mechanistic approach to the world. Many years later Mondrian's Euclidian prejudices are to receive their angry response in the speculations of the talented Austrian painter Friedensreich Hundertwasser. "The straight line," says Hundertwasser, "is a heathen, immoral thing. The straight line is a reproductive and not a creative line. Neither God nor the spirit of Humanity resides in it." And then to assert his own counterclaim he states, "I regard the spiral as a symbol of life. I believe the spiral belongs where matter ceases to be such and begins to be a living thing. . . . My spiral is subject to vegetative growth."[13]

It is certainly true that Hundertwasser has the whole of Chinese culture on his side. Lin Yutang, in a fascinating book written over half a century ago, *My Country and My People,* made this abundantly clear. "We see everywhere in Chinese architecture," he says, "an effort to seek relief from straight lines through some form of irregularity suggestive of animal and plant forms."[14] And he instanced the sagging roof, probably the most distinctive and obvious characteristic of Chinese architecture; the round bridge, which harmonizes with nature because it is in a curve; and the pagoda, which tries to catch and incorporate the rhythm of nature and imitate its irregularity. And he even anticipates Hundertwasser's anger, referring to "our love for rhythmic or wavy or broken lines and our hatred of straight, dead ones."[15]

Hundertwasser's Chinese theory is, of course, only the philosophical expression of his painterly practice. And his marvelous landscapes, often with human faces embedded in them, are great undulating fields of paint, without a single straight line anywhere to be seen and simply appealing to us as some vast contour map of the organic imagination. It is impossible to imagine paintings more dissimilar, more "contradictory," than, say, Mondrian's *Composition in White, Red, and Blue* of 1933 and Hundertwasser's *Spiral Kopf* of 1965. Thus, theoretical opposition between the most Spartan means—namely, the straight versus the spiral or undulating line—becomes two "messages" of painterly creativity. Surely Mondrian and Hundertwasser present two completely opposite creative options, and the profound dissimilarity in their actual creativity mirrors and expresses their equally profound ideological differences. And so we are finally at the very center of the Barzun paradox. Mondrian's truth and Hundertwasser's truth are inescapable contradictories, and yet both of these opposite truths, I think we may say, are equally true.

The contrast between the straight and the curved line is an opposition at the level of the most elementary technical means. A similar opposition is to be found at the level of the source of creative inspiration. In this chapter we have already had some experience of the Impressionist moment in France in the late nineteenth century, when painters like Monet, Renoir, Pissarro, and Sisley—all comrades at the Café Guerbois in Paris—forsook their studios in the capital city and flocked to Normandy, the English Channel, Provence, or the Midi to glory in the opulent tints and tones of the French countryside. Landscapists all, it was Monet who was their ruling prince. Unfortunately, this noble and gifted artist was all but inarticulate, and so it is rather to the voluminous letter writer Cézanne that we must turn for an articulation of the special source of inspiration to which this entire school paid homage. Of course, it is to Nature.

First, in a letter to Zola, Cézanne both describes the outdoor rationale and clearly associates it with nature as the creative source of artistic inspiration. "But you know all pictures painted inside, in the studio, will never be as good as the things done outside. When out-of-door scenes are represented, the contrasts between the figures and the ground are astounding and the landscape is magnificent. I see some superb things and I shall have to make up my mind only to do things out-of-doors. . . . I feel sure that all the pictures by the old masters representing things out-of-doors have only been done hesitatingly, for they do not seem to me to have the true and above all the original aspect lent by nature."[16] Further letters of the much later period of Cézanne's life bristle with a similar sentiment. "Couture used to say to his pupils: 'Keep good company, that is: Go to the Louvre. But after having seen the great masters who repose there, we must hasten out and by contact with nature revive in us the instincts and sensations of art that dwell within us.'" "The strong experience of nature—and assuredly I have it—is the necessary basis for all conception of art" (p. 18). "The Louvre is a good book to consult but it must only be an intermediary. The real and immense study that must be taken up is the manifold picture of nature" (p. 21).

There can be no question of Cézanne's turning to nature for sustained creative inspiration. And to a considerable extent this was also the resource for his Impressionist associates, including even that Postimpressionist van Gogh. Yet already in van Gogh doubts begin to arise, and an alternative source begins to surface—I mean the imagination. "The imagination," van Gogh wrote to Emile Bernard in April 1888, "is certainly a faculty which we must develop, one which alone can lead us to the creation of a more exalting and consoling nature than the single brief glance at reality—which in our sight is ever changing, passing like a flash of lightning—can let us perceive" (p. 31). Van Gogh's reference to the imagination was prophetic, because toward the end of the nineteenth century a new movement arose that rejected the naturalistic conception of art (Cézanne's) that had dominated the preceding generation. Artists now turned away from the external world and looked inward to their own feelings and imaginations as a new source of creative inspiration. Of course this new movement was at first literary rather than artistic: it began with the Symbolists—poets like Verlaine, Mallarmé, and Baudelaire—but it soon spread to the more iconoclastic painters also. In 1908 Edvard Munch was saying: "A work of art can come only from the interior of man" (p. 114), and a year or so later, Odilon Redon was also proclaiming that "there is a method of drawing which the imagination has liberated from those bothersome worries presented by the details of the exterior world" (p. 118).

Cézanne or Munch and Redon? The creative self looking outward to nature or inward to the imagination? Here again, in the matter of creative inspiration, as before in the case of the straight line versus the curve, we are in the presence of contradiction, of the copresence of two opposite truths. And how could anyone doubt that both are equally true? How can an artist definitively choose between the claims of nature and of the imagination? It would be like asking a philosopher to make a choice between the Realism of Aristotle and the Idealism of Kant.

To this brief consideration of two instances of conflicting "creative messages" I must add one sociological footnote. What begins in the nineteenth century in an atmosphere of aesthetic individualism culminates in the twentieth in an atmosphere of dogmatic aesthetic organization. It has in the modern world become artistically fashionable for painters to form themselves into a series of groups, sects, schools, movements, or parties, each making its passionate proclamation about aims, methods, and theories—about "what painting ought to be." Ours is the age of the aesthetic message, the age of aesthetic dogma, and its characteristic mode of expression is the painter's manifesto. This exercise in publicity began its classic operation in France in the first four decades of the present century with Guillaume Apollinaire's *The Cubist Painters*[17] of 1913 and André Breton's *What Is Surrealism?*[18] of

1936, each one, like the examples we have instanced above, announcing an absolutely contradictory approach.

In these manifestos the respective cliques of avant-garde painters exercised excellent literary judgment, for they entrusted their opposite ideological messages not to other artists, but to skillful avant-garde poets. For the Cubists, Apollinaire stressed structure, linear division, mechanism, formalism, and purity, all of which were congruent with the efforts of their academic contemporaries the Cambridge Logicians and with the great *Principia Mathematica* of Russell and Whitehead. For the Surrealists, on the contrary, Breton devoted his attention to the more interior models of dreams, fantasies, and other creations of the imaginative unconscious—and all of *his* debts of gratitude were, of course, owed to the great Viennese physician Sigmund Freud. With the publications of Breton's and Apollinaire's works, the floodgates were opened, and we began to have manifestos devoted to Dada, Neoplasticism, Futurism, Constructivism, Scuola Metafisica, and all the rest, each propounding its own eccentric view concerning the creation and meaning of art. The multiplicity and the sense of intellectual bonding here are astonishing, and, as can also be said, they stand in striking contrast to the individualism of the Italian Renaissance, where the great draftsmen of Florence—Raphael, Leonardo, and Michelangelo; the great colorists of Venice—Carpaccio, Giovanni Bellini, and Veronese; and the great religious painters of Sienna—Duccio, Simone Martini, and Bernardo Daddi, wrote no manifestos, produced no propaganda, and walked their separate ways with confidence, with dignity, and with pride.

I began the writing of this chapter with the statement that the creation of art is ultimately a mysterious thing, and now at its conclusion, after many pages of exploration, cultural history, and philosophic pursuit, the perplexity and the wonder still remain, and I am still of the same opinion. Only, perhaps some little understanding has been added, some grasp of the immensity of the task of coming to grips with the problem, some fleeting insight into the miracle of the creative event.

4

The Tradition of Art:
Art History

It is the function of all art to give us some perception of an order
in life, by imposing order upon it.

Tradition . . . cannot be inherited, and if you want it you must
obtain it by great labor. It involves, in the first place, the historical
sense. . . and the historical sense involves a perception, not only of
the pastness of the past, but of its presence.

—T. S. Eliot

In a description of the disciplines associated with discipline-based
art education, a discussion of artistic creation necessarily comes first.
We must know something about the conditions and modes of the orig-
ination of works of art before we can establish an order of art (art
history), make reasoned judgments of value (art criticism), and reflect
philosophically on art (aesthetics). Accordingly, the last chapter was
devoted to the creation of art. This chapter is about the history of art,
which consists of the study and consideration of works of art under
the aspects of time, tradition, and style. In particular, the essential
purpose of art history is the establishment and consolidation of the
tradition of art. However, as Eliot says, the historical sense involves a
perception not only of the "pastness" of the past, but also of the continuing importance and relevance of the past for us here and now, its
"presence." When art history nurtures such a dual awareness of the
past it contributes significantly to what the report on arts education
Toward Civilization called the first objective of arts education—"to give
our young people a sense of civilization." Everything said in this chapter is also meant to promote this educational end.

Before proceeding, however, we must acknowledge an ambiguity
inherent in the term "art history." In his highly influential *History of
Art*, H. W. Janson points out that the expression "refers both to the
events that *make* the history of art, and to the scholarly discipline that
deals with these events."[1] The first sense refers to the study of the
origin of works of art and the circumstances of their creation. The

second sense refers to the working assumptions, basic ideas, and methods of art-historical investigation. Janson does not distinguish sharply between these two senses, nor does he discuss the effects of different presuppositions and procedures on the nature of art-historical research. Nevertheless, in each of the senses mentioned, art history can itself become the object of inquiry and would then be called either critical art history or the historiography of art history.[2]

We should also distinguish between two dimensions of art-historical study. One is vertical, or serial and sequential, and has temporal continuity as its essence. This dimension (called diachronic) is evident in chronologies or surveys of artistic phenomena from the past up to the present. The second dimension is horizontal and extends itself over phenomena that coexist within a given time frame. This dimension (called synchronic) is typified in cross-sectional or "epochal" studies in which all the arts of a period are examined as they sustain reciprocal relations and influences with the social, economic, political, and religious forces of the time. At this point art history merges with cultural history. This chapter will explore both kinds of study as well as some other types that do not fall clearly into either category.

But first a cautionary word. In framing a philosophy of discipline-based art education one must avoid assuming that theoretical distinctions within the discipline of art history inevitably translate into prescriptions for teaching art history in a program of general education in the schools. "General education" implies schooling for nonspecialists and considers students not as prospective scholars or disciplinary specialists but as young persons in need of general acquaintance with the various segments of what Ernst Cassirer in his classic *An Essay on Man* called "the circle of humanity."[3] This circle is composed not only of such basic forms of human culture as myth, language, history, religion, and science but also the symbolic cultural expression we call art.

Nor is art history as it is taught in the schools directly affected by the scholarly training and research interests of art historians. Having learned how to conduct varieties of art-historical research (some examples of which will be described later in this chapter), art historians expend their energies on structuring and consolidating art-historical events and on enlarging the body of art-historical knowledge. This is not to say that art historians never address nonspecialist audiences; the major textbooks on the history of art are obvious instances of their having done so. But as recent studies of art historians at work clearly indicate, art historians experience difficulty in finding either the time or financial support for enlightening the general public. Perhaps this

difficulty helps to explain the scarcity of articles written by art historians on the teaching of their subject to young persons. Art history,
then, is discussed here primarily for the benefit of those who teach
general art education in the schools. Rarely will these teachers be expected to undertake art-historical inquiry themselves or to reflect
deeply and systematically on art history's theoretical presuppositions.
They do, however, need to know enough about the discipline to feel
secure in their teaching and to be able to structure it effectively for
conveying a sense of art history to the young.

To pull all this together: we will be concerned in this chapter with
four kinds of art-historical study: (1) art history as the imposition of a
historical order on works of art, or the establishment of art's genealogy
and chronology; (2) art history as the study of works of art that coexist
in a particular cultural situation; (3) art history as a self-reflective discipline that meditates on its basic purposes and methods; and (4) art
history as a range of discrete studies that do not fall into any clear
category. To illustrate these kinds of art-historical scholarship I will
first discuss two interesting studies of art history textbooks that reveal
some different ways in which art historians impose chronological order
on art and present its major historical monuments. Second, I will briefly
describe three examples of art-historical research that introduce some
of the typical problems and puzzles confronting art historians. And
third, I will illuminate the nature of art history as a self-reflective
discipline by examining the ideas of Erwin Panofsky, one of the most
distinguished art historians of our time. Once prospective teachers of
art in the schools understand the different senses, directions, and emphases of art history, they will have a better notion not only of what
art history contributes to a general or liberal education but also of what
kind of information about art history to convey to young students.
More will be said about the teaching of art in chapter 7.

Art History as the Survey of Art

The standard art history survey text represents conventional thinking about the nature of art history. The order imposed on works of art
constitutes the chronology or main tradition of art, and the way the
works of the tradition are discussed reflects the ideas and beliefs of
the art-historical thinking of the day. We do well then to begin with
an examination of some texts that have enjoyed the benefit of several
editions to discover what they can tell us about our subject.

In "Art and the Text that Accompanies It," a detailed, systematic,
and comprehensive analysis of basic art history survey texts suitable

for use by high-school students, G. Stephen Vickers, himself an art historian who has contributed to art history texts for adolescents, performs three tasks.[4] He first analyzes descriptions of artworks in order to discover what they reveal about their authors' point of view; he next categorizes the types of information supplied by textbook writers; and last, he compiles a list of three hundred key works suitable for study at the secondary school level. I will concentrate on the first two tasks, beginning with the second one.

After explaining the factors responsible for the emergence of the introductory survey text—the explosion of interest in the creation and appreciation of art, the dramatic expansion of the art world, and the consequent desire for narrowing the gulf between artworks and their new audience—Vickers identifies in general terms the types of information provided by survey texts: (1) external factual information, which consists of such things as the date and title of a work, the name of its artist, its dimensions, theme, and the circumstances of its creation; (2) internal descriptive information, which consists essentially of an inventory of what can actually be found in a work (a description, as it were, of a work's components); (3) formal analysis, which consists of information about a work's web of relations, including color and spatial relationships; and (4) contextual relations, which relate artists' choices to historical circumstances (and which is actually external information of a more complicated kind).

The proportions of the internal, external, formal, and contextual types of information that art history survey texts contain vary according to a writer's purposes and disposition. Discussion of artworks generally moves from description to analysis to interpretation, although this sequence is not always adhered to. Evaluation of artworks does not always enter explicitly into art-historical writing and is sometimes claimed to be the special task of art critics. But a value-free art history is not possible, and, in any case, it would be incompatible with the reasons so many art historians give for writing about art: to facilitate the appreciation of art and to improve aesthetic judgment in the general population. Whether self-consciously or not, art historians express value preferences in their selection of works for study and discussion, in their choice of which relationships within and among works of art they find important, and in their use of language. Still, there is the matter of emphasis: where one writer will openly acknowledge admiration for an artwork, another will try to hew to straightforward description and exposition, however difficult it is to keep evaluative nuances from coloring exposition.

The first major survey text to constitute an improvement over previous art history guides and manuals was Helen Gardner's *Art through the Ages,* first published in 1926 and now in its eighth edition, revised by different authors.[5] In the early editions, especially the third one, Gardner tends first to provide brief accounts of the social, political, and spiritual forces of an era and then to follow with analyses of a few artworks that epitomize the period. The discussion next goes on to a summary of significant artistic developments and their representative works. The early editions of Gardner's book, however, can be faulted for their insufficient integration of external and internal information.

This failure is due to Gardner's decided inclination toward formal visual analysis, an emphasis reflecting the strong influence of Roger Fry, the great English critic. Fry's influence also helps to explain Gardner's reliance on diagrams to reveal the structure of an artwork, a didactic exercise less favored by textbook authors today. One example of Gardner's bent for visual analysis is her description of J.-B.-Siméon Chardin's *Saying Grace.* Having told us that Chardin was a somewhat isolated artist who drew his subjects from social strata different from those preferred by other painters of his time, Gardner writes:

> Not only in theme but in attitude toward form Chardin seemed to continue the tradition of the Le Nain brothers and the "Little Dutchmen" of the seventeenth century. Sometimes it is the interior of the French middle-class home, which Chardin, like the Dutch painters, saw as raw material with pictorial possibilities. The sober dusk of the small room provided an opportunity so to modulate the light that it would create a space in which to place figures that catch the high light from an open door, and form a cylindrical mass cut across by repeated diagonals. The warm, vibrating brown ground modulates the rose, green and yellow of the striped upholstery and garments; a contrasting note is the cool gray-blue of large mass in the apron balanced by smaller areas in the details. The colors are not used with the light sparkling dash of Watteau but with a sober deliberation.[6]

Gardner describes a Chardin still life in similar fashion, saying that in works like these "objects are built into an organization the unity and harmony of which have power of their own quite separate from the representational content."[7] Characteristically, Gardner says little about a work's date, scale, subject, or significance—for instance, in the case of *Saying Grace* about the values dominating middle-class life and its ideal of moderation. This is because Gardner tended to favor internal over external information and to cast a brighter light on a work's from and style than on its period, context, audience, and place in an unfolding historical tradition.

A dramatically different approach is found in E. H. Gombrich's extremely popular *The Story of Art* (now in its thirteenth edition).[8] A distinguished art historian with a strong interest in art's representational and symbolic meaning, Gombrich tends to pay more attention to a work's import and expressiveness than to its form; instead of separating discussions of historical factors from internal descriptions of works, he closely integrates the two. What attracts him is a work's mood and story, which is conveyed to readers by a persuasive description. In contrast to Gardner's somewhat more detached method, we are invited to a more personal and intimate relation to an artwork. Part of the appeal of Gombrich's style is due to the fact that *The Story of Art* was originally written for British adolescents. Gombrich, then, deemphasizes formal analysis and lays greater stress on subject matter and context in a manner that is typical of European writers about art.

The differences between Gombrich and Gardner are clearly brought out in Gombrich's description of Chardin's *Saying Grace*. We are reminded of the tendency of some of the painters of Chardin's time to select episodes from everyday life that could be spun into a story and embodied appealingly in a painting. Hence *Saying Grace* shows us "a simple room with a woman setting dinner on the table and asking two children to say grace." Chardin liked such quiet glimpses of ordinary life and probably felt that he was preserving the poetry of domestic scenes in a manner reminiscent of Vermeer; Chardin, for example, studiously avoided striking effects and pointed allusions. "Even his color is calm and restrained," writes Gombrich, "and by comparison with the scintillating paintings of Watteau, his works may seem to lack brilliance. But if we study them in the original, we soon discover in them an unobtrusive mastery in the subtle gradation of tones and the seemingly artless arrangement of the scene, that makes him one of the most lovable painters of the eighteenth century."[9] Through a set of intimate and casual impressions, then, Gombrich establishes the mood of a painting and an attitude toward it that other viewers may share. He does not discuss the historical setting separately but introduces it directly into the picture via a description of the work's ambiance and story. An explanation of the significant differences between Gardner and Gombrich, then, must take into account not only the passage of time and the waning of Fry's aesthetics but also the national origins of the two writers.[10]

Perhaps it is worth noting that Gombrich's disinclination to emphasize a work's cultural context and position in the sequence of significant artistic events probably stems from his wariness about Hegelian holism. In the philosophy of culture "Hegelian holism" denotes the tendency to see artworks as the inevitable expressions of the mind, soul, and spirit of an age. Conceptions of art history founded on this view are sometimes referred to as *Geistesgeschichte* (history of ideas), which implies the notion of a *Zeitgeist* (spirit of a time). Despite their differences, however, Gardner, Gombrich, and other writers of art history texts generally share the conviction that works of outstanding artistic merit are the major links in the chain of tradition extending from the past to the present. Such works, writes Vickers, "are indispensable data for the construction of a history of art and form part of the artistic patrimony of our civilization."[11] Some contemporary theorists of art history find the notion of artistic patrimony too restrictive and oppressive, but it would be foolish to doubt that masterpieces of art have played, and continue to play, a major role in the establishment and study of the tradition of art.

It was this need for a basic list of artistic exemplars suitable for use in the writing of art history texts that prompted H. W. Janson to select one thousand artworks for his *Key Monuments in the History of Art.*[12] Janson's criteria for admitting a work to the list were its influence on the direction of art, its uniqueness as to kind, and its representativeness of general trends observable within an artistic culture. The list is flexible enough to accommodate a variety of art histories—chronological, topical, biographical, national, and by media.

Since the approaches of different art historians are most easily compared when each discusses the same artist, I quote Janson's *History of Art* on yet another painting by Chardin, *Kitchen Still Life:*

> Chardin can be called Rococo only with reservations. The "Rubenists" had cleared the way for a new interest in the Dutch masters as well, and Chardin is the finest painter of still life and genre in this trend. . . . His still lifes usually reflect the same modest environment, eschewing the "object appeal" of their Dutch predecessors. In *[Kitchen Still Life]* . . . we see only the common objects that belong in any kitchen: . . . But how important they seem, each so firmly placed in relation to the rest, each so worthy of the artist's—and our—scrutiny! Despite his concern with formal problems, evident in the beautifully balanced design, Chardin treats these objects with a respect close to reverence. Beyond their shape, colors, and textures, they are to him symbols of the life of the common man. In spirit, if not in subject matter Chardin is more akin to Louis le Nain and Sanchez Cotan than to any Dutch painter.[13]

In marked contrast to the prominence of formal analysis in Gardner's later writing, we find only a hint of it in Janson's descriptions, followed quickly by a shift to interpretation. Also apparent is a flair for detecting historical relations and analogies of the kind not conspicuous in the

Gardner and Gombrich texts. Perhaps it might be said that the larger and improved reproductions in the subsequent editions of *History of Art* allow Janson to let the images do as much of the communicating as possible while his cool and reasonable yet nonetheless humane and personal narrative provides necessary contextual information.

But the central feature of Janson's writing is its emphasis on the historical antecedents of artworks. Consider, for example, the reference in Janson's introduction to *Luncheon on the Grass* by the nineteenth-century painter Edouard Manet, the predecessors of which include a Renaissance engraving and a Roman sarcophagus. "Manet, Raphael, and the Roman river gods form three links in a chain of relationships that arises somewhere out of the dim and distant past and continues into the future." What is more, "the sum total of these chains makes a web in which every work of art occupies its own specific place and which we call *tradition*." Finally, "whether we are aware of it or not, tradition is the framework within which we inevitably form our opinions of works of art and assess their degree of originality."[14] Hence the title of this chapter, "The Tradition of Art." To repeat, and at the risk of some oversimplification, whereas Gardner's discussions of artworks are notable for her formal analyses and Gombrich's for his symbolic interpretations and capacity for capturing feeling tone, Janson's emphasizes historical linkages and the placement and assessment of a work within a tradition. In this respect Janson's is the most historical of the texts; it underlines the continuity of the art-historical record and the shape and direction of art's evolution. Although all three art historians rely on the comparative analysis of artworks to highlight features they deem important, Gardner does so the least, and Gombrich does so more than Janson. And while all three provide external, internal, formal, and contextual information, each orchestrates and accents it differently.

At the time of its publication Vickers's analysis of the assumptions underlying art-historical texts was untypical of writings by art historians and probably would not have been undertaken but for an invitation from an educational theorist. Today art historians tend to be more interested in such assumptions. Consider, for example, Marcel Franciscono's discussion of fifty years of Gardner's *Art through the Ages*.[15] Franciscono praises the very early Gardner for her clearly expressed sense of values (a quality he regrets is less evident in the later editions). "If," writes Franciscono, "Gardner only occasionally rose to true eloquence, she made up for it by the warmth and general modesty of her descriptions and by her very clear sense of why some things are worth recording; every page shows her belief that works of art are cherishable in themselves, beyond what interest they may have as counters in a stylistic or iconographic progression or as expressions of a particular culture or time."[16]

Gombrich's writing reveals a similar disposition to reveal in a particular artist or work what is important for us in a human sense. For example, Gombrich says of the Flemish artist Van Dyck "that it was he, more than anyone else, who helped to crystallize the ideals of blue-blooded nobility and gentlemanly ease which enrich our vision of man no less than did Rubens's robust and sturdy figures of over-brimming life."[17] If we agree, then we must acknowledge that even an artist like Van Dyck, who stands in rather low regard today, can acquaint us with alternative ideals of human excellence—for example, the ideals of nobility, aristocratic bearing, and the obligations these impose—that even our own egalitarian age can find worth contemplating.

I think it is clear that what Franciscono admires most in the writings of some art historians is their capacity to show how the study of art can expand our sense of human possibilities. Although he does not deny the importance of art history's objective, empirical dimensions, which come into play in such tasks as the authentication of artworks, documentation of subject matter, and verification of causes and influences, his point of view is preeminently humanistic. He prefers an art history of privileged objects that convey values and truths in the ways that only outstanding works of art can and sees an artwork's transcendental significance in its capacity to outlive its own time and remain of interest to later ages. In this way we experience the presence as well as the pastness of art history and recognize the power of art to establish an affinity among minds across time.[18] Indeed, unless human values are kept in the foreground, art-historical writing is in danger of deteriorating into the superimposition of grand schemes that usually have less to do with clarifying the nature and values of art than with bolstering a writer's preferred ideology and interpretive framework. Franciscono would reverse this process: instead of studying art for what it reveals about someone's ideologically colored conception of society, he would study society for how it can help us to understand and appreciate art's aesthetic and human values. Such a view of art history is humanistic in yet another sense: exemplars of rare human accomplishment must constantly be recalled lest we be deprived of the models of excellence they provide. In short, Franciscono's attitude to art history has much to recommend it, and it is congruent with the objectives of discipline-based art education described in this book. Such an attitude in effect expresses Levi's belief, to be discussed in chapter 7, that art history is a humanity and should be taught as such.

A final art history survey text to be dealt with briefly is Hugh Honour and John Fleming's *The Visual Arts: A History,*[19] a relatively recent volume by two British scholars that is now in its second edition. In length, dimensions, character, and style of discourse, the Honour and Fleming volume resembles the Janson book more than it does the other texts discussed in this section. The authors lay even greater stress than Janson does on the contextual understanding of art, and they attempt as much as possible to place the discussion of artists, styles, and groups in their social, political, religious, and intellectual milieux. The text reveals a special effort to show works of art in their original settings rather in their new museum environments. "Great works of art," the authors write, "are more than aesthetically pleasing objects" or "feats of human skills and ingenuity" (p. 15), and they "cannot be fully understood unless related to the circumstances in which they were created" (p. 11). As with reading comprehension, context is all-important.

Another feature of *The Visual Arts* is its more pronounced cosmopolitanism. The text is a word history of art (by which title it is known in Europe), and it presents some interesting juxtapositions of Western and non-Western art. More than most books of its kind it explains why in the West women artists remained a professional minority until well into the nineteenth century. The introduction is also somewhat unusual for mentioning the ways the history of art differs from the histories of craft, technology, and science. Overall, the volume relies quite heavily on visual information, and its extensive use of time lines and maps underlines the importance the authors assign to period and place. The Honour and Fleming text, then, presents yet another way of writing art history, one that highlights information about contextual relations. When we examine what Honour and Fleming say about works described by Gardner, Gombrich, and Janson, we discover that Chardin is dealt with perfunctorily in a manner that emphasizes the social environment of his art over its formal or expressive meaning, while Van Dyck is mentioned primarily in connection with propagandistic uses of his paintings of royalty.

A Sample of Art-Historical Studies

We have said that for purposes of this volume art history is defined as the study of art under the aspects of time, tradition, and style. The first part of this chapter introduced several art historians who pursue this task on a grand scale, that is, as the survey of artworks from past to present toward the end of establishing the genealogy and chronology of art. But it would be misleading to convey the impression that this is how the majority of art historians work and that the discipline of art history can be understood only in this way. I therefore offer a corrective glimpse at some of the other things art historians typically do, the myriad sorts of small-scale, even minute inquiries that are pressed with remarkable patience and tenacity. I deliberately risk shaking confidence in a conception of art history as a unified discipline with a universally accepted structure and perimeter whose basic concepts and ideas of which can (as certain educational theorists in the sixties would have us think) be imparted to young students. Although the study of art history is indispensable to discipline-based art education, teachers of art would be ill served by a simplistic representation of the discipline.

To convey something of the variety and range of activities art historians engage in, we will first look at a recent study of contemporary art historians at work. For a more detailed description of different kinds of art-historical research, we will follow Mark Roskill's account of how art historians cut through mystery and legend to discover facts, interpret disguised meanings in works, and come to terms with a modern picture.

Object, Image, Inquiry: The Art Historian at Work is a report on a project cosponsored by the Art History Information Program of the J. Paul Getty Trust and the Institute for Research in Information and Scholarship of Brown University.[20] It was intended to help devise better information systems (computer technologies, etc.) for use by art historians, but the case studies and interviews incidentally reveal a fascinating cross section of art-historical research and the concerns that preoccupy art historians. The great variety of activities carried on under the banner of art history should dispel any notion that we are dealing with a narrowly conceived field. For example, in the Getty report we find architectural historians crawling through the dirty passages, corners, and towers of buildings in order to ascertain a structure's precise measurements while others precariously mount scaffolds for close-range looks at stained-glass windows; monuments are also examined in great detail in order to gain a fuller, more sensory aesthetic experience than that which can be obtained from a fixed vantage point. Then there are art historians who scrutinize attentively (perhaps for years) the contents of archives in order to document one or another aspect of a work or to prove a connection or influence. Still others may rummage through thousands of photographic reproductions in hopes of detecting the tradition to which an artist or school of artists belongs.

We also find investigators critically reinterpreting the imagery of a particular artist or even a whole period (for example, seventeenth-century Dutch art) with the aim of bringing to light new meanings or the importance of a kind of painting that has gone unnoticed or unappreciated. Others conduct chemical analyses of paintings, a research tool that might ultimately discredit received knowledge about a work. New evidence may also change opinions about principal centers of artistic influence as well as indicate hitherto unsuspected relations among them. But there is more: an intense interest in Gothic architecture and sculpture; puzzlement about incongruous properties of a well-known masterpiece; curiosity about whether the view of modernity embodied in Impressionist paintings may help account for their popularity; a desire to trace the complete life history of a monument or painting; the attempt to reconstruct an artist's exhibition or to show how an artist's studio and working conditions are "reflected" in his or her work; eagerness to understand drapery style in relation to an artist's intention or to discover unity in a seemingly disjointed body of work; efforts directed at understanding the significance of elaborate illustrations in medieval maps or at establishing connections among artists, patrons, critics, dealers, and collectors; a search not only for historical continuities but also discontinuities; and the documentation of an influential structure that no longer exists. All these convey the range of art-historical inquiry, and it is an incomplete one at that, for the studies mentioned are restricted principally to European and American art.

This great multiplicity of art-historical interests can—to use W. Eugene Kleinbauer's distinction in his *Modern Perspectives in Modern Art History*[21]—be sorted into either intrinsic or extrinsic historical perspectives on art. Intrinsically oriented research features the ideas and methods of connoisseurship, stylistic analysis, formal change, and period distinction, while extrinsic studies draw on the ideas and methods of the psychology of perception, psychoanalysis, cultural history, sociology, theology, and intellectual history. As for the diachronic-synchronic differentiation referred to earlier, some of the studies mentioned lie clearly at one or the other end of the spectrum, while the majority probably fall somewhere in between.

Three Art-Historical Puzzles

Having provided some sense of the scope of art-historical investigation, I will now briefly outline three kinds of problems and puzzles that typically concern the art historian, all taken from Mark Roskill's *What Is Art History?*, a highly useful companion to Kleinbauer's volume.[22] Three chapters in *What Is Art History?* help us to form an idea of some of the methods employed by art historians, of the typical character of art-historical concerns, and of the meticulous, often painstaking nature of the art historian's scholarship. Beyond adding to an understanding of the discipline of art history—and hence making us better prepared to use that discipline as a resource in teaching art—the selections from Roskill's book should also engender considerable admiration and respect for art-historical inquiry generally.

Giorgione

In a chapter titled "Cutting through Mystery and Legend: Giorgione," Roskill discusses the Venetian painter Giorgione, an extraordinary artist who poses a number of challenges to the art historian. One challenge stems from the scarcity of documents referring to Giorgione's life and work. Records like registrations of births and deaths, commissions made to artists and payments received by them, and correspondence mentioning their names generally place historians on fairly safe footing. But there is very little such evidence about Giorgione, and what we learn from it is quickly summarized. He was born in Castelfranco, a small fortress city some thirty miles from Venice, in the late 1470s. During his lifetime he was known as Zorzi and came to be called Giorgione around the middle of the next century. The earliest date we have for a work of his is 1505 or 1506. He established himself in Venice. There, in 1507 and 1508, he was paid quite handsomely by the Venetian government for a canvas for the Doge's palace (a work that has not survived and is nowhere described) and was also commissioned to paint frescoes for the German warehouse (lost except for a fragment of a female figure). Immediately after his death in the autumn of 1510 collectors began to prize his pictures even more highly. The last two facts are established in an exchange of letters between Isabella d'Este, a great patroness of the arts, and her agent in Venice. She instructed the agent to purchase, on whatever terms he saw fit, a *Nativity* by Giorgione "in case someone else should take it." The agent replied that Giorgione had died of the plague a short while earlier and that, in any event, no such painting existed. This exchange is evidence of the avidity with which wealthy families bought up works by the most well-known painters.

Giorgione's death, just at a time when he was beginning to enjoy considerable fame, creates particular difficulties, for it has made suspect secondary sources of the kind normally regarded as fairly dependable. These are biographies of artists and journals and diaries prepared by cataloguers of the contents of private collections. The fact that both types of documents were assembled in some abundance from the middle of the sixteenth century on attests to the esteem in which artists were held. In words reminiscent of Levi's earlier remarks about civic pride and humanism in Renaissance Italy, Roskill explains how artists were increasingly regarded as major contributors to a city's greatness and its posterity. They were no longer regarded merely as skilled artisans but as persons with learning and wide interests.

Given the considerable popular interest in artists at that time, it is not surprising that in the case of a painter whose career ended so prematurely myth soon began to embroider the few known facts. This state of affairs was already frustrating for Giorgio Vasari, whose *The Lives of the Most Eminent Painters, Sculptors, and Architects* first appeared in 1550. Although Vasari wrote with assurance about other artists, he was less certain he had separated truth from legend when he dealt with Giorgione, and in several instances he changed his mind about ascribing works to him.

Other factual material art historians use, especially when tracing various influences exerted on an artist, derives from the context or cultural setting in which artists lived and developed their craft. Venice was widely acknowledged as a premier art center in Giorgione's age, and Giovanni Bellini was its most renowned painter. Even if we had not been told by Vasari that Giorgione spent some time with the Bellini brothers, it would be hard to deny that he had adopted and carried forward one of Giovanni Bellini's greatest achievements, that is, the depiction of landscape in terms of both light and atmosphere. Roskill is skeptical, however, about Vasari's assertion that, except for an association with the Bellinis and probable acquaintance with some of Leonardo da Vinci's work, Giorgione was largely self-taught. It is possible to discern the imprint of other artists as well: figures in Giorgione's early works are reminiscent of the style developed by Carpaccio, another prominent Venetian painter; facial features recall physiognomies made familiar by the Dutch painter Hieronymous Bosch, examples of whose art are known to have been on view at Venice; and occasional resort to a complicated, convoluted rendering of drapery recalls northern European engravings.

It should be pointed out that while the validity of external evidence supplied by documents can be established independently of artworks, the question of the impact that various forces and circumstances in artists' cultural environments might have had on their artistic development can be settled only by close inspection of the paintings in question, that is, on the basis of *internal* evidence. Thus far, then, we have seen that the art historian draws on external sources as well as

Giorgione, *The Trial of Moses*, ca. 1500, Uffizi, Florence.

Giorgione, *The Tempest*, ca. 1503, Academy, Venice.

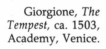

Giorgione, *Castelfranco Madonna*, ca. 1505, S. Liberale, Castelfranco, Veneto.

Giorgione, *Three Philosophers*, ca. 1506, Kunsthistorisches Museum, Vienna.

on knowledge of the cultural context as it is confirmed by internal evidence. But there are some determinations that are made on the basis of the internal evidence alone; these are decisions that "must hinge on what can be inferred from the character of the painting itself," and they are especially important in cases like Giorgione's where we have so few data. Roskill demonstrates this sort of qualitative decision making while establishing the chronology of four paintings, *The Trial of Moses*, *The Tempest*, the *Castelfranco Madonna*, and the *Three Philosophers*, the last three of which are almost universally accepted as Giorgione's.

Consider the judgment that *The Trial of Moses* is Giorgione's earliest work. This belief is supported by reference to aesthetic features that argue for the work's being by Giorgione and for its having been painted by a youthful artist not yet in full control of a personal style. Giorgionian traits are argued for on the basis of resemblances to the painting next in the sequence, for example, the pure poetry of the landscape, the facial characteristics of one of the female figures, and the general appearance and stance of two of the male ones. The artist's relative immaturity, on the other hand, shows in the lack of transition from foreground to background, the additive arrangement of the figures, and their tentative poses and rather unconvincing placement on the ground. "All these points," says Roskill, "suggest an ambitious and highly inventive artist who has not yet reached maturity or become completely sure of himself" (p. 78).

In the case of the *Tempest*, its dating relies solely on qualitative considerations. Because of this small painting's peculiar charm, its very pronounced expression of the dreaminess distinctive of Giorgione's style, and its acknowledged originality—it became, for example, the prototype for the "pastoral idyll" genre—the picture has long been thought to be a mature work of Giorgione's. Yet the figures, though occupying their spatial niches rather satisfactorily, still retain an appearance of being "stuck on" to a landscape backdrop. Since the relationship between figures and space is better realized in the *Castelfranco Madonna*, known to have been completed around 1505, the date 1503 is suggested as the approximate date for the *Tempest*. The *Madonna* also shows progress "in the firm, balanced way in which the figures stand and the way in which their weight is now felt as resting on the ground" (p. 92).

The apogee of the development that began with *The Trial of Moses* is reached in the *Three Philosophers*. In this painting there is a stronger and more consistent harmony between man and nature. "The figures are fuller in physique here and more completely balanced in their gestures and poses, so that the work has what might be called a supernatural lucidity, in the logic of the figures' shapes and their relation to one another and to the landscape" (p. 95). This painting, which dates from approximately 1506, marks Giorgione's entry into what is known as High Renaissance Classicism.

Thus far we have followed a description of how some art historians work and the kind of evidence they employ. It will also be useful to examine the kind of arguments they put forward. When using documents and other external evidence art historians proceed in a factual, empirical, scientific manner; but that is not necessarily the case with internal evidence, that is, the sort deriving entirely from the qualities present within a work of art. To be able to discern the uniqueness of an artist's style or to detect the hand of several artists in a seemingly unified painting (as in the case of Giorgione's *Sleeping Venus*, in which the landscape was contributed by Titian while he was a younger associate of Giorgione's), the art historian must possess a highly developed aesthetic sensitivity and perceptual acuity. And to convince others of the plausibility of aesthetic determinations, the art historian uses a form of persuasive argument that is similar to art-critical discourse. In short, others are invited to look at a painting for themselves to see whether they can agree with an explanation. Persuasive argument also comes into play when the art historian renders evaluative judgments, which even with the best effort, cannot always be avoided. Thus when Roskill speaks of the loveliness of Giorgione's paintings or says they are imbued with a dreamlike pervasive quality and are progressing toward maturity in High Renaissance Classicism, and when he concludes that generally they are fully deserving of the esteem in which they were and are held, he is surely assessing aesthetic excellence and perfection. And in making evaluative judgments, the art historian has something in common with the art critic. I make these points to show that although discipline-based art education draws on four separate fields, sufficient interconnections and overlappings exist among them to prevent overly fragmented, compartmentalized educational experiences.

Vermeer and Velázquez

In another chapter Roskill addresses the problem of meaning in painting, which he had in a sense already previewed in his discussion of Giorgione. This preview was inevitable, for the meanings and even precise titles of several of Giorgione's works have remained obscure. Roskill's attitude seems to be that one can indeed appreciate many works of art even in ignorance of their meaning and that sometimes

(as is the case with Giorgione's *Tempest*) there is good reason for assuming that the artist did not intend one. But that leaves the difficulty
of separating these instances from those others in which the art historian is definitely obliged to ferret out the meaning of artworks. This
task occupies Roskill in "Disguised Meaning in Pictures: Vermeer and
Velázquez."

Vermeer belongs to the northern European tradition of heavy reliance on symbolism, a tradition that has always required the art historian's intercession to make its meanings accessible to later ages. For
example, one of the leading features of fifteenth-century northern European art was the inclusion in still lifes of numerous objects carrying
Christian significance, for example, bread and a glass of water referring
to the Eucharist, an apple to original sin, or cherries to Christ's gift of
heavenly fruit to mankind. Vermeer's contemporaries could still read
these symbols and, of course, were conversant with the newly popular
secular ones that alluded to classical antiquity. By the seventeenth
century, however, painters had developed a flair for hiding and dis-
guising symbols. Thus it had become harder to know when paintings
and the objects depicted in them were meant for prosaic viewing and
when they called for interpretation.

Works labeled allegories always call for an interpretation of their
contents. The female figure in Vermeer's *Allegory of the New Testament*,
for example, is known to represent Faith because she is surrounded
by all the objects that a then popular handbook on symbols prescribed
(although Vermeer did take a few creative liberties). Similarly, trumpet,
book, and laurel wreath make it clear that the woman in Vermeer's
The Artist in His Studio is costumed as Clio, the Muse of History.

But Vermeer was known best for his genre paintings, which were
depictions of Dutch interiors and scenes of domestic life. In several of
these works a woman, bathed in light from a window opposite her, is
shown absorbed in a delicate task. Many of these pictures—*The Lace-
maker* is an example—do not have subtle meanings. A number of them
do, however, and *Woman Weighing Pearls* is among them; Roskill deals
with this work at some length. Here we see a woman carefully operating a small pair of jeweler's scales; pearls are on the table in front
of her, and a fairly large painting hangs on the wall behind her. The
frequent inclusion of paintings in genre works illustrates Levi's remarks
about the great fondness of the Dutch mercantile and middle classes
for this kind of art. Often these "paintings within paintings" are merely
items of home decoration; sometimes, and quite definitely in *Woman
Weighing Pearls*, they are clues for the interpreter. The work behind the

Johannes Vermeer, *Woman Holding a Balance,* ca. 1662–65, National Gallery of Art, Washington, D.C. (formerly titled *Woman Weighing Pearls*).

woman is a *Last Judgment,* and this fact combined with the presence of the precious pearls on the table assigns the work to the *vanitas* type, that is, pictures in which jewels, gold, and mirrors are intended to symbolize human pride and conceit. An earlier interpretation held that this painting was saying, "As you are weighing, so you will be weighed and judged." It may also echo the biblical injunction against laying up treasures for ourselves on earth and the admonition to lay up treasures in heaven instead.

Somewhat unexpectedly, a *vanitas* coloring also suffuses many Dutch still lifes. The observer who revels in the sensuous appeal of

Diego Velázquez, *The Tapestry Weavers*, ca. 1645–48, Prado, Madrid.

gorgeous bouquets of flowers and the abundance of kitchen and table—
baked goods, cheeses, fresh fruit, fish, and venison—is intended to
realize the highly perishable nature of these objects and accept them
as symbols for the transience of human life. Flies and other carriers of
contamination and decay are often painted in to make a point about
imminent decomposition.

Diego Velázquez's *The Tapestry Weavers* introduces, as a subtext,
another sort of art-historical concern: to conserve a record of interpretations of artworks and explain the divergent meanings art historians gave these works in the past. For example, *The Tapestry Weavers*
ostensibly depicts the Santa Isabel tapestry factory in Madrid. The large
figures in the foreground are working women spinning and preparing
yarn. In the background hangs a finished tapestry, and in front of it,
on a stagelike platform, several elegantly dressed women disport themselves. Two additional figures, a helmeted woman and another whom
she addresses, have been read as being either part of the background
tapestry design or as separate from the tapestry and sharing the space
in front of it with the fashionably garbed women. Art historians of the
nineteenth century saw this painting as a realistic portrayal of a particular scene, albeit a work distinctive for certain advanced painterly

effects they pointed out admiringly. This was the age of Realism and Impressionism with its prevailing interest in surface appearances and its preference for recording unposed images of ordinary life; the art historians of the time apparently thought—mistakenly, according to Roskill—that this was also an appropriate stance for encountering the art of the past. In the case of *The Tapestry Weavers* this approach was applied at the obvious cost of leaving quite a number of the picture's features unexplained.

It was not until later that investigators went back to the title this work had in 1664—*The Fable of Arachne*—and took their cues from it. The helmeted figure is now explained as being Athena and as standing in front of the tapestry. (This tapestry is a copy of one of Titian's celebrated paintings, which depicted a mythological scene that did not include Athena or the other female figure.) According to myth, "Athena presided as goddess over the craft of tapestry-making in particular, and in this capacity she was challenged by Arachne, who got herself turned into a spider for her presumption" (p. 146). The myth further tells us that Athena first approached Arachne in the guise of an old woman and later revealed herself in her fury and armed splendor. The painting thus combines both parts of the story, each protagonist being depicted twice: Athena in the person of the old woman in the foreground and again in her goddess regalia in front of the tapestry; Arachne in the young woman winding yarn in the foreground and also in the woman placed just in front of the wall hanging who is turning her head toward the goddess. Velázquez's work is therefore quite a faithful rendition of the fable, as its original title intimated.

That is not all, however. Several decades ago it was discovered that Athena not only appears twice but also officiates in two separate roles: as goddess of craftsmanship in the foreground and as goddess of the fine arts in the background (the art of painting is symbolized by the woven reproduction of a well-known work, while certain traditional attributes identify the female figures occupying the platform with Athena and Arachne as representatives of other art forms). "As goddess of both the major and the minor arts, combining under her surveillance both idea and craftsmanship, she [Athena] symbolically affirms her authority over the process by which the fruits of rough and menial handiwork are turned into the splendors of the finished work of art" (p. 147). It is now evident that this picture can be variously read as an unproblematic depiction or record (of a tapestry factory), as an illustration (of a fable), and, finally, as an allegory (of the arts).

The Tapestry Weavers rewards time spent on it because, first of all, it is an example of a work about which enough can be said to invite

interest, intensify appreciation, and reveal the wide range of background information that art historians must have at their command
(we have now added knowledge of symbols, allegorical attributes,
myths, legends, and the history of interpretations of artworks to their
cognitive stock). Second, I believe Roskill's account of this work permits
us to call into question a chief assumption behind certain contemporary
theories of interpretation: that alternative readings of various "texts,"
in this case artworks, do not represent improvements on earlier ones
but are merely different. But successive interpretations of *The Tapestry
Weavers* demonstrate that, in this case at least, the most recent rendering
is also the best because it is the most inclusive; it explains more elements of the painting than previous readings did. In short, it is justi-
fiable to speak of a cumulative advance in our comprehension of works
of art.

Picasso

Roskill's "Understanding a Modern Picture: Picasso's *Guernica*" is
of interest primarily for what it tells us about the value art-historical
inquiry sets on information concerning the creative process and on
artists' statements about their works. Art-historical investigation (as
Levi mentioned in chapter 3) can recover the creative process that
culminated in a particular painting only with the help of surviving
visual material such as the artist's preliminary jottings, drawings, notes,
and so forth. Mainly because these preparatory efforts were not prized
in their own time, few of them have come down to us. Picasso apparently assumed, however, posterity's interest in wanting to know all
there is to know about the *Guernica,* and so he dated and saved all his

Pablo Picasso, *Guernica*, 1937, Prado, Madrid.

sketches and photographs of the work at its different stages of completion. He thus left a record unparalleled in its fullness and detail that also allows scholars to recognize the novelty of his method. In the past a painter would have tackled such a large project (6½ feet high and 26 feet wide) in phases that included notes and studies, possibly a wax mock-up of the figure layout, a small and freely done version of the whole work, and finally a full-scale "cartoon" for transfer to canvas or wall. When evidence of this kind is used in reconstructions of artistic activity, says Roskill, it usually reveals a logical and steady progression toward the realization of a clearly conceived result. Picasso, by contrast, adopted a procedure that permitted constant major revisions and reconceptualizations while the mural was actually in the process of taking shape.

Because the *Guernica* is so familiar a work, I record only a few of Roskill's observations. First, although the *Guernica* was inspired by an actual event of which news photographs were available, Picasso ignored most of this material. Nor did he really invent a special imagery for the occasion. "Rather the opposite. Each of these images is already found in some equivalent or related shape in prior works of Picasso's of the 1930s" (p. 173). We realize, then, that originality is not always a case of starting de novo; that artists can achieve a powerful impact through realignments and juxtapositions—and hence through transvaluations—of items from their existing repertoire; and that an investigator needs to be thoroughly conversant with an artist's idiom to bring these matters to our attention.

Second, Roskill's interpretation discovers a range of symbols and allegories in the *Guernica*. He thinks the work contains numerous allusions to Western civilization. Originally the fallen warrior wore a helmet and carried a spear in the manner of a Greek god; now he resembles a broken ancient statue. At one stage, the bull had a Zeus-like head. The mother and her dead child bring to mind the Christian theme of the Massacre of the Innocents. The large, strong triangle Picasso uses as the main expedient for organizing the composition recalls the pediments of Greek temples. And the bull and horse are, of course, direct references to Spain and its traditions of the bullfight. The mural can thus be understood allegorically as a statement about the attack launched on civilized Western values by the forces of violence and oppression.

Is this what Picasso meant? He would only say that the horse represented the people and the bull brutality and darkness, and he deflected all further inquiry. That he should have been questioned repeatedly and insistently indicates a new and typically modern relationship between artists and their public. Now, Picasso has been honored and idolized as much as any Renaissance painter. But although eminent artists of that former age were respected as contributors to civic life and men of learning, they were not appealed to for explications of their own work. There was no need for this: artists, their patrons, and the viewers of their works shared the same values and assumptions. In recent times, however, alienation between artists and the art public has sundered these commonalities. Anxious to come to terms with modern art but unsure of their ability to decipher its messages, people today increasingly go to what they consider the ultimate source, the artist. Artists' commentaries on their works have thus assumed an astonishing importance and are taken very seriously. It will be recalled that Levi, too, said ours was the age of the artistic manifesto. But should we give so much credence to the remarks of artists? How much should we rely on their statements and opinions? Roskill writes:

> Obviously the artist is in a privileged position in a good many ways. He is the only one who can tell us the ideas which he had in mind, the state of his feelings at the time, and the problems which came up in the course of the work. But when it comes to the question whether those ideas are in fact communicated, or those feelings put across in the actual work, it is still up to us to decide. Nor is it simply a matter here of determining what the artist intended to do, and then deciding whether or not he succeeded in doing it, because most often the question is whether or not what the artist can tell us is really relevant to the work itself. Artists may be deceived in their thinking about what they are doing or did. Their natural medium of expression is visual, not verbal, and therefore what they say in words may well be parenthetical, or even irrelevant, to the work. They are not immune, just because they are artists, to challenge from us. And most often, in fact, though their statements are helpful, they are helpful in a secondary sort of way—supporting what we get from the work itself but leaving us free to go well beyond them in our interpretation. (pp. 175–76)

We take leave of Roskill with this finding: for the art historian (and, as we shall see, for art critics of a certain persuasion) the work of art is always primary. Its internal evidence—and the external sources, facts, and information that enlarge, sharpen, and enliven the analysis of internal evidence—is decisive. Artists may have their say, but their remarks may be contradicted by the work itself as it finds realization through the scholarship, sensitivity, and perceptiveness of others, including art historians.

Art History as a Self-reflective Discipline

A number of the themes and issues that characteristically occupy art historians when they reflect on their discipline are now more discernible. Among them are questions about the possibility of an objective or scientific (that is a value-free) art history and about the priority to be assigned to either internal or external contextual information. And, with the dominance of external data, researchers must determine the area that their nets must take in to gather sufficient information for understanding an artwork as an expression of a period, era, or civilization. Then, too, what role should formal analysis play in art-historical descriptions? And there are further problems. To what extent should ideas from other fields of inquiry inform the activities and procedures of art historians? For instance, should art-historical inquiry be guided by the methods and orientations of cultural history, psychoanalysis, Marxism, and literary theory? Should scholars confine themselves to *Kunstgeschichte* (art history), or should they see their proper work as *Geistesgeschichte* (the history of ideas, mind, soul, spirit)? How, to refer to T. S. Eliot once more, is order to be imposed on art-historical events? And finally, is it possible to categorize the many themes of critical art history?

One effort at devising an overarching scheme of art-historical explanation is Walter Abell's *The Collective Dream in Art*.[23] Abell begins by identifying at least six traditions of art-historical studies: (1) iconography, which concentrates on the subject matter and the natural or literary sources of art as the basis for comprehending it; (2) biographical determinism, which focuses primarily on the artist's personality; (3) historical determinism, which places strong emphasis on such factors as civilizational and environmental conditions; (4) aesthetic materialism, which relies principally on materials, techniques, and functions in order to come to terms with art; (5) aesthetic teleology, which is associated with the idea of an innate psychological "will to art" (*Kunstwollen*) that finds distinctive expressions in different epochs and races; and (6) pure visibility, an approach that elucidates works of art through the plastic organization of their parts and wholes. Perhaps we may take the liberty of adding yet another critical tradition, that of (7) style, which, according to James Ackerman, lends structure to art history by discovering in artworks more or less stable features and relationships that change over time.[24]

Abell explained how the six critical traditions he identified differ in the value they place on either the properties of works of art themselves (iconography, pure visibility, and aesthetic materialism) or the impetus to art (biographical criticism, aesthetic teleology, and historical determinism). He then tried to correlate salient features taken from each tradition with comparable elements from his own psychohistorical theory. Other writers might describe Abell's six critical traditions differently or use fewer of them, and new categories of art-historical explanation are continually evolving. But for present purposes we need keep in mind only that a comprehensive philosophy of art history would be one that recognizes some truth in each perspective while attempting to integrate aspects of all of them. The prospects for a successful synthesis, however, are rather poor, not least because some perspectives are incompatible.

Since we cannot here record all the discordant voices in critical art history, I give a full hearing to one. It is that of Erwin Panofsky (1892–1968), the acknowledged giant of modern art-historical scholarship. This task is considerably aided by the numerous testimonials to the importance of Panofsky's work that have appeared since his death and by an excellent study by Michael Ann Holly, which for the most part I follow here. Holly's *Panofsky and the Foundations of Art History*[25] serves several ends. It makes available some of Panofsky's untranslated writings that anticipated his later theoretical formulations, and it limns the philosophical and cultural forces that largely nourished Panofsky's views. It draws parallels between these forces and the intellectual climate and trends operating in art-historical scholarship in our own time, and it helps us appreciate Panofsky's immense contribution to art-historical method.

Holly tells the story of how Panofsky's mature vision developed from his early intellectual skirmishes with such influential art historians of his time as Heinrich Wölfflin and Alois Riegl. Also important, although perhaps more indirectly, were the writings of Jacob Burckhardt, Wilhelm Dilthey, and Ferdinand de Saussure, whose ideas, says Holly, formed the soil in which Panofsky's thought took root. Indeed, it is one of the chief merits of Holly's book that it shows the significant impact on art history exerted by ideas and tendencies originating outside the field. Thus she outlines the conflicts that swirled around exponents of both metaphysical idealism and positivism at the turn of the century. These controversies need not detain us except to note that, where art history is concerned, the focus of the debates crystallized into three issues: the relative importance attached to laws said inevitably to determine the course of historical events; the relative significance of form, content, and meaning in describing and explaining works of art; and the appropriateness of concentrating on either diachronic (vertical, chronological) or synchronic (horizontal, periodic) studies of art. Embedded in these three themes are two issues—the importance of the study of form and the importance of synchronic investigations—which became polarized into the formalism-versus-contextualism argument during Panofsky's time. The terms formalism and contextualism are often used loosely in art-historical discourse, and since Panofsky mounted a sustained attack on formalism, a somewhat more careful exposition is in order.

According to Holly, "formalist art history," exemplified in Wölfflin's influential *Principles of Art History*, "is devoted to explicating the work of art by attention to its autonomous aesthetic properties in all their potent immediacy; a history of formal properties often results in a survey of the stylistic modes linking one work to another across time, apart from human content." Conversely, "contextualist art history," exemplified in Panofsky's mature work, "goes beyond the work of art in order to explain its presentation as a product of something else, by investigating such factors as the biography of the artist, the temper of the times, its literary antecedents, and so forth" (p. 13). Yet as Holly emphasizes—and it is a point we came across in our earlier discussion of the methods used by contemporary art historians—many writers are not easily categorized as either formalist or contextualist. Wölfflin did not really believe that style had only one root—autonomous modes of perception determined by underlying historical laws, which art history is supposed to discover—he was simply fascinated by this particular root. And Panofsky himself, who became the contextualist par excellence, acknowledged the limitations of contextualism. Preoccupation with art's environing conditions, he said, may preclude doing justice to a work's feeling qualities or expressiveness—which is also a potential failing of some iconographic descriptions that fit the same interpretations to different works in different styles.

We know that Panofsky championed contextualism as a proper method for art history, but we have not yet learned how he understood the nature and function of art and how he came by his ideas on these subjects. Skeptical of Wölfflin's insistence on an autonomous art history and critical of Riegl's notion of *Kunstwollen*, Panofsky turned to Cassirer's account of the role of mind in culture and was profoundly impressed by it. Cassirer, in turn, had borrowed from Kant and held that reality consisted of such constitutive forms as space, time, cause, and number, to which he added such forms of human culture as myth, language, history, science, religion, and art, all of which, as we have seen, defined for Cassirer the circle of humanity. Panofsky supplemented Cassirer's thought by articulating more fully than Cassirer had done the nature of art as a symbolic form of human culture. Holly suggests that Panofsky's essay on Renaissance perspective effects the bridge between Cassirer's philosophy of symbolic forms and Panofsky's conception of art. Panofsky understood Renaissance perspective as a peculiar product of its time, as a convention for perceiving space and not as the ultimate solution to the problem of representing space on two-dimensional surfaces. Holly quotes him as saying that perspective is "one of those 'symbolic forms' through which a spiritual meaning is joined to a concrete sensuous sign and becomes an essential property of that sign" (p. 136). In this manner Panofsky achieved "a totally comprehensive (formal, cultural, philosophical) treatment of one particular visual form" (p. 145).

Holly writes that if Panofsky's career has been the major "event" in recent art-historical scholarship, his method of iconology has been its major "monument." Strictly speaking, however, iconology is the last of three stages in the interpretation of artworks and presupposes preiconographic and iconographic analysis. Panofsky believed that with this tripartite scheme for the description, interpretation, and explanation of artworks he had established a firm philosophical foundation for art-historical knowledge. Holly summarizes and explains the three stages as follows:

> The preiconographic stage relates to "factual" meaning, to recognition of the work in its most "elementary" sense. For example, to use Panofsky's analogy drawn from the world of gestures, when a man tips his hat in recognition of my passing, I am confined on this level to noting only the objects involved (a hat and a gentleman), and I must leave the matter at that. Applied to Leonardo's *Last Supper*, this reading would factually record only that thirteen men are seated around a table laden with food.
>
> The iconographic stage relates to the "conventional" meaning, to recognition that the man greeting me in this manner is consciously being polite with reference to the world of articulated values that he has acquired as a member of a community. Similarly, Leonardo's *Last Supper* is observed at this stage to have its conscious source in the Christian ethos as manifested in the biblical story.
>
> The iconological stage involves a reading of the work as a possibly unconscious bearer of meaning beyond what the creator might have intended; this level involves an analysis of the meaning in terms of underlying cultural principles. For example, the gesture of lifting a hat in greeting indicates a whole range of twentieth-century world views, both conscious and unconscious, while also providing a biography of the man who interacts with the world when he greets me in this manner. The *Last Supper* is now seen not only as a "document" of Leonardo's personality but also as an expression of the world view of the High Renaissance. The act or object is resituated in the context from which it was first extracted for examination in isolation on the initial level. (pp. 41–42)

This brief sampling should have made it clear that Panofsky is writing *Geistesgeschichte* and not merely *Kunstgeschichte*. Iconology is thus a highly complex and difficult method, requiring a solid grounding not only in art history but in cultural history and philosophy as well. Although Holly thinks that iconology is the most important art-historical approach of our time, its forbidding demands and the essential impossibility of completing iconological investigations (Panofsky himself, she says, seldom fully realized the goals of iconology in his own studies) made it unlikely that it would be practiced as widely as, for instance, iconography. Holly mentions some of the method's complexities. She refers to Panofsky's definition of content as but one example of the problem of prying out a work's deepest meanings. In Panofsky's scheme content does not mean interpreted and transfigured subject matter, as it does in some aesthetic theories; rather, content is "that which a work betrays but does not parade. It is the basic attitude of a nation, a period, a class, a religion or philosophical persuasion—all this *unconsciously* qualified by one personality, and condensed into one work" (pp. 166–67).

Though critical of certain of Panofsky's ideas, Holly finds much to admire in his work. She remarks on his readiness to transcend the boundaries of art history and his deftness in drawing on other areas of knowledge. It is in this interdisciplinary bent that Panofsky approximates the disposition of contemporary art historians who are currently mining various fields of inquiry and considering different points of view—semiotics, psychoanalysis, feminism, deconstruction, and Marxism among them[26]—in order to devise new methods for the study of art history. Whether these novel perspectives will ultimately revolutionize art history cannot be known at this time; the ferment in the field will have to subside before we can make a reasoned judgment.[27]

But what Holly seems to have responded to most sympathetically in Panofsky's writing is the quality of his scholarship, the personality that shines through his work, and his belief in the necessity of the imaginative recreation of artistic intentions which do not lend themselves to verification by scientific methods alone. The notion of imaginative re-creation helps us to understand what Panofsky means when he says that the history of art is essentially a humanistic discipline and that a work of art is a created object demanding to be experienced aesthetically.

This brief review of Panofsky's contribution to art history does scant justice to the nature and importance of his work, but it does allow us to return with greater understanding to some of the questions raised at the beginning of this section. One of them was whether art history should be value-free, more like science than like one of the humanities. Once more, the role he assigns to imaginative re-creation clearly places art history within the humanities—with the proviso that art-historical research must be constrained by factual evidence whenever it is available. In my opinion Panofsky's respect for both the empirical ethos and the humanistic imagination is what enabled him to span with ease the alleged gulf between the sciences and the humanities that C. P. Snow dramatized at mid-century in his provocative and much-discussed lecture *The Two Cultures and the Scientific Revolution*.[28] (Roskill writes—unfortunately without elaboration—that although art history is one of the humanities, it is also a science.) Being thoroughly at home in the two cultures, Panofsky was able to be explicit about the essential differences, as well as the similarities, between scientific and humanistic inquiry. Indeed, in his iconology he forged an exemplary mode of humanistic interdisciplinary investigation. He has given us contextualism writ as large and as eloquently as possible.

As for the diachronic/synchronic distinction, Panofsky's work reveals the interplay between the two toward the end of a configurational, synchronic interpretation that attends to cultural patterns, qualities, and meanings as much as it provides a genealogical account of an art object. His *Gothic Architecture and Scholasticism* exemplifies this kind of comprehensive interpretation.[29] Perhaps we may say that, as embodiments of cultural attitudes and bearers of meaning, works of art are the figures in the field of culture and the works' circumstances their inseparable ground. (Chapter 7 will explore the educational relevance of diachronic and synchronic approaches to art history.) There is no doubt that the method of iconology deploys all the kinds of information mentioned earlier in this chapter (internal, external, formal, contextual), with a strong emphasis on contextual information.

Finally, while there may be no overarching theory or unanimously accepted philosophy of art history, there is still the question of the humanistic purposes it serves. I think that Panofsky would have agreed, as will many others, that all the disciplined intellectual effort expended in amassing and interpreting art-historical facts would be for naught if it did not, as John White puts it in an essay titled "Art History and Education," provide a "foundation for a broader, richer, deeper, intuitional response to the experience of a work."[30]

I should point out that an important lacuna in the foregoing discussion is the role of artists in shaping the history of art. By this I am not referring to the obvious, that without artists there would be no art history, but the fact that artists themselves are sometimes art historians. And not only that: by taking an interest in the arts of other cultures and in artists forgotten or insufficiently valued, they have drawn them into the history of art and have thus helped to shape its development.

While ideas about the history of art were expressed as far back as antiquity—there was, Francis Sparshott reminds us, an antiquity of antiquity—it was principally during the Italian Renaissance that artists turned to writing art history. Indeed, the Renaissance painter and architect, Giorgio Vasari (1511–74), is regarded as the first art historian worthy of the name. His *Lives of the Most Excellent Painters, Sculptors, and Architects* (1550) "stands alone," writes Luigi Salerno, "as the first real and autonomous history of art, by virtue not only of its monumental scope but also of its organization—the integration of the individual biographies into a whole."[31] The writing of art history in terms of artists' biographies, however, declined after the Renaissance and began to take the forms discussed in this chapter. John Canaday's *The Lives of the Painters* (1969) does, however, recall this way of writing art history.[32]

As for artists drawing on the arts of other civilizations for artistic inspiration and thus ultimately effecting the development of art history, we may point to numerous instances of assimilation by Western artists of the crafts and fine arts of Asia. Theodore Bowie speaks of many such instances that have taken place for the last three thousand years.[33] Yet with rare exception the works assimilated were works of ceramics, metalwork, and fabric, the typical products of artisans. In the eighteenth century these works became known as *chinoiserie, turquerie*, and later *japonaiserie*. The influence of Eastern painting, printmaking, sculpture, and architecture, on the other hand, was not significant until the nineteenth and twentieth centuries when European artists such as Whistler, Degas, Lautrec, Manet, and van Gogh and American artists such Morris Graves, Mark Tobey, Walter Barker, Ulfert Wilke, and Isamu Noguchi came under the influence of Asian art forms and philosophy. The influence of African art on Picasso and other twentieth-century artists is, of course, a well-known story.

In this chapter I have distinguished different sorts of art-historical scholarship. One kind of study imposes a historical order on works of art and establishes art's genealogy and chronology. To illustrate this approach, I discussed the methodological assumptions and values of several writers of art-history textbooks, Helen Gardner, E. H. Gombrich, and H. W. Janson. The differences among these authors were found to be a function of their objectives in writing art history, their aesthetic presuppositions, their disposition toward internal, external, and contextual relations, and even their nationality. Descriptions of the same artwork by each of these writers brought out their distinctive points of view. There then followed references to research and inquiry ranging from chemical analyses of artistic materials to the preparation of catalogues documenting the oeuvre of particular artists. Art-historical puzzle solving was illustrated by the efforts of art historians to cut through rumor and legend in order to report as objectively as possible what is known about an artist's life and the dates of his works, to unravel the meaning of symbolism in works that defy easy interpretations, and to assess the relevance of knowledge of artists' procedures and verbal statements in gaining an understanding of their work. Yet another type of art-historical scholarship, which scrutinizes the premises of art-historical inquiry itself, was examined through the methods of one major art historian, Erwin Panofsky.

5

The Critique of Art: Art Criticism

The function of criticism is the re-education of perception of works of art; it is an auxiliary in the process, a difficult process, of learning to see and hear.

—John Dewey

Presumably . . . criticism will consist not merely of evaluation but of reasoned evaluation, and will typically consist in the skillful deployment of good reasons for evaluation.

—F. E. Sparshott

The major function of the critic is to improve the intellectual environment in which the creation of art takes place.

—Harold Rosenberg

Art . . . must be defended and pursued and relished not for any political program it might be thought to serve but for what it *is*, in and of itself, as a mode of knowledge, as a source of spiritual and intellectual enlightenment, as a special form of pleasure and moral elevation, and as a spur to the highest reaches of human aspiration . . . as the very medium in which our civilization either lives and prospers . . . or withers and dies.

—Hilton Kramer

In other words, the functions of criticism are many: to cultivate artistic perception, to make a reasoned assessment of artistic quality, to improve the intellectual environment in which we think about art, and to appreciate art's multifarious values. Art criticism cannot be the sole prerogative of art critics, however, for it is clear that art historians, philosophers of art (especially in their more speculative moments), and teachers of art also perform these critical acts. Indeed, professional art critics typically gain experience in other fields—for example, literature, art, art history, philosophy, and political history—before turning to the criticism of art, and not a few of them are also active as artists and art historians. In short, great breadth and depth of experience are required to be a good critic. Since artists express the full range of human experience, the interpretation and evaluation of their work calls for uncommonly percipient respondents.[1]

All the critics discussed in this chapter are wise in the ways requisite for good criticism. Each contributes something important to our understanding of art and life. Bernard Berenson's notions of ideated sensations and life-enhancement play a central role in our appreciation of Italian Renaissance painting. Roger Fry's insights are still relevant to an appreciation of Postimpressionist art. Harold Rosenberg's descriptions of the new social and cultural conditions of modern society have created an atmosphere that has made the purposes of avant-garde art more intelligible. Hilton Kramer's articulate intelligence and steady reflection on the quality of the aesthetic experience that artworks afford helps to keep our interest centered on the inherent values of art. Charles Jencks, on the other hand, is the most interesting writer today about artistic developments subsumed under the rubric "postmodernism." Surely if we want to know what art criticism is, we will find out in the writings of these critics.

Bernard Berenson (1865–1959): Ideated Sensations and Life-Enhancement

As I write I have before me three essays about this extraordinary critic and lover of Italian Renaissance painting. One is by Meyer Schapiro, a distinguished art historian and critic in his own right, written shortly after Berenson's death in 1959.[2] Though impressed by Berenson's exceptional perceptual power—he had a "wonderful eye"— Schapiro is mainly concerned to raise questions about Berenson's ethics, the limitations of his connoisseurship, and his failure to appreciate the accomplishments of twentieth-century art. In particular, Schapiro notes the conflict of interest caused by Berenson's connoisseurship and his business relations with his dealer. These are observations and problems that any examination of Berenson's life must consider, but they are not what interest me here. Rather it is Schapiro's acknowledgment of Berenson's lasting contribution to our understanding of Italian painting. "Berenson," writes Schapiro, "told his readers and hearers what to enjoy and how to enjoy it. His early writings on pictures—authoritative, resonant with lofty conviction and explanation—presented a model of aesthetic response, intense and refined, as well as a method of discerning the works of the great artists."[3]

That says it all, and it is this Berenson—Berenson the "sage and teacher who has a supreme message for the reader"—that I present here. This supreme message concerned the life-enhancing effects of figure painting, which consist of an increased sense of reality and human capacity and of a heightened self-consciousness. Berenson describes the nature of these values in the appreciative essays he wrote during the 1890s that introduced his studies and lists of Italian Renaissance art, all of which were later collected into a single volume. No one who reads the essays on Titian and Giorgione, on Giotto and Masaccio, or on Leonardo, Michelangelo, and Raphael, says Schapiro, can fail to profit from Berenson's perceptiveness. Indeed, Berenson's accounts of his experiences of paintings dissolve any doubt that one significant locus of aesthetic value resides in the work of art as it unfolds in the experience of a sensitive beholder.

The second essay on Berenson is by Kenneth Clark, who also observes that Berenson's commitment to culture and aesthetic perfection was tarnished by his need to earn a living, which included authenticating pictures and giving advice to dealers and collectors.[4] But if Clark's assessment is a more positive one of Berenson's major contributions and continuing relevance, it is perhaps because Clark recognized a kindred spirit in Berenson. Clark thinks that Berenson's stature as a critic is the result of the interdependence of four major activities: the use of principally internal evidence to clarify the personalities of Italian Renaissance painters; the establishment of a scale of values for Italian painting from Duccio to Veronese; the formulation of nonmystical propositions about the nature of our aesthetic responses to works of art; and the correlation of the facts of culture and art history.

Like Schapiro, who believed Berenson's assessments in his essays on Renaissance painting were often "arresting and true," Clark thinks these same essays "contain extraordinarily accurate and durable judgments."[5] In contrast to Schapiro, however, who held that Berenson's thinking revealed no development and that his aesthetic principles eventually became personal clichés applied indiscriminately to any sort of artistic problem, Clark maintains Berenson's aesthetic theory still provides a viable base for art criticism. And he adds that we admire Berenson for the same qualities that we admire any important critic: a rare combination of learning, intelligence, sensitivity, and faith in humanity that results in fresh historical intuitions, new directions of thought, and revelations that enlarge human sympathy and imagination. Berenson's failure to extend his aesthetic appreciation to a number of modern and twentieth-century artists does not invalidate his insights into Renaissance painting. But Schapiro found it strange that Berenson did not by and large recognize the merits of modern artists, for Berenson's appreciation of tactile values, movement, and space composition, as well as the high seriousness he associated with art, are consistent with the impulses that produced modern painting.[6]

S. J. Freedburg, at one time chief curator of the National Gallery of Art, is the author of the third essay about Berenson.[7] Freedburg's aim is to restore Berenson's reputation as an authenticator of paintings and to recall connoisseurship to its former role in art-historical studies, a role that had diminished with the increasing popularity of Impressionism and the influence of iconography as a way of describing and interpreting paintings. After expressing his belief that Berenson's contribution to our understanding of Italian painting is "the most embracing, and possibly the most influential, of this century" (p. 7). Freedburg discusses at some length the discipline of connoisseurship and the need to supplement internal evidence with archival documentation and information revealed by modern restorative procedures, which can often correct the more intuitive judgments of connoisseurs (both of which Berenson tended to disdain). The details of connoisseurship can be set aside here, but it would seem that a renewed interest in judgments of authenticity and quality, in Freedburg's view, is needed to counteract the disproportionate emphasis current criticism places on art's social and political aspects. Thus Freedburg alludes to Berenson's remarkably impassioned and far-ranging capacity for visual experience. He had a gift for experiencing and appreciating particular, concrete things and an ability, already remarked, to convey the character of the lived intensity of his aesthetic experiences—all qualities that prompted Freedburg to include Berenson among the great critics of modern times.

I can provide here only one example of Berenson's appreciative criticism, one that illustrates the application of his aesthetic principles, his tone and personal style, and his method of description. In his essay on the Florentine painters of the Renaissance, published in 1896, Berenson first describes the objectives of the great artists of Florence, who, unlike most Venetian painters of the time, were also architects, poets, sculptors, and even scientists—hence the expression "the Renaissance man."[8] Giotto was such a Renaissance man, yet he had a "peculiar aptitude for the essential in painting *as an art*" (p. 62). This aptitude, says Berenson, cannot be appreciated without an understanding of what is essential to the art of figure painting. For Berenson the function of figure painting is to give an abiding impression of artistic reality with only two dimensions. In order to do this works of art must arouse the tactile sense. "I must," writes Berenson, "have the illusion of being able to touch a figure. I must have the illusion of varying muscular sensations inside my palm and fingers corresponding to the various projections of this figure, before I shall take it for granted as real, and let it affect me lastingly" (p. 63). Therefore, "the art of painting . . . is somehow to stimulate our consciousness of tactile values, so that pictures shall have at least as much power as the object represented, to appeal to our tactile imagination" (pp. 63–64). This capacity to appeal to the tactile imagination raises the works of Giotto above the status of mere symbols or messages and gives them their perennial value. It is not, that is, what a work illustrates or the pleasurable associations it evokes or even its color, but rather its form that is important and the principal source of aesthetic enjoyment.

How does our perception of form in art differ from our sensory experience of form in nature? Berenson's answer is that artistic form stimulates to a higher pitch the physical processes that are the origin of our ordinary pleasures. The form of a painting "lends a higher coefficient of reality to the object represented, with the consequent enjoyment of accelerated psychical processes, and the exhilarating sense of increased capacity in the observer" (p. 67). We thus take greater pleasure in a painted object than we do in an actual object. I think that what Berenson is saying about artistic pleasure is, though phrased differently and in less ambiguous terms, precisely what later theorists of aesthetic experience have asserted to be an important feature of aesthetic enjoyment (to be discussed in the next chapter). The point is that by virtue of the tactile imagination's being stimulated by artistic form, our consciousness and mental functioning undergo amplification, and we experience a heightened sense of capacity. A work's color, composition, movement, and associations may provide satisfaction, but "*unless* it satisfies our tactile imagination, a picture will not exert the fascination of an ever-heightened reality" (pp. 68–69). Clark thinks that in this assertion Berenson is essentially correct.

Having informed us of the aim of Florentine painting—the making of an appeal to the tactile imagination—and having described the character of the pleasure we may derive from it, Berenson goes on to explain Giotto's unique genius. To bring this out he compares two versions of the enthroned Madonna: one by Cimabue, *Madonna and Child Enthroned with Angels* (ca. 1285–90), and the other by Giotto, *Madonna Enthroned* (ca. 1310). And Berenson finds that although the difference between the two is striking,

> it does not consist so much in a difference of pattern and types, as of realization. In the "Cimabue" we patiently decipher the lines and colors, and we conclude at last that they were intended to represent a woman seated, men and angels standing by or kneeling. To recognize these representations we have had to make many times the effort that the actual objects would have required, and in consequence our feeling of capacity has not only not been confirmed, but actually put in question. With what sense of relief, of rapidly rising vitality, we turn to the Giotto!

Cimabue, *Madonna and Child Enthroned with Angels*, ca. 1285–90, Uffizi, Florence.

Giotto, *Madonna Enthroned*, ca. 1310, Uffizi, Florence.

Our eyes scarcely have had time to light on it before we realize it completely—the throne occupying a real space, the Virgin satisfactorily seated upon it, the angels grouped in rows about it. Our tactile imagination is put to play immediately. Our palms and fingers accompany our eyes much more quickly than in the presence of real objects, the sensations varying constantly with the various projections represented, as of face, torso, knees; confirming in every way our feeling of capacity for coping with things—for life, in short.

By what means does Giotto so engage our tactile imagination?

With the simplest means, with almost rudimentary light and shade, and functional line, he contrives to render, out of all the possible outlines, out of all the possible variations of light and shade that a given figure may have, only those that we must isolate for special attention when we are actually realizing it. This determines his types, his schemes of color, even his compositions. He aims at types which both in face and figure are simple, large-boned, and massive—types, that is to say, which in actual life would furnish the most powerful stimulus to the tactile imagination. Obliged to get the utmost out of his rudimentary light and shade, he makes his scheme of color of the lightest that his contrasts may be of the strongest. In his compositions he aims at clearness of grouping, so that each important figure may have its desired tactile value. Note in the "Madonna" we have been looking at, how the shadows compel us to realize every concavity, and the lights every convexity, and how, with the play of the two, under the guidance of line, we realize the significant parts of each figure, whether draped or undraped. Nothing here but has its architectonic reason. Above all, every line is functional; that is to say, charged with purpose. Its existence, its direction, is absolutely determined by the need of rendering the tactile values. Follow any line here, say in the figure of the angel kneeling to the left, and see how it outlines and models, how it enables you to realize the head, the torso, the hips, the legs, the feet, and how its direction, its tension, is always determined by the action. There is not a genuine fragment of Giotto in existence but has these qualities, and to such a degree that the worst treatment has not been able to spoil them. (pp. 69–71)

Now, given the engagement of our tactile imagination and the means by which it is stimulated, what, more specifically, is the clue to Giotto's genius? It is, says Berenson, Giotto's profound instinct for *the significant*, his feel for the materially significant as well as his facility for capturing the significant in the attitudes and expressions of figures representing various kinds of symbols, as in his great cycle of paintings in the Arena Chapel at Padua. Giotto's sense for the significant enabled him to paint objects in such a manner as to make us realize his representations more quickly and more completely than we realize the things themselves.

We feel confirmed in that sense of capacity, which is a genuine source of aesthetic pleasure, and we can understand why it is sometimes said that art is better than life itself: the contemplation of works of art engages powers and pleasures rarely called forth in everyday existence.

To be sure, Berenson is often accused of making too much of "the moment of ecstatic perception." And the unashamedly lofty and noble style in which he expressed his delight in certain qualities of art is at odds with contemporary sensibility. Yet at a time when discourse about art tends to be intolerably dense and pervaded with ideological rhetoric, it is refreshing to read accounts of artworks that convey a genuine love of art's intrinsic qualities. Berenson's descriptions of his aesthetic experiences of Renaissance masters (grounded, we should not forget, in a disciplined method of observation and judgment) suggest that we need to pay more attention to our physiological responses to art. The concept of disinterested attention or detached affect that we take to be central to aesthetic experience also needs at least some qualification, for both Berenson and Clark make much of such sensations in their reports of personal response to art. It will be recalled that Clark too spoke unapologetically of the incandescence of moments of vision and sympathetically said of Berenson that "one could almost see his frail little body reacting physically to the tactile values or space-composition of the work before him."[9] Clark suggests that just as we must take Wordsworth at his word regarding the intensity of his experiences of nature, so we should take Berenson at his regarding the intensity of the pleasure he felt in looking at pictures.

Berenson, then, is our first type of critic—the critic as connoisseur who, like all great critics, makes reasoned judgments of value while cultivating perception and improving the intellectual climate in which we think about art. So far as Italian Renaissance painting is concerned, Berenson is our incomparable mentor. Yet even great critics can have blind spots, and while Berenson is given some credit for recognizing the merits of the Impressionists and Postimpressionists and even, some say, for discovering Cézanne and Matisse, his sympathy clearly failed to encompass later modern art. So it is not to Berenson that we must go for an appreciation of, say, Postimpressionism, but to the great English critic Roger Fry, who, as Kenneth Clark remarked on the dedication page of his *Looking at Pictures*, taught a whole generation to see.

Roger Fry (1866–1934): The Values of Form

One of the culturally important events of our time is the series of A. W. Mellon Lectures in the Fine Arts delivered annually at the National Gallery of Art in Washington, D.C., which is published as part of the Bollingen Series by Princeton University Press. Among the impressive volumes in this series are *The Nude* by Kenneth Clark, *Art and Illusion* by E. H. Gombrich, *Nicholas Poussin* by Anthony Blunt, *Art as a Mode of Knowledge* by Jacob Bronowski, *The Use and Abuse of Art* by Jacques Barzun, *The Burden of Michelangelo* by Leo Steinberg, and, more recently, *Painting as an Art* by Richard Wollheim. Also included in this distinguished series is Jacob Rosenberg's *On Quality in Art: Criteria of Excellence, Past and Present,* a volume that is especially pertinent to a discussion of criticism.[10] Rosenberg is primarily concerned to discover the nature of artistic excellence and how judgments of excellence are made. To gain this information Rosenberg does not engage in abstract philosophical speculation but goes to the writings of the great critics themselves, both traditional and modern, such as Giorgio Vasari, Roger de Piles, Sir Joshua Reynolds, Théophile Thoré, and Roger Fry. In this section I will first summarize some of Rosenberg's observations about criticism and critics before discussing Fry in more detail.

Rosenberg asks two questions at the outset: What is the meaning of artistic quality? And can judgments of artistic value be objective? "Artistic quality" implies the degree of artistic excellence of a work and should not, says Rosenberg, be confused with such notions as beauty, taste, and style. As for the objectivity of artistic value assessments, Rosenberg finds it in the "common agreement among artistically sensitive and trained observers" (p. xxi). The role played by tradition is especially important in the formulation of criteria of excellence. In words that recall the method of the great Berenson, Rosenberg quotes Panofsky as saying that "when a 'masterpiece' is compared and connected with as many 'less important' works as turn out, in the course of investigation, to be comparable and connectable with it, the originality of its invention, the superiority of its composition and technique, and whatever features make it 'great' will automatically become evident" (p. xxii). Rosenberg further emphasizes that there can be no judgment of quality without direct experience and that a reasoned method of analysis is prerequisite to a full and intense experience of artistic value.

Because of the importance he attaches to tradition and its cumulative wisdom in matters of judgment, Rosenberg discusses assessments of quality made by a number of earlier critics. He credits Vasari (1511–74) with the insights that judgment should not be unduly restricted by the dominant art theory of a period or dogmatic historical concepts and that leeway should be given to one's intuitive reactions and instincts. To Roger de Piles (1635–1709) he attributes the recommendations that critical standards should not derive from one great master or period alone but from several and that any critical theory should be broad enough to take advantage of comparative analysis. The critical writings of Sir Joshua Reynolds (1723–92) exemplify this dual capacity, for despite his deep-seated commitment to classicism and the Academy as its characteristic institution, Reynolds was also able to perceive the merits of other styles, for example Dutch and Flemish painting. Théophile Thoré (1807–69), also known as Thoré-Burger, recognized not only the uses of attribution in judging quality but also the need to locate works in both their historical context and the artist's development. But it was left to Roger Fry, says Rosenberg, to provide "an instructive example of how to penetrate into a deeper understanding of works of art through an incisive and perceptive analysis of the formal organization and the technical means employed. In this way he was able to reveal to us the full stature of Cézanne and to extend our understanding of modern art" (p. 124). What now was Fry's special contribution to the critical act?

Fry, whom Kenneth Clark considered the best-known English writer on art and the most influential figure since John Ruskin, was born in 1866, only a year later than Berenson, but he did not enjoy as long a life (he died in 1934), and the circumstances of his life were vastly different. Whereas Berenson's career as a connoisseur and critic of Italian Renaissance painting progressed with a consistency that gave it pattern and style, Fry's was restless, explorative, and more individualistic. Fry was active as an artist and business entrepreneur as well as critic, connoisseur, and lecturer. But he is perhaps most closely associated with the organization of a Postimpressionist show of paintings in London in 1910 that for the first time acquainted the British public with the art of Cézanne, van Gogh, and Gauguin, the early Picasso and Matisse, and the Cubists and the Fauves. The reaction to this exhibition was as notorious as that to the Armory Show in New York in 1913, which presented new forms of modern art to the U.S. public. It was during this time, says Rosenberg, that Fry formulated a theory of art that derived largely from his understanding of Cézanne's work, a theory that toward the end of his career he used to reinterpret and reevaluate the entire history of art. Although Fry's life unfolded differently from Berenson's, he shared Berenson's deep and lasting appreciation of the Renaissance masters. It is particularly to Giotto, Masaccio, and Raphael that Fry was indebted for his notion of plastic values, which played so large a part in his estimation of Cézanne's significance. In Fry's scheme of things Cézanne occupied the same position in relation to the achievements of modern painting that Berenson assigned to Giotto in relation to Renaissance painting. And it is to Fry's critical principles and his study of Cézanne that I now turn.

Like Berenson, Fry often expresses impatience with theory and abstract speculation. Rosenberg points out that Fry nonetheless tends to rely on a few basic theoretical notions and seldom departs from them. These ideas revolved around a "formalism" that postulates a basic distinction between reality and pure art and holds that access to pure art and its distinctive aesthetic effect is possible only through the aesthetic sense. Fry regards the aesthetic sense as a kind of sixth sense that is not distracted by nonartistic associations, whether literary, psychological, social, or political. Fry even asserts that the representational aspect of art detracts from a pure aesthetic effect, which derives from the clear expression of volume, plastic continuity, and coherence in space. Moreover, unity and order are indispensable to the design of every artwork, while rhythm, texture, and color are essential elements of a work's animation, along with, of course, all-important plastic expression. Fry thus comes close to rejecting as irrelevant what Berenson calls the illustrative aspects of art. And Fry is also wary of art that is too intellectual, for such art subdues intuitive and subconscious impulses. Excessive finish, since it seems to derive from nonartistic impulses, has a similar effect.

Works of art that express "sensibility" and "vitality" are critical to Fry's reevaluation of the history of art, a reassessment that leads him to devalue Egyptian, Greek, Medieval, and High Renaissance art (e.g., Raphael and Fra Bartolommeo), since the pursuit of ideal beauty sacrifices the quality of vitality (a charge he brings especially against Greek art and one with which Berenson, we might add, would never have concurred). On the other hand, it is primarily the possession of vitality that raises African sculpture and Chinese bronze vessels high in Fry's estimation. What is it for a work to exhibit "sensibility" and "vitality"? "Sensibility" is bound up with the unconscious of the artist and the artist's manner of execution and is to be distinguished from a work's design or organization. "Vitality" refers to the strong illusion that works of art possess a life of their own. To intuit vitality we need to perceive the difference between a "statement" about an emotion and the representation of the emotion itself. Though vitality is not always positively related to a work's artistic worth, it is likely, writes Fry, that "if we find aesthetic satisfaction in a work of art it is probable that our satisfaction will be heightened if the images which arouse it suggest vital energy."[11] Rosenberg believes the ideas of sensibility and vitality are too vague to be very helpful, and Clark was thinking of Fry's vagueness on this point when he spoke approvingly of Berenson's nonmystical propositions about the nature of art. Yet perhaps vitality need not be such a vague notion after all if we can take it to be the same as the different magnitudes of intensity ascribed to aesthetic qualities by subsequent aesthetic theorists.[12]

Fry's criticism is generally considered exemplary of a formalist aesthetic, an approach to the evaluation of art that acknowledges only plastic features as relevant to pure and worthwhile art and as primarily responsible for generating aesthetic enjoyment. Without question a work's form can be an important source of aesthetic gratification. Take it away (which is, of course, impossible) and little interest remains in an object as a work of art. In numerous instances expressive form is all that a work presents to perception, and certainly for many artists finding the right form in which to express their feelings, intuitions, and ideas is a crucial phase of their creative efforts. (Think back to Levi's discussions of Mondrian and Hundertwasser in chapter 3.)

Formalism as a theory of art is currently not held in high esteem, but those who discount form in art are in effect admitting that they are not really interested in art but in something else. Fry simply went too far in his exclusiveness and the restrictions he placed on what can count as aesthetically relevant. Nonetheless, in an influential essay, Morris Weitz has wisely counseled that it behooves us to explore all strands of aesthetic theory for what they can tell us about the excellences of works of art, however limited such theories may be in certain respects.[13] Furthermore, one must consider the cultural context in which Fry was writing. Like Berenson he was cognizant of the superficial criteria that the large majority of persons tend to rely on in judging artistic excellence. Both Berenson and Fry therefore realized that a job of teaching had to be undertaken. We are familiar with Berenson's achievement in this regard. For a sample of Fry's "educative" criticism we may turn to his monograph on Cézanne. Yet as Rosenberg points out, this monograph is something of an exception to the stereotypes that have developed about Fry's beliefs and writing. It does not confine itself to an analysis of the formal or plastic values of Cézanne's work, for it discusses Cézanne's artistic intuition, the circumstances surrounding his life, and his reactions to the work of his contemporaries. If Fry provides an excellent model for the proper evaluation of a work art by a great master (which Rosenberg contends), what can we learn from this model?

I select for illustrative purposes Fry's discussion of *The Cardplayers* (1890–92) from Cézanne's mature period. In language reminiscent of the praise that Berenson lavishes on Giotto for his sense of the sig-

Paul Cézanne, *The Cardplayers*, 1890–92; Museum d'Orsay, Paris.

nificant, Fry remarks that in no work of art since the great Italian Primitives or the later efforts of Rembrandt had an artist achieved such extraordinary monumental gravity and resistance. And unlike that of his nineteenth-century contemporaries, these qualities emerged in Cézanne's work quite naturally and inevitably from his interpretation of commonplace situations. Regarding the formal and plastic values of *The Cardplayers*, Fry writes that Cézanne

> seems to have carried the elimination of all but the essentials to the furthest point attainable. The simplicity of disposition is such as might even have made Giotto hesitate to adopt it. For not only is everything seen in strict parallelism to the picture plane, not only are the figures seen in almost as strict a profile as in an Egyptian relief, but they are symmetrically disposed about the central axis. And this again is, as it were willfully, emphasized by the bottle on the table. It is true that having once accepted this Cézanne employs every ruse to render it less crushing. The axis is very slightly displaced and the balance redressed by the slight inclination of the chair back and the gestures of the two men are slightly, but sufficiently varied. But it is above all by the constant variation of the

movements of planes within the main volumes, the changing relief of the contours, the complexity of the color, in which Cézanne's bluish, purplish and greenish greys are played against oranges and coppery reds, and finally by the delightful freedom of the handwriting that he avoids all suggestion of rigidity and monotony. The feeling of life is no less intense than that of eternal stillness and repose. The hands for instance have the weight of matter because they are relaxed in complete repose, but they have the unmistakable potentiality of life.[14]

Again, Fry remarks that the work's gravity, reserve, and weighty solemnity bring to mind some monument of antiquity. A little café and its habitués take on a Homeric cast and amplitude. And finally: "If, by reason of the helplessness of language, one is forced to search for poetical analogies even to adumbrate at all the emotional effect of this design it is none the less evident that this results from a purely plastic expression. There is here no appeal to any poetical associations of ideas or sentiments. It is a triumph of that pictorial probity which it is the glory of modern art in France to have asserted—its refusal of the assistance which romantic interpretations offer. And the reward of this difficult attempt is seen here, for Cézanne's purely plastic expression reaches to depths of the imaginative life to which consciously poetical painting has scarcely ever attained."[15] In these words Fry notes the power of figurative language to draw attention to a work's special values, a tactic that recalls Jacques Barzun's realization that words and their correct use are indispensable to critical judgment and the teaching of art.[16]

In his educative capacity Fry follows Berenson, from whom, as mentioned before, he had learned a great deal about formal and plastic values. Fry's pedagogical aim, as it were, was to inform viewers of Cézanne's art that the quality Berenson had found so valuable in the art of Giotto had at long last been rediscovered by modern masters like Cézanne and other Postimpressionist painters. As I have noted, Fry's appreciation of the work of the Postimpressionists further evolved into a fondness for African and Asian art. At a time when the field of art education is given to sympathetic consideration of non-Western cultural and artistic values it is worth noting that Fry anticipated this interest by almost seventy years. Any doubts about Fry's relevance, then, stem from the limitations of his aesthetic theory, not from the catholicity of his taste.

Harold Rosenberg (1906–78): The Premises of Criticism

The question of critical language and rhetoric is central to any discussion of criticism, but it is especially important to an understanding of the writings of Harold Rosenberg, who believed that it was necessary to coin a new terminology for discussing the ideas, personalities, and content of avant-garde art. There have been doubts about his success in forging this new vocabulary and employing it effectively—it is said that he too often let rhetoric perform the actual business of criticism—but that question is of less interest here than Rosenberg's statement of his critical premises, which, interestingly, was first presented at an art education conference.

Confining himself to a discussion of modernism (that is, post-nineteenth-century academic art), Rosenberg writes that to gauge modernism's gains and losses accurately criticism must be serious and relevant to the art under consideration as well as sensitive to the changing social, cultural, and political situation in which artistic creation occurs. This point is important since the inflections of criticism can affect the experiences and attitudes not only of appreciators of art but also of artists, and they can further influence the terms of the debate that attends new creations. Here, simplified and paraphrased, are the eight critical propositions to which Rosenberg subscribed:

1. Criticism must recognize that the creation of art in the twentieth century takes place within a political-cultural drama of a world in the process of remaking itself.

2. Since this political-cultural drama has a global dimension, the artist works in an environment unbounded by time and space.

3. In contrast to traditional modes of creation, modern styles tend to originate in abstract ideas and idea-based movements.

4. Given the norm of change in modern life, the capacity for innovation and the renewal of old forms become a primary value in art.

5. A break between past and present creates a state of uncertainty in which the future is unknown.

6. As a result of vast social changes in the movement, composition, and potentialities of populations, the problem of individual and collective identity has become a dominant theme of contemporary cultural forms.

7. Given our civilization's commitment to archaeological, psychoanalytical, and philological excavation, contemporary culture now contains the culture of all ages.

8. The mass media and their characteristic products create a need to clarify the relation between traditional forms of art and their substitute products in the media.[17]

Rarely has a critic set out his premises so precisely, systematically, and comprehensively, and nothing could indicate more clearly the importance Rosenberg assigns to the changing social, political, and cultural milieu of modern civilization. Moreover, Rosenberg's critical credo does not feature criteria of artistic excellence so much as it betrays a keen eye for the changed context for creating and thinking about art. Not that Rosenberg lacked a sense of artistic values, but he was more concerned that we approach the products of contemporary artists with a proper awareness of the altered conditions under which they were created.

We have moved quite a distance from the temperaments and dispositions of Berenson and Fry. Though both believed that criticism should be relevant, serious, and sensitive to the art under consideration, Berenson and Fry kept their attention firmly on the internal evidence of works of art (Berenson on tactile values, movement, and space composition and Fry on sensibility and vitality) at the expense of the relevance of a work's social context. More conspicuously than either Berenson or Fry, Rosenberg moved back and forth between the political-cultural drama of modernity and the work of artists, many of whom were his friends. In describing the relations of society, art world, works of art, artists, and appreciators, Rosenberg brilliantly exploited the resources of rhetoric. Some of his more colorful phrases will not soon be forgotten, for example, "the tradition of the new," "the anxious object," "action painting," "art and its double," "de-aestheticization," MOMA and Dada," "the herd of independent minds," "D.M.Z. vanguardism," "redcoats and coonskinners," and many others he used in his portrayal of modern culture.

But, once again, it is not Rosenberg's colorful rhetoric that is important here but the way he helps us understand what is going on in the work of a particular artist. Rosenberg's essay about the American artist Jasper Johns exemplifies his conviction that one of the characteristics of contemporary art is its self-conscious break with tradition, its acceptance of innovation as a cultural norm. Furthermore, it reflects Rosenberg's conclusion that criticism must concentrate on the works of individual artists since we can no longer assume that groups or schools of artists are attempting to solve shared problems within a continuing tradition. In contrast to the Renaissance artist, for instance, who tended to address common difficulties—such as how to represent solid three-dimensional forms on a flat two-dimensional surface or to project linear and atmospheric perspective—from within the tradition they had inherited, the artist today creates in an atmosphere in which he thinks of himself as a "one-man culture." This means that artists must be assessed on the originality of their appropriation of elements from both the remote and immediate past and from any other source that can satisfy their creative impulses. Their success will depend, as

Leo Steinberg once put it in his own writing on Jasper Johns, on whether the "flinting together" of diverse elements produces something that is novel and arresting and not merely interesting, as demonstrated by the haunting effects of some of Johns's work. His images of desolate waiting were actually achieved with quite banal and commonplace objects such as targets, numbers, coat hangers, and flags.[18] An aura of interpretation now surrounds Johns's work. What does Rosenberg contribute to this literature of interpretation?

Although Rosenberg cautions against taking artists' statements at face value (along with Mark Roskill in chapter 4), he does find one of Johns's remarks about his own work relevant. Johns once said, "I don't want to express myself on the canvas, and I'm not trying to evoke on the canvas a mysterious sign. I'm prepared to paint things that everybody already knows."[19] By way of evidence Johns points to his paintings of the American flag, targets, numbers, and letters of the alphabet: they have nothing to do with him personally since he did not invent them. It is as if, recalling a line from Ortega y Gasset's *The Revolt of the Masses*, Johns knew himself to possess a commonplace mind and therefore felt no compunction about introducing commonplace components and techniques into the art of painting.

What compelled him to do so? Rosenberg points out that artistic acts like these were a reaction against the art of Abstract Expressionism and its high seriousness, against artists who worked hard at realizing an artistic vision at often great psychic cost and sacrifice. This strenuousness derived its impulse from an idea about the nature of the artistic process, namely, that the subject of a work could never be known in advance but had to be discovered in the act of painting itself—an approach to creation, Rosenberg observes, consistent with Picasso's remark that the purpose of creating was to find, not to seek. (Recall also Levi's discussion of the Platonic theory of artistic creation in chapter 3.) Johns's work then, which represented the most significant break at the time with the high seriousness of Abstract Expressionism, was in effect a parody of Expressionism's attitude and intent.

Yet, while mocking Abstract Expressionism, Johns did not so much reject it entirely as put certain aspects of it to his own uses. First of all, he still held to the idea of a subject so long as it did not emphasize the highly evocative and often mysterious allusions that Abstract Expressionists believed could only be discovered in the act of painting. Johns's subjects were once again what "everyone already knows." And to a limited extent his work retained the characteristic manner of painting it was ridiculing and reacting against, for example, manipulating pigment to wring from it all the allusive magic the medium itself could

Willem de Kooning, *Asheville*, 1949, The Phillips Collection, Washington, D.C.

Jasper Johns, *Target with Four Faces*, 1955, Museum of Modern Art, New York.

yield. By and large, however, Johns's work shows little or no working over of materials, no transfiguration of subject into content, no magic or mystery, Rosenberg noted. Pigment and other materials are merely there as components of the work and nothing more. Leo Steinberg had made similar observations about Johns's early work.

After indicating Johns's intention to remove himself from his paintings so that he could achieve a cool detachment and impersonality that was in striking contrast to the psychic investments of the Abstract Expressionists, Rosenberg states that the effect of Johns's painting was to reduce the strain of both thinking and feeling on the part of the artist and the viewer. If Abstract Expressionist painting implied completion by a spectator's thought and psychological involvement, the new article required nothing of the sort. "At one stroke," says Rosenberg, artists like Johns and the post–Abstract Expressionist painters who followed him, "extinguished speculation about the meaning of individual paintings and directed attention to them as objects among other objects."[20] Not that such a program could be wholly successful, for indefatigable symbol hunters and seekers after meaning (like Steinberg in his interpretations of Johns's paintings as images of desolate waiting) will find significance where none was intended. And one cannot de-aestheticize art by fiat. But it is clear that Johns's purpose is radically different from that of the Abstract Expressionists, which, according to Rosenberg, he was ridiculing.

> Johns's subject matter did not need to be invented or discovered, nor did it have to be evoked out of psychic states that were difficult to maintain—for example, Pollock's "contact" with the canvas or de Kooning's "inspiration." It lay ready to hand. Better still, his flags, numbers, and targets were already on the way to being paintings, in that they were signs inscribed on a flat surface, apt for placement and handling in any manner the artist chose. Banners of sorts had appeared among the Abstract Expressionists: Gottlieb's three solid ovals above a horizontal field of black; Pollock's "Blue Poles," which one could easily imagine being adopted by a Third World republic. Dispensing with riddles, Johns's subjects were ideally suited to reduce the strain of both thinking and feeling in painting. Confronted by images that it had had no part in creating, painting was as if struck dumb—its guiding axiom after Johns became "You see what you see." (pp. 134–35)

And he goes on:

> Johns had split Abstract Expressionist painting into two halves: its signs and its agitated handling. Thus divided, both halves were emptied of meaning. Having ceased to embody the artist's psyche, the signs on the canvas joined the order of insignia outside of art—for example, the in-

signia on packing cases, from which Johns has tended to derive his
lettering. Deprived of its goal of discovery, the liberated brushwork of
de Kooning, Hofmann, Kline became merely a newly fashionable mode
of ornament. As put together in Johns's flags, targets, and numbers, the
two halves of Abstract Expressionism become substances of an art completely manageable by the artist, and entirely void of meaning. Every
attempt at interpretation was thrown back by the artist's disavowal of
purpose. The principles he was prepared to proclaim consisted exclusively of negations of Abstract Expressionist truisms. No more romantic
fumblings, supported by declarations that "when I am in my painting,
I'm not aware of what I'm doing." No more pretensions of invading the
Unknown. No more "self-expression." (pp. 134–35)

Rosenberg thinks that discussions of Johns do not stress enough that
"in his paintings both sign and method have become subject matter,
modelled on the canvases of his predecessors but transformed by his
determination to keep himself out of the picture. The contrast between
the agitated surfaces of Johns's flags and targets and the inertness of
these motifs presents a lesson in the illusory effects of style considered
as expression, since the flags and the surface textures were chosen with
the same detachment. Johns's cold-blooded rearrangements of the in-
gredients of America's passionate postwar abstract art amount to a
double parody" (pp. 135–36).

So much for a representative sample of Rosenberg's criticism, one
that we may agree has succeeded in improving the intellectual atmosphere in which we think about and experience art and has met
the aim of making relevant and intelligent statements about artists and
works of art. Rosenberg, it should be emphasized, did not take these
objectives lightly, for he believed that it was important to have intelligent reactions to works of art. In the case of explaining the works of
Johns, at least the early ones featuring targets, numbers, letters, and
flags, and so on, this involved first trying to come to terms with a
creative innovation by comparing it to what it parodies and seeks to
counteract.

What about an assessment of Johns's work? As I said, Rosenberg
was reluctant to make his criteria of excellence explicit, but we can
infer something about his values from at least three references: his
endorsement of a Baudelairian concept of modern art, the importance
he attached to doing and making, and his awareness of the seriousness
of the artist's undertaking. Regarding Baudelaire, Rosenberg is on record as approving his remarks about modern art. "What is pure art
according to the modern idea?" asks Baudelaire. His answer is that "it
is the creation of an evocative magic, containing at once the object and

the subject, the world external to the artist and the artist himself."[21] Accordingly, Rosenberg thought that Johns's attempt to remove himself from his creations, to eliminate all traces of individual temperament, was a basic misapprehension and thus something to be counted against his works. So far as artistic making is concerned, Rosenberg placed much weight on it, and this helps explain his reservations about conceptual art, in which process plays such a minor role.[22] Insofar as Johns's early works may be regarded more as "statements" about Abstract Expressionism than anything else, these paintings too may be said to fall into the class of conceptual art. Part of what Rosenberg valued in artistic creation was the artist's existential encounter with materials and the ensuing struggle to realize a personal vision. Johns and his followers largely abandoned this struggle in their self-conscious attempt to remain aloof from their paintings and to create works out of commonplace objects that reduced the strain of both making and beholding. By contrast Rosenberg believed that the creation of art was the last bastion of genuine freedom and individualism in a mass society. But what Rosenberg lamented most of all was the fact that Johns and his followers had no important artistic ideas. Though he admired creative originality, Rosenberg was hardly speaking sympathetically when he said that Johns's *Coat Hanger,* which consists simply of a wire hanger suspended against a ground of black crayon, "is an idealized self-portrait of Johns as Mr. Anything."[23]

I have selected Rosenberg's discussion of the art of Jasper Johns because I think it is less controversial than some of the essays with which Rosenberg is often associated, for example, his writings about action painting. It also reveals a certain disinterested approach, for although there is much in Johns's work that is not to Rosenberg's taste or expressive of his values, he nonetheless tries, consistent with his critical premises, to make serious and relevant statements about it. Rosenberg's analysis of Johns's achievement, moreover, raises questions about the direction art has taken in the latter half of the twentieth century and whether this direction is in the best interest of art, artists, and the art public.

Hilton Kramer: Modernism and the Reaction to It

If in Bernard Berenson we discover a highly evolved capacity for appreciating the values of Renaissance painting but a somewhat less positive attitude toward modern art; and if through Roger Fry we realize that an appreciation of formal and plastic values can reveal the genius of such a painter as Cézanne but may obscure the aesthetic relevance of subject matter; and if through Rosenberg we learn how an art of high seriousness that struggles to realize a personal vision can be set on end through parody; then our next two critics, Hilton Kramer and Charles Jencks, provide us with insights into "modernism" and "postmodernism." For an explanation and assessment of modernism I turn to Hilton Kramer, perhaps the most intelligent and articulate critic active today, whose writings also fulfill all the functions of criticism mentioned thus far—the reasoned assessment of quality that simultaneously cultivates perception and improves the intellectual climate in which we think about art. Unlike Rosenberg, Kramer has not, so far as I know, expressed his critical credo in a number of propositions. Rather, his intent, premises, and values must be culled from his writings, from which I select the introductory essays to his two collections of criticism, *The Age of the Avant-Garde: An Art Chronicle of 1956–1972* and his more recent *The Revenge of the Philistines: Art and Culture, 1972–1984.*

The Age of the Avant-Garde contains reviews and commentaries on the critical conventions and social institutions that attended the era of the avant-garde, a period that in Kramer's view lasted roughly from the 1850s to the 1950s, from Courbet's one-man show to the heyday of the Abstract Expressionists in the 1950s.[24] The avant-garde, in other words, has passed into history and is no longer a vital force or part of a living modern tradition. Kramer's criticism, then, is about the avant-garde but not of it; it reflects the current period, which has begun a far-reaching review of the avant-garde. This review has a dual character. On the one hand, it consists of a creative and critical commentary on the heritage of the avant-garde; on the other, it involves an effort to come to terms with its basic achievements. In his 1973 collection Kramer construes his own contributions "as initiating a revisionist view of the avant-garde era—an attempt to see the classic accomplishment of the avant-garde through the lens of a post-avant-garde sensibility" (p. x). In particular, he is concerned to separate the avant-garde's attainments from what he considers to be the sentimental myths that continue to surround it. What then is the reality and what is myth?

The reality was a period of genuine change in the cultural climate in which works of art were created, a time when the idea of revolution against established standards and the status quo gradually became accepted by those very same bourgeois or middle-class institutions that had initially served as the targets of the revolutionists. This is part of the irony of the present-day situation: wholly bourgeois institutions, the vast conglomeration of cultural organizations and networks of communication, reproduction, and dissemination that make up the contemporary art world, now embrace a revolutionary rhetoric of the new. It is a classic case of a cultural establishment coopting its erstwhile bitter antagonists. But once this victory over middle-class institutions was accomplished, the raison-d'être for a genuine avant-garde disappeared. That is, although the reality has changed, the rhetoric lives on.

This now obsolete ideology, says Kramer, exploits what the literary critic Lionel Trilling once called art's subversive adversary relation to bourgeois culture, the expression of which continued long after the avant-garde had made its accommodation to bourgeois society. A pervasive hatred of middle-class values thus became institutionalized, and today it finds ironic expression in the lives of many who by virtue of social position, income, and personal style are really paragons of middle-class living but who still continue to think of themselves as rebels. As distinct from the motives that propelled genuine artistic revolt against philistine standards and intolerance, we now have merely a taste for the new, a situation that, in Kramer's view, should be an occasion for despair rather than celebration since it washes away the true revolutionist's reason for being.

What were the aims of the cultural revolution of the new? What was the character of its adversarial disposition? What role did the bourgeoisie actually play in the drama of the avant-garde? What, more specifically, has been its aftermath? Kramer thinks that as a historical phenomenon and not as a permanent fixture of cultural life the

> avant-garde belongs ineluctably to the world of the middle class and is barely conceivable in isolation from it. The avant-garde has been, from the start, a vital coefficient of bourgeois culture. Beginning as an avowal of the life of feeling that the defensive and insecure institutions of the middle class could not bring themselves to acknowledge, lest its precarious hold on its own self-esteem be shattered, the avant-garde developed into the critical and increasingly combative conscience of bourgeois civilization. The cultural history of the bourgeoisie is the history of its gradual and painful adjustment to this conscience—an adjustment that made the bourgeoisie, despite its own worst inclinations, the moral and aesthetic beneficiary of the avant-garde's heroic labors. (p. 6)

Kramer follows this interpretation with some positive remarks about bourgeois society, which, despite its worst reactionary tendencies and cruelties, was really the first modern class. Its furtherance of the industrial revolution and acceptance of the principles of a democratic society showed it to be something of an avant-garde itself. Kramer's point is that the bourgeois ethos has a progressive side that is as significant as its reactionary side. What Kramer is also saying is what

Jacques Barzun points out in his *The Use and Abuse of Art:* the bourgeois is a much more complicated type than persistent caricatures suggest.[25] And Levi, in an essay that pays homage to what Kramer calls the progressive side of the middle-class mentality, has likewise remarked how much the achievements of modern culture owe to the bourgeois ethos.[26]

In Kramer's view the avant-garde, like the bourgeoisie, also had a progressive and a reactionary side.

> At one extreme, there is indeed an intransigent radicalism that categor-
> ically refuses to acknowledge the contingent and rather fragile character
> of the cultural enterprise, a radicalism that cancels all debts to the past
> in the pursuit of a new vision, however limited and fragmentary and
> circumscribed, and thus feels at liberty—in fact, compelled—to sweep
> anything and everything in the path of its own immediate goals, what-
> ever the consequences. It is from this radical extreme, of which Dada, I
> suppose, is the quintessential expression, that our romance of the avant-
> garde is largely derived. But the history of the avant-garde is by no means
> confined to these partisans of wholesale revolt. It also boasts its cham-
> pions of harmony and tradition. It is actually among the latter that we
> are likely to find the most solid and enduring achievements of the modern
> era—among those tradition-haunted artists (Matisse and Picasso, Eliot
> and Yeats, Schoenberg and Stravinsky) who are mindful, above all, of
> the continuity of culture and thus committed to the creative renewal of
> its deepest impulses.[27]

Kramer is especially astute in observing that both a radical outlook and terminology and a certain accommodation to tradition frequently coexisted in the same artists (his examples are Futurists). That is, tra-dition was being renewed at the same time that it was being deplored. It is at this point that Kramer departs from Rosenberg's interpretation of the avant-garde, for Rosenberg had stressed more emphatically its break with tradition. Yet Kramer does not think the major plot of mod-ernism is to be found in those tendencies that have been accorded the greatest attention and publicity, for example, the radicalism of Dada, Futurism, and Constructivism. Rather, it unfolds in the careers of Ma-tisse and Picasso, artists "who were working their way toward those fundamental revisions of established pictorial practice that proved to be the very basis of modernist painting in the twentieth century" (p. 8). Kramer takes the artistic development of Picasso and Matisse to represent the main plot of modernism because these artists understood that it is far easier to proclaim a disjunction between present and past than to implement it. Once more the Futurists are evoked, who, despite their radical rhetoric, actually worked their way through existing modern styles while forging their own marginal and incremental contributions to Cubism. But, like other instigators of aesthetic revolt, Kramer thinks their talent was expressed less in artistic innovation than in ideology.

If the adversarial intentions of revolutionary artists and their ideological nihilism constituted one term in the dialectic of the avant-garde, the other term was shaped by creative engagement with tradition and by the belief that tradition had to be mastered before it could be added to and extended. Tradition had to be *felt* before new emotion could emerge and be given a new form. "Thus," writes Kramer, "the impulse to act as the creative conscience of a usable tradition was as much a part of the avant garde scenario . . . as the impulse to wage war on the past, and the artists who aligned this ambition with this tradition-oriented function faced an infinitely subtler and more difficult task." For the intention of such artists was not to subvert tradition but "to rescue it from moribund conventions and redefine it in the most vital terms—terms that spoke directly to the sensibility of the age" (p. 12). Paradoxically, however, the effort to subject tradition to constant reevaluation led to the dissolution of any sustainable relation to it and hence to our current cultural malaise. Without a viable tradition or formidable antagonist, there was nothing left for the avant-garde to do.

Kramer clearly makes the artist's creative engagement with tradition a principal consideration in assessing the achievements of the avant-garde. This position reflects his attitude toward the role of tradition in culture and civilization. And it is interesting to note that, like Levi's epigraphs in chapter 4 on art history and Charles Jencks's discussion of postmodernism in the next section of this chapter, Kramer too calls attention to T. S. Eliot's essay "Tradition and the Individual Talent" and its treatment of the place of tradition in the history of culture. Note, however, that Eliot, Kramer, Levi, and Jencks stress a dynamic and creative, rather than a static, relation to tradition, one that extends and invigorates it—an attitude that enables us to speak of a living, changing tradition. It was precisely this dynamic relation to tradition that initially made the avant-garde insufferable to the established tastes of bourgeois society. Yet that society's inherent liberalism eventually enabled it to accept avant-garde revisions on its own terms. All the more pity, remarks Kramer, that it did not recognize in the avant-garde's efforts "the democratic option implicit in the bourgeois ethos and explicitly guaranteed in the bourgeois polity" (p. 15).

Since the principal activity of the progressive side of the avant-garde, however unconsciously pursued, was the creative engagement and transformation of tradition but not its obliteration, it was only natural that the museum would succeed the Academy as the representative institution of the avant-garde. In contrast to the stability associated with the Academy, the modern museum was animated by an ethos of dynamism. It embraced and placed under its supervision both the past and its current revisions, a function, it might be noted, that is quite consistent with Eliot's idea of tradition. It was a museum, for example, that was pivotal in irreversibly altering the traditional function of art when it exhibited Marcel Duchamp's urinal and in effect bestowed on it the status of art. After Duchamp a great tidal wave of anti-art swept over the cultural landscape causing great devastation, for his assault and assaults launched by his followers effectively demonstrated "that there is no such thing as an object or a gesture that, within the magical museum context, cannot be experienced as art." But, asks Kramer, at what cost to existing monuments of art and those to come? He replies, "It deprives them—and us—of their essential seriousness" (p. 18). Whether we call this attack on seriousness parody, ridicule, or vandalism, it is but one more instance of what Jacques Barzun has referred to as the principle of systematic inversion, a major tactic of post-avant-garde art that has by now used up its credit.

The "new academy" of modernity, then, is not an updated version of the one disestablished by the avant-garde, that is, the official Academy of the nineteenth century that set the standards for taste and ultimately withered under the onslaught of revisionist artists; rather, it is the museum culture committed to a principle of innovation. On this point Rosenberg and Kramer are of a single mind. Yet so long as it exists solely to satisfy a taste for novelty, the new Academy can no longer serve its public by interpreting the changed realities of artistic experience. In light of this situation Kramer thinks that the only course for criticism is to renegotiate our relation to the avant-garde, with an eye particularly on rediscovering the contributions of its progressive, rather than its revolutionary, members. "The task of criticism today," says Kramer, "is, in large part, an archaeological task—the task of digging out a lost civilization from the debris that has swamped and buried it" (p. 19). Only through such excavations can we separate the myth of the avant-garde from the reality of its achievements.

Kramer wrote these words in the early seventies. The extent to which criticism has in his estimate accepted this task can be gathered from the introductory essay, "Postmodernism: Art and Culture in the 1980s," to his *The Revenge of the Philistines*, published twelve years after the previous collection.[28] If Kramer's 1973 essays are the expression of what he then called a post-avant-garde sensibility, the later collection contains reflections on a period commonly referred to as "postmodern." The term, says Kramer, is not without its irony since modernism is now firmly established in the cultural mainstream and functions as a tradition that is constantly evoked with general approval. But just as modernism subjected the tradition of the nineteenth-century Academy to radical criticism and thus considerably loosened its hold, so modernism itself is now under attack. The assault has come not from traditional philistines but from modernism's former friends and the insiders of the current art world. It is as if the very success of modernism implies that something irredeemably corrupt must lie at its center. Whatever the causes, modernism has come under the intensive scrutiny that Kramer thinks is characteristic of the postmodern outlook. Kramer's more recent essays, then, can be seen as attempts to help us understand the basic premises underlying the postmodern critique of modernism.

What are some of the reasons for the subversion of modernism from within? Ironically, it stems in part from a nostalgia for the old bourgeois culture that modernism worked so hard to discredit. In this respect Kramer's excavation metaphor has proved extraordinarily prescient, for the immediate past as well as the near-century preceding it were, in a sense, ploughed through, but what was gleaned from the overturned layers were not works reflecting modernism's progressive impulses but rather the nineteenth-century academic works against which it had originally set itself. Kramer writes:

> The revival of nineteenth-century Salon painting and Beaux Arts architecture, the sweeping revaluation of German Romantic painting and of the American artists of the Hudson River School, the elevation of Victorian and Pre-Raphaelite art, and the boom in Art Nouveau design and even in Art Deco ornament—these are but the most spectacular symptoms of a craving that is central to the whole aesthetic outlook of postmodernist art. About these revivals of bourgeois art and design, which now enjoy such impressive critical favor, it is sometimes said that they signify little more than the gyrations of the art market and the special tastes of a generation of art historians too young to have participated in the classic battles of modernism. There may be some truth in this, but as an explanation it does not take us very far. Neither the art market nor the world of scholarship on which it depends functions in a void. They too are subject to the pressures that shape the life of culture. A reversal of this magnitude requires a larger perspective. For what, after all, is being sought out in these revivals of bourgeois styles? What, indeed, does it mean to revive a discredited style? (pp. 3–4)

And Kramer answers his own question by saying that it is the present condition of culture itself in which the attitude and high seriousness of the modernist outlook has been discredited, a feat accomplished in large part by the "pop" culture that flourished in the 1960s:

> In this altered atmosphere, the traditions governing nineteenth-century bourgeois art and architecture were seen to embody a great many envied qualities and capacities. They were taken, indeed, to represent a better world than ours—specifically, the world as it was seen to exist before it had been systematically stripped of its pretensions and extravagances (and thus of its fun!) by the dour moral injunctions of modernism. What was now admired in these rediscovered styles of the last century had nothing whatever to do with a strict aesthetic probity, the traditional hallmark of the modernist outlook. On the contrary, it was their freedom from modernist constraints—from modernist "conscience"—that commended these styles to their new admirers. The productions of bourgeois art were now admired for their amplitude and flamboyance, for their easy access to grand gestures and a showy sociability, even for their mediocrity and frivolity. What appealed also was their high technical proficiency combined with an unembarrassed espousal of sentiment, anecdote, and declamatory rhetoric. In the period that saw Andy Warhol emerge as the very model of the new artist-celebrity, moreover, sheer corniness was no longer looked upon as a failure of sensibility, nor was superficiality—or even vulgarity—regarded as a fault. Bad taste might even be taken as a sign of energy and vitality, and "stupid art"—as its champions cheerfully characterized some of the newer styles that began to flourish in the late seventies and early eighties—could be cherished for its happy repudiation of cerebration, profundity, and critical stringency. Try to imagine Arshile Gorky or Mark Rothko or Robert Motherwell countenancing such a turnabout in attitudes and you have a vivid sense of the differences separating the last stages of modernist orthodoxy from the very different moral climate of postmodernist art. (pp. 4–5)

For an explanation of the postmodernist revival of bourgeois cultural values, Kramer turns to the attitude toward life and culture called "Camp," an attitude that in effect strips art of its content in favor of an infatuation with style. Unlike true irony, which wounds and ridicules, the irony of Camp contains a large element of praise, accommodation, and affection. It creates a relation of comic intimacy and finds something redemptive in absurdity. In one sense the postmodernist Camp outlook serves to identify an avant-garde composed of those possessed of special insights denied the philistines The latter think they understand and enjoy this art, but they are not really getting the point of the joke, for that is the prerogative of persons endowed with the new sensibility. But not only the lay public is duped by the Camp sensibility. "The whole apparatus of curators, dealers, critics, art historians, and collectors . . . promptly goes into action, organizing, exhibitions, making 'discoveries,' creating new reputations and new markets, etc., while remaining oblivious to the comic implication of its new role in the postmodern scenario and indifferent to the corruption of standards that results from its efforts" (p. 7).

Kramer thinks much is at stake, most importantly artistic standards and the ideal of the seriousness of art against which Camp invokes the criterion of the facetious. But facetiousness is a highly dubious norm for charting the course of culture, for it implies, says Kramer, an easy strategy of inversion rather than one of direct attack or creative reinterpretation. Though temperamentally and politically at some distance from each other, both Rosenberg and Kramer voice concern at this turn of events. Kramer in fact sees the dethroning of the serious as the definitive expression of the special temper of postmodernist culture. This principal animus of Camp sensibility was also recognized by one of the preeminent cartographers of postmodernism itself, Charles Jencks (to be discussed shortly). Kramer quotes Jencks as saying that "the Camp attitude is essentially a mental set towards all sorts of objects which *fail from a serious* point of view" (p. 8). And Jencks continues:

> Instead of condemning these failures, [the Camp attitude] partially contemplates them and partially enjoys them . . . . it tries to outflank all the other stereotyped views of failure which are morbid or moralistic and substitute a sort of cheerful openmindedness. It starts from failure and then asks what is left to enjoy, to salvage. It is realistic, because it accepts monotony, cliché and the habitual gestures of a mass-production society as the norm without trying to change them. It accepts stock response and ersatz without protest, not only because it enjoys both, finding them "real," but because it seeks to find those usually disregarded moments of interest (the fantastic hidden in the banal). Thus the epitome "it's so bad that it's good," which accepts the classifications of traditional culture but reverses the verdict. (pp. 8–9)

In other words, Jencks, whom Kramer considers an exceptionally intelligent critic, well understands not only that Camp represents a collapse of standards but also what this collapse portends. Perhaps most chilling of all is architect Philip Johnson's (postmodern) conviction that believing in good things is futile, an opinion he expressed in an interview referred to by Jencks. "I think it much better," says Johnson, "to be nihilistic and forget all that" (p. 10). Kramer thinks that such an attitude leads back to the spiritually impoverished culture of T. S. Eliot's wasteland. Kramer points out, however, that even an age dominated by self-consciously stylish pluralism cannot repeal its history, however much it attempts to do so. Quality, standards, and seriousness insistently assert themselves, for example, in the recent magnificent exhibitions of Cézanne and Picasso, which stand in sharp contrast to the facetiousness and casualness of Camp.

It is apparent that Kramer thinks postmodernism has brought high culture to the brink and that the widespread endorsement this outlook has received from the art world calls for a searching examination of postmodernism's premises. We do well to keep Kramer's discussion of modernism and postmodernism in mind when we consider our next critic, Charles Jencks, who must now be regarded as the preeminent theorist of postmodernism. On the basis of Jencks's earlier work, Kramer has credited him with important insights into the origins of postmodernism. But I follow here Jencks's more recent *Post-Modernism: The New Classicism in Art and Architecture,* which he acknowledges to be more systematic and comprehensive than his previous more tentative presentation of his views on the subject.[29]

Charles Jencks: The Values and Rules of Postmodernism

We have remarked that although the disciplines in which discipline-based art education grounds itself are distinct enough to warrant drawing their boundaries, several of their concerns nonetheless overlap. This overlap is quite apparent in the ideas and writings of the critics we have just discussed. Charles Jencks, a contemporary English writer, is yet another critic whose work is informed by a range of associated interests, for Jencks is an architect, an architectural historian, and a theorist as well as a critic. But it is primarily in this last role that we will consider him here. How does Jencks see the role of the critic?

He believes it is the function of the critic to construct interpretive frameworks that do justice to the characteristics and values of new movements arising in culture, in the instance at hand, the emergent qualities of postmodernist art and architecture. The task is to define postmodernism's key concepts, tropes, and preferences; to discriminate major artists and works from minor ones; and in general to build "a new structure which, if effective, changes the historical landscape, the relation between present and past figures and between key terms" (p. 36). These remarks reflect the functions of criticism this chapter has emphasized: making reasoned judgments of quality that simultaneously cultivate perception and improve the intellectual atmosphere of critical talk about art.

Worth noting in Jencks's characterization is the intention he attributes to criticism to modify the historical landscape and force works of art, both past and present, into new orders of relationship. The language is familiar and recalls the use Levi made of T. S. Eliot in his discussion of tradition and the sense of history in chapter 3, and Kramer's reference to Eliot in his assessment of the accomplishments and limitations of the avant-garde. Jencks also appeals to Eliot's famous essay in explaining the motivation behind much postmodernist art and architecture. There is a kinship, in other words, between Eliot's idea of tradition, which includes the belief that the creation of significant new works alters, however slightly, our perception and appreciation of existing relationships among works of art, and Jencks's explanation of postmodernism as the reweaving of the tradition of modernism with strands of classical Western humanism. Far from seeing postmodernism as postulating a break with the past or as negating modernism, Jencks sees it conducting a creative dialogue with both the remote and the immediate past. His discussion of postmodern art and architecture introduces the notion of a reversible history as a key element and concentrates on a distinctively postmodern style—Free-Style Classicism. "Since the end of the 1970s the majority of Post-Modern artists and architects have taken a diverse tradition and consolidated it with what I call Free-Style Classicism—a rich, broad language of form, going back to Greece and Italy, but also to Egypt and so-called 'anti-classical' movements such as Mannerism. In effect they have returned to the archetypes and constants which underlie Canonic Classicism, those that are familiar to everyone who has looked at a Poussin or strolled through a Palladian house. The result is an eclectic mixture which freely combines elements of Modernism with the wider classical tradition" (p. 7).

That Free-Style Classicism is "free" does not imply a lack of direction, order, or rules. Nor is it to be confused with simple revivalism because it combines ideas, materials, and forms from the past in creative and surprising ways. Finally, it is not the only artistic or architectural game in town since late modernism and vernacular, regional, and revivalist traditions continue to flourish. In short, Jencks thinks that a commitment to both modernism and classicism is necessary for any creditable postmodern art, the broader implications of which interest him more than any particular fashion.

I must pass over many of Jencks's interesting remarks about the nature of postmodernism and his classification of its principal streams—five in painting and sculpture (metaphysical classicism, narrative classicism, allegorical classicism, realist classicism, and classical sensibility) and four in architecture (fundamentalist classicism, revivalist classicism, urbanist classicism, and eclectic classicism). That is, Free-Style Classicism draws on the language of canonic classicism and shares some of its assumptions, but it is more eclectic, hybrid, and pluralistic.

Motives vary for the postmodernist return to history, but underlying them "is the idea that, in its continuous evolution, the classical language has been transformed over time and ties generations together in a common pursuit" (p. 317). Moreover, like their forebears in the Renaissance and the nineteenth century, postmodern classicists are quite self-conscious and verbal (which recalls Levi's observation in chapter 3 that modern artistic movements are characteristically idea-based and prone to issuing credos and manifestos). Jencks even goes so far as to suggest that the discovery of tradition by "Born-Again Classicists" is not unlike the conversion experiences of born-again Christians. It is as if "the tradition of the new" is being replaced by "tradition as an organic continuum." This sense of discovery permeates Jencks's study of postmodern classicism and is expressed this way: "Post-Modern Classicism evolved out of the modernist classicism of Le Corbusier, Mies, and Louis Kahn; Carlo Maria Mariani evolved from de Chirico; Kitaj and Hockney owe a debt to the cubism and classical work of Picasso; and the work of Lennart Anderson and Milet Andrejevic springs from Morandi, Balthus and other Modernist painters" (p. 329). But what, more specifically, does Jencks see as the emerging rules of the creative combination of modernism and classicism?

After remarking that rule-governed behavior is the basis of all creativity and understanding (inasmuch as making and perceiving presuppose some set of conventions), Jencks sets out eleven rules that he thinks are implicit in emerging postmodern classicism (pp. 330–49). These principles are not universally adopted by postmodern artists and architects, nor need all postmodernist works show evidence of their having been followed. Since they evolved in a world governed by fragmentation, pluralism, and inflation, they are of necessity relative rather than formulaic. Briefly stated and summarized, these rules stress:

1. dissonant beauty and disharmonious harmony, in contrast to Renaissance harmony and modernist integration, which tend to spawn asymmetrical symmetry, syncopated proportion, fragmented purity, unfinished wholes, and dissonant unity;

2. pluralism, both cultural and political, which is the occasion for disharmonious harmony and the begetting of a radical eclecticism that often favors a collage of motifs and materials;

3. urbane urbanism, the chief feature of which is an urban contextualism that believes new buildings should not only be integrated with works in its immediate environment but should extend it as well;

4. anthropomorphism, which refers to the ways postmodernist classicism uses the human figure to evoke a human presence;

5. anamesis, which is essentially historical memory and the imaginative use of parody, nostalgia, and pastiche, as well as enigmatic, plotless allegory (especially in painting and sculpture);

6. a return to painting and content that is as variegated in content and style as the pluralistic society whose values it reveals but that overall betrays a general will to meaning through divergent signification;

7. double-coding, which is essentially the extension of the uses of irony, ambiguity, and contradiction in literature and painting, sculpture, and architecture;

8. multivalence, which is a result of double-coding and consists of the meshing of diverse meanings that may interact and form a greater unity;

9. the reinterpretation of tradition, which is neither mere replication nor canonic revivalism but the creative transformation of conventions;

10. rhetorical novelty, or the means by which creative reinterpretation of traditional ideas, forms, and conventions is carved out, such as paradox, oxymoron, ambiguity, disharmonious harmony, amplification, complexity, contradiction, irony, eclectic quotation, anamesis, anasthrope, chiasmus, ellipses, elision, and erosion (all of which suggest the aptness of the metaphor of a postmodernist language); and

11. the absent center, which reflects uncertainty and ambivalence about the symbolic character of centers of interest in works of art while acknowledging the strategic importance of a center and harboring an affection for some of its traditional manifestations (but nevertheless appreciates its problematic status in the modern world and contemporary artistic creation).

In Jencks's words, "Post-Modernism is in this sense schizophrenic about the past; equally determined to retain and preserve aspects of the past as it is to go forward; excited about revival, yet wanting to escape the dead formulae of the past. Fundamentally it mixes the optimism of Renaissance revival with that of the Futurists, but is pessimistic about finding any certain salvation point, be it technology, a classless society, a meritocracy or rational organization of a world economy (i.e. any of the answers which have momentarily been offered in the last hundred years). . . . The mood on board the ship of Post-Modernism is that of an Italian and Spanish crew looking for India, which may, if it's lucky, accidentally discover America; a crew which necessarily transports its cultural baggage and occasionally gets homesick, but one that is quite excited by the sense of liberation and the promise

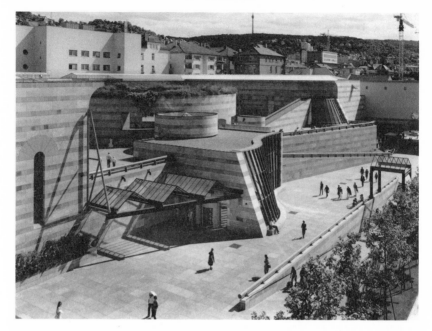

James Stirling and Michael Wilford, *Neue Staatsgallerie*, 1977–84, Stuttgart, Germany.

of discoveries" (p. 349). In short, Jencks is saying that we live in an age of anxiety whose cultural expression is replete with ambivalence.

One outstanding example of postmodernist classicism in architecture will bring out several of the points made above. Jencks thinks that the *Neue Staatsgallerie* (1977–84) in Stuttgart, designed by James Stirling and Michael Wilford, illustrates most of the ideas and principles of postmodern classicism. Jencks discusses the Stuttgart Museum in his chapter on urban classicism, a style that stresses historical and functional diversity and urban contextualism. He traces this emphasis to the influence of Jane Jacobs's *The Death and Life of Great American Cities* (1961), which made a plea for a greater multiplicity of city functions, shorter blocks, a mixture of old and new buildings, and a proper population density.

A series of photographs would be required to adequately convey an impression of the museum's special features, but at least we can indicate here what is distinctive about this museum compound, for it is a compound rather than a clearly demarcated building. Jencks writes that the museum—which in essence is architecture based on the principle of the collage—speaks directly with a kind of fractured beauty and acknowledges "our fragile position of departure, where we have left the certainties of an integrated Christian culture, where we gain a certain identity from the past but are dependent on, and enjoy the fruits of, a fast-changing technology." He goes on to say that "our sensibilities have been formed by these fragmentations and discontinuities but, far from disliking the heterogeneity which they entail, we enjoy the resultant hybrid aesthetic for its continuity with our daily life. By contrast, integrated systems can seem artificial and constricting" (p. 271). How does the Stuttgart Museum reflect this sensibility?

To repeat, the museum is not a single building but a series of fragments placed on an acropolis (which conceals a parking garage) that invites visitors either through or over the site. At the taxi drop-off point is a templelike entrance whose features recall primitive, classical, and modernist styles. The exterior of the parking garage, on the other hand, reveals the battered portico of an Egyptian pylon and is both underlined and highlighted by handrails containing lighting fixtures. While these handrails serve to direct traffic and help hold together a stylistically diverse site, their variegated colors also refract the many hues of the clothes worn by museum visitors. There is a multiplicity of functions as well: the complex is used not only as a museum but also as a social center, so it occasionally takes on a bazaarlike atmosphere. Multiple references constantly remind the observant and knowledgeable visitor of the distant and recent past—sandstone and travertine, modern concrete, Romanesque arches and windows, Egyptian cornices, rustication and classical motifs—all of which constitute, in Jencks's view, eclecticism in its most highly developed form. Eclectic choices and ironic dualisms abound, but no synthesis is achieved, for that would require more than an interesting combination of diverse components. Nonetheless, Jencks considers the Stuttgart Museum a fitting tribute to the dichotomy between traditionalism and modernism; it is indeed dichotomy dramatized and celebrated. The remote and the more immediate past are forced to confront each other on their own terms.

Perhaps nothing reflects the museum's inherent ambiguity better than what Jencks calls its absent center, a characteristic feature of many postmodern structures. In the middle of the museum compound is an outdoor sculpture court; insulated against noise and traffic, it resembles a piazza or public space. It has, however, no symbolic significance. Instead we find at the ground center of a rotunda (which, open to the sky, is in effect a domeless dome recalling classical sources)—a drain. This drain is inscribed with three circles and thus represents nothing more than the cross section of an electric cable. It is as if, Jencks remarks, this drain confirms Henry Adams's conjecture that the essence of the modern era is more fittingly symbolized by the dynamo than by the Virgin. For added contrast a sinking Doric portico on one side of the open rotunda faces a modern stairway on the opposite side.

Jencks thinks that the absent center exemplifies the principle of collage on which the museum appears to be based, a principle that realizes the lack of any compelling symbol that could make sense to a heterogeneous and pluralistic society. This principle explains why the Stuttgart Museum is a mixture or combination of components and not a synthesis, and although Jencks thinks that for this reason the building is flawed, he persists in believing that as of 1984 the Stuttgart Museum is the most impressive structure of postmodernism. He clearly approves of what Stirling and Wilford have accomplished. The museum has, he says, the virtues of its urban strategy and is a very popular and profound building: "It appeals to many different tastes, the prime if not the only goal of Post-Modern architecture, and illustrates many of its strategies, including ironic representation and contextual response" (p. 274).

I chose to feature Jencks's interpretation of a work of architecture, for architecture is his forte. His observations about painting and sculpture impress me as less cogent, however commendable may be his effort to achieve something of a synthesis of postmodernist thought. He has wisely refrained, however, from bringing postmodernist philosophy and literary theory into the picture. Much of this theory and philosophy advocates a radical disjunction with Western humanism and would thus make a mockery of the values of the new classicism that in Jencks's view are an important ingredient of the postmodernist movement in art and architecture.

This concludes my discussion of the critique of art, or art criticism. My strategy has been to examine criticism in terms of a number of characteristic functions that critics themselves regard as important rather than to provide a systematic analysis of the concept—proper work for the philosophy of art, to be discussed in the next chapter. Thus not much has been said about the intertwining of the phases of criticism—description, interpretation, evaluation, and so on—that makes it so difficult to distinguish among them in critical talk about art. The volume on art criticism in this series will address the role of these critical acts in teaching and the use of art criticism in the classroom. Rather, my purpose here has been to convey some idea of the typical concerns of critics and of what they actually do.

The important resemblances between the art critic and the art teacher are, I think, quite evident. Both are knowledgeable guides to the worthwhile in the world of art, both try to enlighten the mind and point out important sources of aesthetic satisfaction, both care greatly about quality in art and in the lives of individuals, societies, and civilization. The principal difference between them is that the art critic tends to assume an educated audience whereas the art teacher faces the preeminent and formidable task of helping to bring the young to an appropriate level of understanding and appreciation. Still, the values and activities of the art critic, no less than those of the artist, art historian, and philosopher of art, provide a model for teacher and learner alike.

6

The Philosophy of Art:
Aesthetics

In recent years aesthetic inquiry as a philosophical discipline has become essentially the philosophy of art, being concerned primarily with the nature of the work of art as the product of artistic creative activity and as the focal point of aesthetic appreciation and art criticism.

—Donald W. Crawford

Aesthetics is concerned with the way we ordinarily think and talk about art. It considers conceptual problems surrounding the meaning of terms such as imitation, realism, representation, expression, form and content, intuition, intention, and work of art, and attempts to understand and clarify these artistic concepts and terms.

—H. Gene Blocker

Since contemporary scholarship understands aesthetics to be a branch of philosophy, I use "aesthetics" and "philosophy of art" synonymously in this chapter, although, strictly speaking, aesthetics as an area of inquiry extends farther in its concerns than the philosophy of art does. In addition to examining questions about the nature, meaning, and value of art, aesthetics also considers what is involved in taking up an aesthetic point of view toward objects of practically any kind. Aesthetics may inquire into the beauty of natural phenomena as well as that ascribed to mathematical proofs and well-wrought arguments.

It is also possible to speak of scientific aesthetics. In contrast to the methods employed by philosophical analysis, scientific aesthetics draws on the empirical methods of psychology and the social sciences. Indeed, it was the hope of Thomas Munro, who did so much to advance the study of aesthetics as an independent area of inquiry in this country, that aesthetics might one day become a fully empirical and scientific discipline. Yet the current literature of aesthetics attests to the field's retention of an essentially philosophical character. Thus it is as philosophical reflection on the variety of human experience called art that aesthetics will concern us here.

Philosophical reflection, however, can assume different forms. One form consists of systematic observations about art by such major philosophers as Plato and Aristotle in antiquity, St. Thomas Aquinas in the Middle Ages, Immanuel Kant in the eighteenth century, Arthur Schopenhauer, Hegel, and Friedrich Nietzsche in the nineteenth, and John Dewey, Susanne Langer, and Nelson Goodman in our own time. In the works of these philosophers discussions of art occur within larger philosophical systems that seek to articulate the unity and wholeness of human experience.

Another variant of philosophizing is less concerned to advance a particular view of life in which art has an important place than to structure the domain of aesthetics itself, to map its characteristic ideas, theories, and problems. This may be done historically, as in Monroe C. Beardsley's *Aesthetics from Classical Greece to the Present,*[1] or systematically, as in Francis Sparshott's *The Theory of the Arts,*[2] a work that classifies and analyzes all the theories that must be taken into account by anyone wanting to think seriously about art. In this connection, it discusses four lines of aesthetic theory: the classical, the expressive, the mystic, and the purist.

In addition to these kinds of writing, which we may call philosophy of art in the traditional or grand manner, there is a smaller-scale, less ambitious type called conceptual analysis, which attempts to clarify and improve our intellectual grasp of a large number of aesthetic concepts—for example, those mentioned by H. Gene Blocker in his epigraph to this chapter. Teachers of art who come to understand the different senses of aesthetic concepts and the issues they raise for aesthetic learning will be much better prepared to deal with them when they surface in classroom talk about art.

Both kinds of philosophical reflection referred to above seem to invite attempts at formulating a definition of art that would make it possible for us to know when we are actually in the presence of a work of art. But in what does the essence of art consist? Is it to be found in a special set of properties or qualities of artworks that are there to be perceived by anyone who makes the effort? If so, what are they? Or are clues to the essence of art to be found in certain intentions and functions that art bears witness to or fulfills? Though they seem quite sensible, questions like these are rejected as misguided by certain aestheticians, who believe that no definition is capable of capturing art in its true complexity and changing character. Rather, they advise us to regard all attempts to capture the essence of art (and many of its subconcepts) as, in effect, suggestions to favor some aspects of art over others. In a modern classic of conceptual analysis, Morris Weitz writes that

> it behooves us to deal generously with the traditional theories of art; because incorporated in every one of them is a debate over and argument for emphasizing or centering upon some particular feature of art which has been neglected or perverted. If we take the aesthetic theories literally . . . they all fail; but if we reconstrue them, in terms of their function and point, as serious and argued-for recommendations to concentrate on certain criteria of excellence in art, we shall see that aesthetic theory is far from worthless. Indeed, it becomes as central as anything in aesthetics, in our understanding of art, for it teaches us what to look for and how to look at it in art. What is central and must be articulated in all the theories are their debates over the reasons for excellence in art—debates over emotional depth, profound truths, and natural beauty, exactitude, freshness of treatment, and so on, as criteria of evaluation—the whole of which converges on the perennial problem of what makes a work of art good. To understand the role of aesthetic theory is not to conceive it as definition, logically doomed to failure, but to read it as summaries of seriously made recommendations to attend in certain ways to certain features of art.[3]

Weitz is saying that all definitions of art are in effect honorific or persuasive definitions framed with a view to influencing the character of beholders' responses, and perhaps also to affecting artistic creation. Israel Scheffler, a philosopher of science and education, agrees. He sees a close resemblance between the logic of the concept of art (and many of its subconcepts) and the logic of the concept of education (and many of its subconcepts, such as teaching, learning, curriculum, and so forth). Like definitions of art, definitions of education are actually recommendations to value certain educational activities and outcomes more highly than others. Scheffler calls these definitions programmatic definitions because they carry practical implications for teaching and learning and curriculum design.[4] The definition of discipline-based art education propounded in this volume can likewise be regarded as a programmatic definition grounded in a persuasive definition of art that stresses certain of its aspects over others.

This is not to say that philosophers have abandoned the search for art's essential character. Recent efforts to specify the nature of art in relation to the institutions of the art world, for example, have generated considerable interest and aroused debate that has been responsible for the progressive refinement of institutional definitions. Their general idea is that the way social or cultural institutions confer art status has much to do with what is considered to be art. One might think that since institutional definitions are content to explain how certain things come to be called works of art, they would have nothing helpful to contribute to reflections on art education. That is not quite the case; insofar as the ability to recognize some objects as candidates for the conferral of art status builds on a sense of art history and theory—or, as Arthur Danto puts it, insofar as knowledge of art is needed to create the atmosphere in which we experience works as art—institutional accounts can become relevant to education by suggesting content that needs to be taught.[5] Most fruitful for educational purposes, however, are theories that attribute humanistic functions to artworks. Among them, as we have seen, are the provision of a high level of aesthetic gratification, the expansion of perceptual powers, and the communication of insights into the human condition.

Attempts to formulate either essential or persuasive definitions of art inevitably generate other questions about art. Some of these basic questions are nicely brought out by some remarks in Ellen C. Oppel's introductory essay to her very informative *Picasso's Guernica*. "In 1937, Picasso was asked to design a mural for the Spanish Pavilion at the international exposition in Paris. The result was *Guernica*—named after a Basque town that had been bombed some months before, during this first year of the Spanish Civil War. It is Picasso's best-known painting, and one of the masterpieces of our time. Yet it is a problematic work, stylistically complex, with images difficult to decipher, whose meaning is unclear."[6] In these few sentences Oppel refers to all the components of what Alexander Sesonske calls the *aesthetic complex*: an artist who creates a work of art, to the exhibition of which an audience responds, and also the interpretation and judgment of this work, which take place within a society where the work continues to be of interest.[7] Donald W. Crawford writes similarly that "there are five main clusters of concepts to which aestheticians direct their attention and which thus serve to define the discipline: (1) the art object, (2) appreciation and interpretation, (3) critical evaluation, (4) artistic creation, and (5) cultural context."[8]

Which component of the aesthetic complex—creation, object, response, or society—receives the larger share of an aesthetician's attention depends not only on individual preferences and temperaments but also on prevailing cultural attitudes. Hence there is a history of changing emphases in theorizing about art. The concept of *mimesis*, for example, loosely translated as imitation, figured centrally in the writings of Plato and Aristotle and became the chief legacy of ancient aesthetics. This interest in the imitative function of art raised the nature of the art object to a position of primacy. It was insisted that art objects should bear a striking resemblance to reality—although, as we shall see, Aristotle's views on the matter were much more flexible than Plato's. By the eighteenth century, however, in the writings of English and German philosophers, interest in art had begun to move from the object to the beholder's experience. The concept of imitation yielded its place of preeminence to that of imagination, which was analyzed in terms of taste and disinterested pleasure. Philosophical interest that had once centered on the object now concentrated on the nature of aesthetic experience, to which the art object was instrumental. The next shift of focus within the aesthetic complex occurred in the nineteenth century in the writings of Friedrich Nietzsche who, as Levi noted in chapter 3, conferred extraordinary significance on the artist's powers. Accordingly, writers scrutinized the artistic personality for hints as to the nature of art.

Contemporary aestheticians appear to distribute their attention among all the components of the aesthetic complex, although on closer inspection a trend of sorts is discernible. After a period during which considerable theoretical effort was expended on the problems of critical evaluation, interest now seems to have turned to the relations of art and society. The work of the late Monroe C. Beardsley is symptomatic of this change in direction. Beardsley, who in his earlier writings had much to say about the concept of criticism, wrote in one of his last essays that "the fundamental task of the philosophy of art in our time . . . is that of providing a coherent and judicious account of the relationships between the arts and the other components—or segments— of culture."[9] To be sure, not all contemporary aestheticians address this "fundamental task." Many continue to analyze such traditional concepts as style, expression, aesthetic judgment, and so forth, so that catholicity of interest characterizes contemporary philosophy of art. Invariably, the writings of aestheticians affect in various ways the thinking of art-educational theorists who, after a time of preoccupation with the artist and artistic creativeness (or creativity generally), are now pondering other constituents of the aesthetic complex as well.

Whatever may be the prevailing emphasis in the philosophy of art, the theory of discipline-based art education assumes that all the components of the aesthetic complex are important. Still, a strategic position is reserved in the interpretation of this approach in this volume for the standpoint of the beholder, that is, the outlook of the educated nonspecialist who attempts to understand and appreciate works of art with the interpretive power acquired in a program of general art education. How to bring a person to this level of response is the challenge faced by a theory of discipline-based art education.

I will now discuss some of the issues typically addressed by philosophers of art, and I will pay as much attention to the manner in which they deal with questions as I do to the conclusions they reach. This procedure allows us to benefit from both the insights of aestheticians and their methodology; it is the latter, after all, that distinguishes aesthetics most clearly from the other disciplines of discipline-based art education. We will now consider briefly the concepts of representation, artistic expression, aesthetic experience, and critical evaluation.

Representation

In *Philosophy of Art*, one of the best nontechnical introductions to the field, H. Gene Blocker takes an approach to understanding and appreciating art that is quite compatible with that of discipline-based art education.[10] For example, he writes that his views are "built on the assumption that there exists an active interchange between philosophical theories about art, art criticism, art history and the history of taste and ideas generally" (p. vii). The theory of discipline-based art education assumes the same. More specifically, Blocker examines a perennial aesthetic conundrum: how can the autonomy or independent character of works of art that we prize so highly—the ways, for example, in which artworks draw attention to themselves and seem to function as self-sufficient, self-enclosed objects—be reconciled with their relevance, with the ways in which artworks draw attention away from themselves to something to which they refer or which they represent? Blocker calls this the autonomy-heteronomy problem of art.

To illuminate the autonomy-relevance problem, Blocker analyzes the concepts of representation, expression, and form. Since it is difficult to come to terms with concepts like these in the absence of a controlling definition of art, Blocker supplies one.

A work of art is composed of materials taken from the world outside of art. But these materials are transformed within the art work to express a new vision or point of view unique and internal to that particular work of art, a vision or point of view which casts its light back onto the external world from which the original materials were borrowed. Ironically, what holds a work together is its representation of the world, the coherence of its vision or interpretation of what it is about—its content! Understanding the general meaning of the "subject matter" presupposed in daily life outside the art work is *necessary* to understanding its transformation into the content of the art work, but it is not *sufficient*. What must be added to this to understand the content is an understanding of its formal composition within the art work, and this can come only from direct experience of the work itself. (p. 198)

We will here recount Blocker's philosophical story of how in aesthetic thinking the concept of representation came slowly to displace the notion of imitation. Before tracing the genealogy of the concepts of imitation and representation, Blocker points out that both are strongly related to the idea of artistic realism and to attitudes about the relation between art and reality. To clear up any confusion that may exist about the nature of artistic realism, Blocker gathers from current literature evidence of a continuing belief that the most significant values of art lie in its realistic properties and that art is indeed inseparable from reality itself. This view places the emphasis wholly on art's heteronomous effects; what matters most is realistic portrayal, not interpreted subject matter appearing as content embedded in an expressive form that conveys something of the artist's creative imagination and unique contribution. The renewed interest in artistic realism thus recalls the classical concept of imitation, or *mimesis*, articulated in the writings of Plato and Aristotle, an idea that had enormous influence on subsequent theorizing about art and which held sway until well into the nineteenth century, when it was supplanted by the concept of artistic expression. But to return to our main line of inquiry: imitation ceded primacy to representation in the practice and philosophy of art because, as we shall see, artists began to have different ideas about reality and philosophers began to have a better understanding of the nature of visual perception and artistic representation.

Blocker begins in characteristic philosophical fashion by drawing some initial distinctions that clear a path for further exploration. First he distinguishes imitation from resemblance; for instance, a stone found on a beach may resemble a particular person, but it cannot imitate that person. Any successful imitation, on the other hand, presupposes some sort of resemblance. Imitation implies striving to achieve a likeness, whereas resemblance may just be a coincidence. What is more, in appraising imitations we assess not only their correctness but also the worth of the thing imitated. A successful imitation of a person, therefore, is valued more highly than that of an earthworm. Further, imitation goes in only one direction: if x resembles y, then y resembles x; but x's imitating y does not imply y's imitating x. Imitation thus involves an asymmetrical relation in which an imitation looks as much as possible like the thing imitated, which in turn provides the criterion for evaluating the imitation. This is to say that the valued properties and qualities of the original are reflected back onto the copy, lending it some value, though not as much as that possessed by the original. Thus "the *goal* of imitation is an object which is simply interchangeable with the original without being the same thing; in short, to create the illusion that the copy is not a copy at all, but the original" (p. 34). And the history of art abounds with stories about artful copies of objects that fooled people into thinking they were seeing the real thing. This objective of imitation, says Blocker, was given classic expression in Plato's *Republic* and Aristotle's *Poetics*.

Both Plato and Aristotle accepted the idea that art is essentially imitative. But Plato was driven to derogate art (or at least certain kinds of art) by his view of reality and the priority he assigned to gaining knowledge. For Plato, true knowledge of a thing derives from an intuition of its concept or form, and that can be achieved only through logical definition, argumentation, and proof. To use Plato's famous example from the *Republic:* the bed the carpenter makes is only an imitation of the form or concept of a bed and is thus already once removed from reality. An artist's picture of a bed would therefore be merely an imitation of an imitation, incapable of leading viewers to knowledge and hence of no cognitive value. Plato condemned pictorial art because it was parasitic on actual objects. Because it held up a mirror to reality, it had the potential to mislead people. Now in a mirror-image theory of art, works are judged solely on the basis of the accuracy with which they reflect things in real life, and since we take the same attitude toward the reflection as we do toward the thing itself, Plato forcefully denounced all imitations of undesirable acts; to condone such depictions would be morally deleterious. Conversely, portrayals of worthy activities, though still not providers of true knowledge, could be morally efficacious.

Plato's view of imitation is an extreme version of a realist theory of art, yet after a period of relative neglect during the Middle Ages, a variant of it was revived in the Italian Renaissance. The renewed emphasis on the imitative capacities of art was an effect of the period's intense interest in the study of nature and in scientific investigation. Somewhat ironically, however, although Renaissance artists strenuously strove to imitate nature, many of their works do not look very realistic to us today; the paintings of Giotto and Botticelli in particular appear quite formal and highly stylized. This fact forces us to acknowledge, says Blocker, that the meaning of realism is culturally relative. "Every age thinks its art is totally realistic and the art of every other age is completely unrealistic" (p. 39). What accounts for this cultural relativity?

For answers to this question Blocker looks not to philosophers of art but to the psychologist Rudolf Arnheim and the psychologist–art historian E. H. Gombrich. These two distinguished scholars on the topics of visual perception and representation have concluded that an accurate copy of reality is not possible inasmuch as there can be no neutral mode of imitation or mechanical duplication of reality. Instead of faithfully duplicating reality, artists translate or transpose physical objects, or they provide structural equivalents of them in a given medium. During this process the artist's mind is active and constructive as it selects, organizes, synthesizes, and integrates aspects of things imitated or represented. A naive theory of realism is thus opposed by a more sophisticated one, which posits that the portrayal of reality involves not copying or exact duplication but the interposition of stylistic conventions in acts of artistic interpretation. This is not to say that the connection between art and reality has been completely severed, only, says Blocker, "that the relationship is not one of copying, but of representing or interpreting reality from a given human perspective or set of cultural connections. We can never see an object just as it is in itself, but only as it appears to us from our biological and cultural standpoint; similarly, we cannot translate a three-dimensional object onto a two-dimensional surface except in one of many possible conventional, stylized ways" (p. 43). Thus the naive or primitive conception of imitation in the sense of producing a replica of reality has been discredited by the now generally accepted idea of the impossibility of a neutral or innocent vision. It was a chimera, then, that philosophers projected and artists adopted when they tried to actualize the Platonic version in their work. Occasions when artists earned high praise from their contemporaries for works that looked exactly like "the real thing" are explained by the fact that artists and audience were seeing the artwork through the same culturally conditioned lens.

One observation that can be made at this point is that since there are many possible styles in which an object may be recognizably depicted, no one mode of representation is necessarily more valid than others. Recall how Barzun said that styles cannot contradict one another; each may result in representations that are equally effective while expressing different attitudes toward their subject and reality. It would be foolish, for example, to criticize a work of Romantic art for failing to conform to the canons and conventions of the classic style. In summary, writes Blocker, there are "four main reasons why artistic representation deviates from reality—the artist's personality, the cultural outlook of the times, the art style of the period, and the artistic materials used; each of these can interpose itself between reality and the representation, significantly affecting the outcome. Works of art, we may conclude, do not copy reality but interpret or represent it. But representing an object is representing it in a certain light, interpreting it from a given point of view. The object is always represented, in other words, according to some general idea, or meaning." (p. 438)

A second observation follows from the finding that naive imitation theories of art have undeniably fallen into disrepute. Unlike styles of art, which are not invalidated by incompatibilities and contradictions, art theories are often rendered obsolete by new ones that are truer to the facts of the matter. In other words, a measure of cumulative progress is possible in aesthetics.

Third, Blocker exposes the narrowness of the human disposition to regard only a certain manner of depiction as *the* correct and accurate way to portray reality when he argues that all representations are culturally relative. That is, they represent a particular, often ethnocentric, point of view. In the process Blocker has performed yet another typical philosophical function: the critical analysis of unexamined beliefs.

Still, we have not advanced very far toward solving the autonomy-heteronomy problem. Even if we no longer think of art as striving to imitate, just what does it "represent"? The representational objectives of some artists seem modest indeed. Georgia O'Keeffe, for example, was quoted in chapter 3 as having remarked that her painting of a white barn was meant to represent nothing more than her vision of a simple structure, that is, of a particular, concrete thing. Is this all that "representation" can mean in the visual arts?

To discover an answer to this question, and at the same time to gain insight into the autonomy-heteronomy tension, we follow Blocker in taking a closer look at Aristotle's *Poetics*. Its central thesis was framed in reaction to Plato's theory of imitation, which held that artists can only produce deceptive copies of individual concrete things. Aristotle, by contrast, believed that artists were capable of representing general truths through portrayals of actual objects and events as well as ideal types and things that could happen. Even depictions of the imaginary, however, must bear sufficient similarity to the real world to be credible.

But to admit this much is to free the artist to alter reality in accordance with the internal needs of a work of art. The artist is no longer forced, as the primitive realist view would have it, to try to imitate things as they really are but may represent them either as they are now or as they were in the past, as they are thought to have been or as they might be. In terms of the aesthetic problem that concerns Blocker, interest has shifted from "heteronomous conformity to the world to the internal and autonomous requirements of a good work of art" (p. 50). Of course, says Blocker, the imitation of reality remains an important critical standard for Aristotle, "but its nonaesthetic teeth have been removed. What really counts now is what is convincing or likely *within the work of art*" (p. 51). This means that greater rein has been given to the imagination. Blocker concludes that the artist's concern "is not to *duplicate* scenes from real life, but to *represent* certain aspects of life as he sees them from his own special standpoint" (p. 53).

Blocker carries his analysis of realism and representation forward into the modern period of photography and film, but his strategy remains the same—to show that seemingly realistic works of art like photographs and films also rely on stylistic conventions for the portrayal of reality. In these no less than in other representational art forms "the perception of art requires attention both to the artistic medium and to the object represented therein. The art work not only represents an object, but it also displays the artist's rendering of that object in the artistic media. If the medium were totally transparent, the artist would have nothing to say about the object. Art exists in a tension between these two factors and can never separate itself entirely from one or the other" (p. 67). Another way to put the matter is to say, with Virgil C. Aldrich, that an artist is someone who composes the special qualities of materials and subject matter into a work of art that features not only the aesthetic qualities of transfigured materials but also an interpretation of subject matter that appears as the content of the work, all embedded in a form constituting the work's web of relations and exhibiting qualities of its own.[11]

Finally, Blocker shows how his analysis of representation sheds light on the autonomy-relevance problem in art.

> We need to draw an important distinction between the subject matter as it is known outside of that work of art and the subject matter as it is portrayed within that work of art. We will call the first "subject matter" and the second "content." The subject matter lies outside the art work, while the content is internal and autonomous. This resolves the autonomy/heteronomy problem. The art work can refer beyond itself and yet remain autonomous. How? It is based on and comments on an independent subject matter through its unique interpretation of that subject. The artist uses as elements independently interpreted subject matter (the human couple, mother and child, a tree or a chair, and so on). These are already understood and already have representational meaning. Second, the artist composes a context of such elements which does not exist independently of that work of art. Artistic creativity enters at this second stage. Because of the first the artist can communicate with other people about a commonly shared world; because of the second he can say something new. Third, because of the relation of these two, the second sheds light back onto the first. That is, the artist's individual, fresh point of

view becomes an interpretation of ordinary reality, and thus a new way of looking at that reality is created.[12]

I mentioned Blocker's belief that an understanding of art involves an active interchange between philosophical theories about art, art criticism, and the history of art, taste, and ideas. His discussion of the concept of artistic representation is an excellent example of just such an interchange. Beginning with statements by contemporary artists about the importance they attach to realism, Blocker weaves back and forth between discussions of aesthetic theory in antiquity, the Renaissance, and the modern period, revealing along the way a sound knowledge of art history, art criticism, artistic creation, and the psychology of perception. He undertakes all of this not as an exercise in philosophical analysis for its own sake but rather as a means of resolving an aesthetic issue—the reconciliation of art's autonomy and relevance. In the process Blocker makes us witness to an intellectual drama—how the concept of representation came to replace that of imitation. He also demonstrates why aesthetics is often called a second-order discipline: its basic work consists of a critical analysis of statements already made by others about works of art.

Artistic Expression

John Hospers's *Understanding the Arts* is perhaps the best available summary of the conventional wisdom of aesthetics.[13] Like Blocker, Hospers thinks the most effective way to come to terms with aesthetic theory is to indicate its relevance to specific problems that arise in our attempts to understand art. Indeed, *Understanding the Arts* is distinctive among books on aesthetics for opening with a literary work, Stephan Zweig's short story "The Royal Game" (about chess), which Hospers uses to examine a number of aesthetic concepts. But he also makes ample reference to works of visual art and lends significant credibility to his arguments through numerous quotations from artists, critics, and philosophers.

If Blocker told the story of how in aesthetic theory interest in representation gradually supplanted interest in imitation, the account Hospers provides shows how interest in expression came to displace interest in representation; how, that is, the emphasis shifted from the ways artworks represent external reality to speculations about how art expresses the artist's inner world of feelings, emotions, intuitions, and attitudes. As with Blocker, Hospers's manner of going about his task and reaching his conclusions will receive equal attention.

In ordinary discourse we take "expression" to refer to some outer manifestation of an inner state, to the way we make others aware of our everyday moods, feelings, and emotions. This is, of course, too unsophisticated a conception of expression to apply to art, and John Dewey submitted it to considerable refinement in his *Art as Experience*. Dewey first differentiated between expression as emotional discharge, that is, as impulsive behavior and a sudden "boiling over," and the act of expression. Inner agitation "must be clarified and ordered by taking into itself the value of prior experiences before it can be an act of expression." Moreover, "these values are not called into play save through objects of the environment that offer resistance to the direct discharge of emotion and impulse." When the objects of the environment that offer resistance to spontaneous emotional release are artistic materials, inner agitation must work itself out through these and will in the process become ordered and clarified and eventually embodied in a work of art. "Such transformation," writes Dewey, "marks every deed of art."[14] I draw attention to the crucial importance Dewey assigned to the artistic medium in expression, for, as we will see shortly, other theorists have not shared this concern.

It is, I think, possible to speak of a standard interpretation of the act of artistic expression in its most extended form: the clarification of feelings and emotions and their embodiment in the medium of a work of art for the sake of eliciting an emotional response in beholders. To put it somewhat differently, artistic expression consists of the artist's inner state; the artistic medium in which the artist's interior perturbation is regulated and transformed; the work of art, which embodies the artist's affective condition in the medium; and the viewer, who reacts to the work in a certain way. Each of these components can assume focal importance in different expression theories.

The idea that the function of art lies in the expression of feeling has had a relatively short history; prior to the nineteenth century it would have been considered quite alien. But like the theory of art as imitation-cum-representation that exerted a powerful influence over aesthetic thinking and artistic creation, expression theories in their turn became highly influential, beginning with the Romantic era. Most of these theories have been focally concerned with the nature of affective life: the expression of feelings, emotions, and attitudes rather than ideas, ideals, or themes. As Eugene Véron wrote in his *L' Esthetique* (1878), "Art is the manifestation of emotion, obtaining external interpretation, now by expressive arrangements of line, form, or color, now by a series of gestures, sounds or words governed by particular rhythmic cadence."[15] The more celebrated proponents of this approach in the modern period include the Italian philosopher Benedetto Croce (1866–1952) and the British philosopher R. G. Collingwood (1889–1943). The main contribution of recent American and British philosophers has been to clarify some of the inherent ambiguities in the views of these and other expression theorists.

At a time when the "standard" interpretation of expression in art is seldom challenged, it requires an effort of the historical imagination to realize the distance that separates us from Croce's and Collingwood's understanding of it. Hospers helps us through these difficulties, and he does so within the framework he adopted for explaining the concept of expression generally. He organizes his discussion around four senses of artistic expression: expression as a process, which emphasizes the artist, his inner states, and his interaction with the medium; expression as communication, which usually spans the gamut from artist to percipient; expression as the arousal of feeling, which concentrates on the nature of the percipient's response; and expression as the properties of a work of art. Hospers assigns the writings of Croce and Collingwood to the process category of expression theories, and we begin there.

To repeat, it is taken as axiomatic today that an artist is someone who expresses ideas and feelings in a medium that offers some resistance to being manipulated and that in the manipulation of materials during the process of creation the artist's feelings undergo transformation. This is not how Croce views the matter. What is important to him is that the artist has intuitions or ideas that are considered to have been "expressed" when they have been pushed about and transfigured in the artist's thinking and achieved there a definite formulation or clarification with which the artist rests content. In other words, for Croce an act of expression is complete as soon as an initially vague intuition has assumed a satisfactory shape *in the artist's mind*. Externalization in an artistic medium, that is, the creation of an artwork that makes the artist's intuition accessible to the public, usually follows because artists like to share what they have expressed, but it is *not* a necessary phase of expression per se. Croce's theory thus appears to severely curtail the act of artistic expression as it is usually understood, relegating to a subsidiary status several elements usually included in it (i.e., artistic media and materials, the finished work, the audience). It also alters the criteria that would normally be used to judge whether a person is an artist. "The painter is a painter, because he sees what others only feel or catch a glimpse of, but do not see."[16] What sets the artist apart is, therefore, an internal power of intuition, not merely the ability to give public manifestation to that vision, no matter how excellently the latter may be accomplished. Some further observations might explain his views and perhaps render them less startling.

First, visions and intuitions do not come to the artist's mind full-blown; they may originate in momentary glimpses or impressions but require further development and elaboration in the artist's imagination to realize their full artistic potentialities. This may involve a lengthy and strenuous but mainly mental process, one during which many avenues may be tried and found futile and in which steps are retraced and new beginnings made. It is thus clear that the Crocean artist is fully subject to the frustrations and vexations we think of as befalling creative people.

Second, and this is very important, the artist shapes and transforms rudimentary ideas by thinking them through in terms of the media and techniques of a particular art form—in terms of words, tones, pictorial images, shapes, hues, and so forth. Croce tends to be rather dismissive of artistic technique because he thinks it is something anyone can learn, while the ability to intuit, to see in the special way referred to, is the artist's gift alone; no techniques exist for generating ideas that promise successful elaboration into expressions ready for externalization. But, as Hospers points out, we now realize how crucial it is that artists be the master of a technique and intimately acquainted with the possibilities and limitations of an artistic medium. Without skill, training, and prior practical experience artists would not only be unable to execute in a public form the intuitions that have been fully "expressed" in their minds, they would not even be able to perform the mental labor of shaping intuitions in terms of an artistic medium—they would be just like the rest of us who possess neither talent nor technique.

Third, it would, even in a Crocean account, probably be incorrect to think of the artist as someone who sits in an armchair cogitating, then after a while, finally in possession of the full expression of an intuition but dimly glimpsed at first, gets up and unhesitatingly puts it down on canvas. Croce does allow for sketches and trials and for tentative manipulations of actual art materials. But these are only an aid to the artist's mental activity; they help to clarify ideas, and often they generate new ones as well.

Fourth, in Croce's thinking artistic materials and techniques have a strange dual existence and function, or, rather, they are being worked over in two separate arenas: as mental media in the artist's imagination and as physical media in preliminary work as well as the externalization of the finished expression. But their most important role is the first. Fifth, Croce goes somewhat against the grain of expression theories generally in his relative neglect of the affective dimension. Intuitions are not identical with emotions, although the process of expressing intuitions may be accompanied by feelings. Finally, in Croce's view, intuition, from an initial faint hint to a completed formulation in the artist's mind, is synonymous with expression. And it is always self-expression, that is, it is undertaken for the artist's personal satisfaction and no one else's. Hospers writes that "expression is always a solo process." It "is a coming-to-consciousness about one's own emotions; it is not directed at an audience." The poet writing down a poem merely provides an opportunity for someone to "overhear" what the artist has expressed, but the poem is not consciously addressed to that reader.

A twist is given to Croce's theory of artistic expression by R. G. Collingwood, who accepts Croce's basic premise concerning the artist's mind being the primary locus of artistic expression. Collingwood's departure lies in an emphasis on the artist's feelings and their management by the artist. Hospers writes that for Collingwood "expression is a matter of making clear the exact nature of one's emotions to oneself." This struggle to get a firm grasp on one's emotions progresses haltingly and gropingly and is not strongly goal-directed. The reason for this is that the end cannot be previsioned; no methods are available for directing this mental process. "The artist," says Hospers, "doesn't know what he's going to say until he has said it, doesn't know what he's going to express until he has expressed it."[17] (Recall Levi's similar remarks in chapter 3.) To underline the point, Hospers quotes a famous passage from Collingwood's *Principles of Art*: "The description of the unwritten poem as an end toward which [the poet's] technique is a means is false; it implies that before he has written his poem he knows, and could state, the specification of it in the kind of way in which a joiner knows the specification of a table he is about to make. This is always true of a craftsman; . . . [but] the artist has no idea what the experience is which demands expression until he has expressed it. What he wants to say is not present to him as an end toward which means have to be devised; it becomes clear to him only as the poem takes shape in his mind, or the clay in his fingers."[18]

How well does the Croce-Collingwood theory of artistic expression hold up under scrutiny? Both Croce and Collingwood downplay technical skill in art, but technique is so undeniably a part of actual art making and artistic performance that Hospers thinks it unwise to sever it from creation. "Technique," he insists, "is not a *sufficient* condition for good performance and creation, [but] it surely is a *necessary* condition."[19] The same can be said about artistic media as opposed to their mental representations, which supposedly are the sole locus of expression. Surely materials are not a matter of relative indifference to the artist. It is often said that an artist is someone entranced with materials not only because their manipulation is enjoyable but also because new ideas constantly emerge from it. Hence note taking, tryouts, and sketches are much more important than they would be if they were incidental rehearsals for mental operations. It is straining, therefore, to assert that artists are done with expression when they have completed it in their minds. This view would demote the creation of the art object to something of an anticlimax, and that cannot be true even in the rare instances of artworks that were not made for a public; externalization always matters deeply to the artist. As for Hospers's critique of the role of emotions, intuitions, and other inner states, it applies to most expression theories, not only those of the process type.

If process theories of expression of the type just discussed cut the act of artistic expression short at its beginning stages, communication theories take in its whole span: the process of expression is not considered complete until the audience has responded to the work—and responded in a narrowly prescribed way, that is, by experiencing the same emotions the artist felt during the act of creation. The most famous advocate of artistic expression as the communication of feeling was the great novelist Leo Tolstoy. Tolstoy's belief, stated in *What Is Art?*, is that art consists of "one man consciously handing on to others by means of external signs feelings he has lived through in order that others may be infected by these feelings and also experience them."[20] Yet this communication sense of expression does not seem to withstand close examination any better than the process sense does. It is not plausible, says Hospers, to claim that an audience is necessary in order for artistic creation to run its course to consummation. Furthermore, it is far from certain that the communication of feelings as Tolstoy imagined it—where a state of equivalence is reached between what the artist puts in and the beholder takes out—ever actually takes place, or could ever be demonstrated to have taken place, in artistic expression. Hospers remarks that it is next to impossible to know exactly what an artist feels while creating a work; all we have to go by is the work of art, from which it is extremely difficult to infer the mental states that supervened the artistic process. Nor is it clear that we need such knowledge in order to appreciate art, but more on that later.

It is equally doubtful that the beholder of art can, or should try to, replicate the artist's feelings. The creation of a work of art may be an agonizing and frustrating experience for an artist, but why should the beholder suffer similarly? Indeed, a percipient's conscious efforts in that direction would be quite at odds with the mood of authentic contemplation, which is characterized by detached affect and which, as will be suggested in the next section, should be maintained if experience is to have aesthetic character. In short, says Hospers, "It would be difficult to find a reason why the *aesthetic* process, experienced by the consumer, should match the *artistic* process, undergone by the creator of art."[21]

Then there are questions about the value of communicating a particular feeling. Is the importance or scope of the emotion commensurate with the effort that went into creating the work of art and the effort necessary to experience it appropriately? And if so, has it been communicated well? Tolstoy uses the artist's sincerity as a criterion for assessing the worth of a communicated emotion. But again, there is no necessary correspondence between sincerity and significance. Many immature or shallow artists are convincingly sincere, but their products are not artistically worthwhile on that account. The standard of spontaneity falters on similar grounds: the history of art affords too many examples of artistic creation being anything but spontaneous and none the worse for it.

Finally, one must ask whether it is true that artists are always or usually trying to communicate their feelings. If we are to believe Jasper Johns's statements, such was not the case with him, and we know of composers, writers, and painters who have said they kept their emotions deliberately in check while working and even distrusted them. Yet this choice does not seem to have affected the stature of their work nor falsified its description as "expressive." Hospers quotes Richard Strauss on the composer's characteristic mental state while composing: "I work very coldly, without agitation, without emotion even. One must be completely master of oneself to organize that changing, moving, flowing chess-board, orchestration."[22] Communication theories, then, fail to convince for several reasons.

As we have seen, communication theories command the entire territory of the act of artistic expression, including the portion occupied by evocation theories, that is, those concentrating on audience response. Evocation theories of expression assert that what a work of art expresses is what is being evoked in a beholder and, further, that the evocation is affective in character. These theories therefore pronounce the percipient's emotional reaction as the most important feature of artistic expression. Yet evocation theories are perhaps the easiest to refute because they either distort responses in the direction of extreme naivete or impoverish the expressive potential of works of art. For example, only very unsophisticated beholders (very young children, perhaps) would feel saddened by music expressive of sadness, cringe before a painting expressive of foreboding, give up hope while reading a poem expressive of despair. Rather, works that express emotions that we try to avoid in real life are, when they are successful, typically responded to with admiring appreciation, even delight in their unique articulation of these feeling states. This may seem paradoxical, but it conforms to the realities of aesthetic experience, for instance, the fact that we can derive great satisfaction from tragic art. But how is this possible? Hospers suggests that

> in life, experiences of grief and sadness are always *tied to particular events*, such as the death of a loved one, which evoke the sadness of grief; because we do not like loved ones to die, we do what we can to avoid the situations which produce the emotion. But the sadness of music (and art in general) are not like that: we can experience the emotion *without* the situation that in life would bring it on; we experience it in detachment from a life-situation, and abstracted from that occasion we can enjoy and savor it: we get the frosting, so to speak, without having to eat the unappetizing cake. Whatever the true account is of the difference, we can at least distinguish *life-sadness* from *art-sadness*: we do not seek to cultivate the first, but we may well cultivate the second.[23]

It is of course something of a mystery why the experience of sad and tragic happenings and depictions in art should be enjoyable, but evocation theories of expression will not dispel it.

Lastly, if the expressive qualities of artworks do not necessarily evoke corresponding emotions in beholders, it is equally questionable if whatever affective reactions beholders do experience are sufficient to indicate wholly what a work expresses. If the emotions of pity and fear, as Aristotle believed, constitute the proper response to tragedy, are these feelings all that can be expressed in tragedies? If certain songs and marches stir feelings of patriotism, is patriotism the only expressive potential they can have? It would appear then that the evocation theory of artistic expression breaks down rather severely.

Having analyzed the many difficulties with the process, communication, and evocation senses of artistic expression, Hospers settles on the properties sense as the most reasonable. We now concentrate on the central portion of the spectrum of artistic expression: the work of art as the artist's product and the expressive properties it ends up possessing—no matter how, precisely, they have come to be in the artwork. This formulation cuts out as unnecessary any guessing about the process side of artistic creation, about emotional states the artist may have undergone and given embodiment to. But no great loss has been suffered as far as understanding art is concerned. "Perhaps,"

Hospers suggests, "we should say . . . that the *creation* of a work of art is one thing, and the expression of emotions is another—something which may or may not *accompany* the process of creating the work. In that case, it would not be true to say that the creation of the work *is* the expression of emotions or of anything else; expression would simply have no place in the account" (p. 203).

With a properties emphasis, simplification has also become possible at the audience-response end of artistic expression. Since the artist's emotions have become irrelevant, we should not expect percipients to duplicate them. We need not even think that beholders should respond to art with feelings that somehow parallel a work's expressive content. All that is expected of astute viewers is that they pay close and appropriate attention to the properties an artwork has to offer, including its expressive qualities; that they enjoy and appreciate these properties as well as the complex whole into which they compose themselves; and that they estimate the success of the whole. We now see that the notion of expression in art, although it may continue to have life as a theoretical problem, has largely disappeared as a category as far as the percipient's experience is concerned, for it is simply not true that one notices the work of art first and then pays attention to its expressiveness, or vice versa. Hospers makes the following crucial point about works of art and our experience of them: "When we hear a composition, we do not merely experience combinations of sound, and when we see a painting, we do not merely experience combinations of shapes and colors; sounds and colors are *percepts*—they are what we perceive with the senses—and one of the most remarkable things about art is that *in art all percepts are suffused with affect,* or feeling-tone. Not merely that when we see or hear X we feel Y, but that we perceive X as *having* the quality Y. It is not geometrical shapes we see first, it is the *expressive quality* of those shapes" (p. 212).

In this connection, recall Levi's characterization of art in chapter 3 as an image of human import suffused with feeling. And it is only fair to mention that views of this nature, in addition to being verified by our commonsense experience of art, gain authority from the theory of gestalt psychology, especially as reflected in the writings of Rudolf Arnheim. He realizes that expressive qualities are the artist's main means of communication (though not necessarily of the artist's feeling) and that this realization is fraught with consequences for teaching both artistic creation and aesthetic appreciation.[24] Hospers, too, recognizes that coming to terms with expression is extremely important for teaching and learning in art. Yet it is to Hospers's credit that, having said this, he does not simply recommend adoption of the properties version of expression theory, the one he finds most acceptable, without indicating some problems that still remain.

Many of these difficulties stem from the poor match between language and aesthetic features, a situation especially vexing to teachers (and, of course, critics) who are trying to talk about art as helpfully as possible. They soon discover that our vocabulary of expression or mood words is far too limited to capture many of the subtle qualities of works of art. (This accounts for Fry's recourse to poetic figures in describing Cézanne's paintings.) The best we can hope to do with the descriptive terms we use is to indicate a range within which a work's expressive properties would fall. But even with these more modest ambitions our accounts are likely to be contested, for it is a fact that people tend to disagree most sharply when it comes to the description of expressive qualities, while consensus is often quite easily obtained regarding a work's composition or style.

Yet Hospers cautions against assuming automatically that because our descriptions of expressive qualities differ, our experiences of them are also radically different. There is yet another side to the problem with language: we often hear it said that "the same" emotion or feeling can be expressed or embodied in myriad artworks, and in different art forms at that. But is this really the case, or are we confronted with finely differentiated expressions to which we apply the same adjectival phrases merely for lack of more precise ones? A deficiency also obtains on the part of art, for some very important human emotions do not seem to find easily recognizable expression in works of art. What, for instance, is the shape of hope, inspiration, fear, and love? But that is not the end of perplexities to challenge us, for the apparent relativity of expression also calls for an explanation. Hospers acknowledges that expressiveness varies from culture to culture, and it is also true that different eras of the same civilization have attributed different expressive import to the same work of art. The ultimate mystery, of course, is how inanimate things such as artworks can have human emotional qualities as properties at all. To say that they possess these qualities only metaphorically and not literally does not take us very far, for we still have not explained what it is in artworks that appears to justify such metaphorical ascriptions.

Even if, despite the remaining difficulties just mentioned, we accept the properties sense of expression in art as the most viable, we must still address the question of whether an artwork's expressiveness contributes decisively to its value. Opinions vary, but I think it is safe to say that expressiveness is but one criterion of artistic excellence (unity, complexity, thematic import being others). Many justly celebrated works are not expressive of anything, or else they are only indefinably or vaguely expressive. On the other hand, expressiveness cannot save an otherwise weak artwork. It is even possible that if artists strive too hard for expressiveness, they succeed only in making it trite, obvious, or sentimental. Furthermore, changes in an artwork may destroy its beauty or artistic value while leaving its expressiveness intact. Still, expression has earned the space devoted to it here not mainly because it is intriguing but mainly because it is important to our understanding of art. It would be nearly impossible to teach art meaningfully in a program of discipline-based art education without tackling the notion of expressiveness.

Another purpose of this lengthy account of Hospers's survey of artistic expression, however, has been to convey a sense of the multiplicity of meanings an aesthetic concept can have and a sense of the questions and complications to which it gives rise when we reflect on its role in our appreciation of art. Once again, we have seen that philosophers of art do not go to work until others—artists, critics, philosophers, generalists—have made statements and taken positions, which philosophers of art then examine to determine the grounds of their truthfulness or usefulness. We admire Hospers's careful method, that is, the way in which he first distinguishes different senses of expression—process, properties, communication, and evocation senses—and then systematically examines the strengths and limitations of each sense, making a number of important distinctions along the way. He treats the concept of expression as a puzzle and unfolds an analytical drama that ultimately gives reasoned preference to one sense of expression, the properties sense, over others.

Thus far we have considered two concepts that are central to a grasp of art, concepts that bear principally on our understanding of the art object: what it represents or is expressive of. We now consider two concepts that bear on the nature of our engagement with art and our judgment of it, the concepts of aesthetic experience and critical evaluation.

Aesthetic Experience

Is there really something we can call aesthetic experience? And if so, can we talk clearly and intelligently about it? Moreover, is the idea of aesthetic experience of particular importance to our experience of art? Or is it more common to speak of the aesthetic experience of nature and ordinary objects?

In examining the concept of aesthetic experience, and the notion of critical evaluation to follow it, I will summarize two essays by philosophers who were regarded during their lifetimes as the respective deans of American and British aesthetics, the late Monroe C. Beardsley and Harold Osborne. The concept of aesthetic experience held an important position in the philosophies of art of both, but I shall here concentrate on Beardsley's version of it. In the next section I will discuss Osborne's ideas on critical evaluation.

In "Aesthetic Experience," published in Beardsley's *The Aesthetic Point of View*, Beardsley begins by assuming that it is still an open question whether there is a peculiarly worthwhile experience called "aesthetic" that is discernible in the wide range of our encounters with the world, including first and foremost our encounters with works of art.[25] The problem is to identify those features that lend a more markedly aesthetic nature to some experiences than to others. In view of the difficulty of this enterprise we should not expect more clarity or exactness than is attainable under the circumstances. But Beardsley thinks the task is manageable if we look for a complex rather than a simple description of aesthetic experience, one that will have the added advantage of possibly reconciling some of the positions and discoveries of other philosophers, past and present.

Beardsley notes how his initial attempts to record aesthetic experience drew inspiration from John Dewey's aesthetics, particularly from what Dewey implied by his notions of "having an experience" and of that experience's distinctive consummatory value. Yet although Beardsley admired Dewey's general aesthetic outlook, he also felt that his descriptions were unduly confusing. For example, Beardsley thought Dewey's definition of the work of art was misleading since Dewey did not identify it with the object of art but with the process of realizing it. Furthermore, Beardsley did not believe that in order for experience to have an aesthetic character it had to satisfy Dewey's ideal of "an experience." Beardsley did retain, however, Dewey's insistence on the hedonic character of aesthetic experience, which he described variously in terms of satisfaction, pleasure, and gratification, all testifying to the widely held belief that experiences with aesthetic character are intrinsically enjoyable. But he also cast about for a broader conception of aesthetic experience that would accommodate more than the very special occasions featured in Dewey's aesthetics.

Beardsley suggests there are five criteria of aesthetic experience. He believed that although the criteria should be applied together, not all of them need be at any given time; only the first is indispensable. At least three others should be present, however, and the last one he thinks is very important. The five criteria are as follows:

1. *Object directedness.* A willingly accepted guidance over the succession of one's mental states by phenomenally objective properties (qualities and relations) of a perceptual or intentional field on which attention is fixed with a feeling that things are working or have worked themselves out fittingly.

2. *Felt freedom.* A sense of release from the dominance of some antecedent concerns about past and future, a relaxation and sense of harmony with what is presented or semantically invoked by it or implicitly promised by it, so that what comes has the air of having been freely chosen.

3. *Detached affect.* A sense that the objects on which interest is concentrated are set a little at a distance emotionally—a certain detachment of affect, so that even when we are confronted with dark and terrible things, and feel them sharply, they do not oppress but make us aware of our power to rise above them.

4. *Active discovery.* A sense of actively exercising constructive powers of the mind, of being challenged by a variety of potentially conflicting stimuli to try to make them cohere; a keyed-up state amounting to exhilaration in seeing connections between percepts and between meanings, a sense (which may be illusory) of intelligibility.

5. *Wholeness.* A sense of integration as a person, of being restored to wholeness from distracting and disruptive influences (but by inclusive synthesis as well as by exclusion), and a corresponding contentment, even through disturbing feelings, that involves self-acceptance and self-expansion. (pp. 288–89)

These criteria are invoked not only to ascribe aesthetic character to an experience, but also to use their opposites as negative reasons that explain why our experiences of certain works of art are often unsatisfactory.

The first feature of aesthetic experience, object directedness, is perhaps the least controversial of the five. Before there can be an aesthetic experience, there must be something to be experienced—a painting, a musical performance, a novel—something, furthermore, that is of such a nature as to keep our attention focused on it. For Beardsley this criterion is broad enough to include conceptual art (a fact often overlooked by his critics) inasmuch as a work of conceptual art directs us to a possible state of affairs the artist wants to bring to our awareness. Our attention remains aesthetic so long as we feel "that things are working or have worked themselves out fittingly." If we turn away in disgust or if something repels us, it is because the experience lacks aesthetic character; we have in effect said that we have failed to discover either fittingness or rightness in the object.

Felt freedom, the second criterion of aesthetic character, may not always be present. What Beardsley means by this term is the way some things suddenly command our interest by virtue of their sheer compelling quality, such that whatever else we were thinking about loses its dominance over our awareness, and we feel freed from ordinary concerns, free to give ourselves over to the aesthetic. This effect cannot be consciously produced and, once again, may happen quite unexpectedly. Beardsley gives the example of our turning on the radio and hearing part of a Mozart string quartet that immediately brightens our mood. Guy Sircello has something similar in mind in his essay on beauty when he mentions that beauty (aesthetic character for Beardsley) is, in effect, an attention getter. He writes that beauty typically breaks in upon us, and we freely yield to it for the sheer enjoyment of doing so and for no other reason.[26] And Kenneth Clark seems to tap the same vein when he describes his characteristic pattern of response to works of art (to be discussed in chapter 8) and says of the period of impact or first impression that it may occur even while we are riding on a bus and suddenly notice a painting in a store window that captures our eye. This appears to come close to what Beardsley speaks of when he states our spirits can be lifted by things that we had not consciously selected for attention.

Detached affect is another feature that is not a necessary condition of aesthetic character. Yet something like it seems to be typical of many of our aesthetic experiences, and artists generally make a point of providing for it through conventions that keep us from confusing even the most realistically rendered works with actuality itself. To be sure, there have been instances in which artists appear to have erased the border between art and reality. In even some of the more bizarre cases, however, we can observe some distancing techniques that affect the character of our response. For example, the artist who had his father sit in a rocking chair in a museum (my example, not Beardsley's) might be thought to have made any feeling of detached affect impossible by using a real person instead of a model or robot, but here the museum gallery setting itself proved a sufficient distancing device. Beardsley refers to Gaetano Zumbo's sculptures of corpses which, however gruesome we may find them, we do not confuse with actual dead bodies.

Regarding the feeling of active discovery—"of insights into connections and organizations" or "the elation that comes from the apparent opening up of intelligibility"—Beardsley acknowledges that he had always assumed that the aesthetic experience of art, its hedonic character notwithstanding, is basically a cognitive act but that he appreciated this fact better after reading E. H. Gombrich, Nelson Goodman, and Rudolf Arnheim. Of course, artworks differ greatly in the magnitude of the feeling of active discovery and insight they are able to generate; relatively simple ones probably cannot afford much in the way of intelligibility. However, those works that make it appropriate to speak of feelings of discovery and insight would have obvious pedagogical importance. (It should be noted that this aspect of aesthetic experiences also occurs in cognitive disciplines like history, the empirical sciences, and mathematics.)

Finally, Beardsley attaches significance to the feeling of wholeness or reintegration. In his view this characteristic ranks almost as highly as object directedness, the only necessary condition Beardsley stipulates for aesthetic character. Wholeness implies unity not so much in the dimension of completeness as in the dimension of coherence. And by this Beardsley means, first, "the coherence of the elements of experience itself, of the diverse mental acts and events going on in one mind over a stretch of time," and, second, "the coherence of the self, the mind's healing sense . . . of being all together and able to encompass its perceptions, feelings, emotions, ideas, in a single integrated personhood." Feelings like these may occur in areas outside the arts, but when experience is of a more concentratedly intellectual kind, coherence is normally achieved by narrowing the focus and pushing away extraneous elements. Beardsley thinks it is primarily in our aesthetic experience of art that we find a "widening and deepening of a pattern or network of relations to take in contrasting elements."[27]

With typical modesty Beardsley acknowledges that the five criteria of aesthetic character he discusses may "well prove to be not unuseful." Although he stresses the compound character of aesthetic experience and its disjunctiveness (aesthetic experience tends to separate itself fairly well from other types of experience), he does indicate how aesthetic character can also be found in experiences outside the arts. Beardsley concludes with some examples of contemporary art criticism that illustrate "the sort of discrimination that critics are called upon to make—distinguishing as clearly as possible between those works that push aesthetic experience into new directions, expanding the range of qualities it can encompass, and those works that renounce their interest in aesthetic experience and abandon it in favor of something else, something quite different" (p. 297). And what Beardsley is alluding to here is not only the particular examples of "art" he mentions—chickens having their heads cut off with scissors and human combatants struggling to the point of actual injury—but a general principle he has stated elsewhere: "When the experience is largely painful, when it consists more in blowing the mind than in revitalizing it, when it involves no exercise of discrimination and control, we must frankly say that what it provides is not much of an *aesthetic* experience, however intense it may be. And so its goodness, if it has any, cannot be strictly artistic goodness."[28] Indeed.

Beardsley hoped his analysis might not only prove to have some practical use but that it might also open up exchanges in which writers might discover more or fewer criteria of the aesthetic—if, that is, there is anything to the idea of aesthetic experience in the first place that is worth defending. I should now like to suggest one more way Beardsley's scheme is useful in a pedagogical context. I have often presented Beardsley's criteria of aesthetic character to students and pointed out how they are features in our experience of both traditional and modern works of art. After that we would move toward borderline cases and discuss these. Yet I have also on occasion asked students what seemed to be some of the reasons for their having had an unsatisfactory experience of a work of art. What caused them, for example, to walk out of a movie or to endure it with little enjoyment? Why did they turn away with indifference or distaste from certain paintings and sculptures? What seemed to them to be missing in a dramatic or musical performance?

I discovered that their impatience, dislike, or lack of interest invariably had to do with the lack in their experience of one or more of Beardsley's criteria of aesthetic character. Of course, these students did not yet have a clear idea of aesthetic experience itself. In one way or another the reasons the students gave included the following: things did not work out in fitting and appropriate ways (absence of object directedness); no dramatic kindling of interest had occurred (absence of felt freedom); and art objects were experienced as too menacing or intimidating to be enjoyed aesthetically (absence of detached affect) or as mundane and stereotyped (absence of active discovery). All of these problems, or some of them, produced a state of dissatisfaction or frustration in the students (absence of personal wholeness or integration). Even if, as Beardsley remarks, the whole idea of aesthetic experience will eventually have to be scrapped (although I do not think he seriously entertained this possibility), attempts to discover its nature nonetheless enhance and expand our reflections on the phenomenon of art and what might be involved in enjoying and teaching it.

Critical Evaluation

Clues as to what constitutes a favorable critical evaluation of art are already contained in the discussions of Blocker, Hospers, and Beardsley. For example, a work of art will have merit if it effectively inter-animates medium, form, and content (Blocker), if it is rich in expressive power (Hospers), and if it has the capacity to bring about a high level of aesthetic experience (Beardsley). Yet we may ask whether all critical criteria are of equal importance. Are some irrelevant, aesthetically speaking? How much value should we place on what a work of art says in contrast to how it says it? These are just some of the questions that arise in connection with critical evaluation, a topic on which an extremely large literature exists.

I should like to focus on Harold Osborne, the longtime editor of the *British Journal of Aesthetics* and author of several books on aesthetics. Osborne's view, in contrast to certain tendencies in modern analytic philosophy, was that aestheticians ought to have the progress of humanity constantly in mind when addressing the problems of their field. In one of his major books, *The Art of Appreciation*, he took the improvement of our aesthetic experiences of works of art as his principal aim and concern.[29] However, my selection for discussion here is Osborne's presidential address titled "Assessment and Stature,"[30] delivered to the British Society for Aesthetics, in which he attempts to put the question of critical criteria and reasons in philosophical perspective.

Osborne argues there is a need for a better understanding of critical evaluation because contemporary society continues to be confused about the nature and value of art. Not knowing what to think, persons tend to accept just about anything done in the name of art. Marcel Duchamp's signing and exhibiting of an actual urinal was just the beginning. More recent art-world happenings have included the slaughter of animals, self-inflicted wounds, humans wrestling in a pile of manure, and obscene and pornographic acts, to mention only a few of the more extreme exhibitions to which the art public has been treated. Surely, if the philosophy of art has any uses, one of them should be to sort out the problems that frustrate our attempts to come to terms with art and form estimates of its value. It is Osborne's intention to provide guidance in just this way. He is not concerned in this instance to tell people what to judge or how to judge.

Osborne distinguishes three principles that govern our assessments in all the arts—artistic excellence, aesthetic satisfaction, and stature. The last one is composed of three subsidiary principles—the promotion of understanding, the presentation of nonverbal thought, and the expression of embodied feeling. Consider the first principle: we value artistic excellence in the arts for the same reason that we admire the display of skill and technique elsewhere; in appreciating a thing's beauty and distinctiveness we admire the elegance, unobtrusiveness, assuredness, and directness with which it was brought about. We may also relish the skill evident in exploiting the potentialities inherent in materials. By "artistic excellence," then, Osborne means "a capacity for judgment and a sense of appropriateness inherent in skills and accomplishments that are inseparable from mastery of the artistic materials . . . and the successful employment of this mastery to create a work which manifestly achieves its own particular purpose" (p. 5). Yet comparisons of degrees of artistic excellence cannot be made across art forms and may be of limited use even within the same genre. It would be foolish to compare, say, Picasso's visual draftsmanship with Milton's craftsmanship in the use of words. On the other hand, judgments about the relative merits of Picasso's and Raoul Dufy's draftsmanship are possible. In fact, this is just the sort of comparison that Jacob Rosenberg makes in his *On Quality in Art: Criteria of Excellence, Past and Present* (discussed in the preceding chapter).

Osborne's second principle of assessment (after artistic excellence) is the capacity of a work of art to provide aesthetic satisfaction. In the course of his discussion of this power of artworks Osborne calls attention to certain human faculties that were once essential for survival but which, in the course of evolution, gradually came to be cultivated for their own sakes. In such cultivation lies the origin of most of the spiritual or higher values that have since developed into human needs. Art, that is, is a response to "a specific aesthetic need, which combines a love of perfection for its own sake with the cultivation and expansion of the faculty for direct apprehension that underlies all our cognitive powers. For vague though the term is, there is general agreement that aesthetic contemplation demands primacy for direct perceptual awareness above theoretical and practical interests" (p. 6). Accordingly, we now regard a work of art as "a complex unity for perception with a hierarchy of emergent properties whose apprehension extends perceptual activity to an unusual level of alertness." There is no denying that we may experience this type of satisfaction and its benefits in our encounters with nature and in certain religious experiences, but for Osborne and many others "it is at its most intense in our contact with the arts and the provision of artifacts suitable for sustaining this kind of experience at a high voltage is the proper aim of the arts as such" (p. 7).

Now from the fact that these two principles of assessment loom large in our evaluation of artworks it does not follow that a work must satisfy both criteria in order to be evaluated positively. Evidence of artistic skill does not ensure aesthetic satisfaction, just as great aesthetic satisfaction may often be derived from works somewhat deficient in artistry. Similarly, many acclaimed works of contemporary art eschew the stimulation of aesthetic gratification in favor of other values. Yet there is no gainsaying the wide use of these two principles of judgment. In his *The Aesthetic Experience,* Jacques Maquet, an anthropologist, shows how they are applicable not only to the judgments of traditional works of Western art but, contrary to some views, also to the cultural expressions of non-Western societies.[31] When, of course, a work does exemplify both principles, we generally ascribe aesthetic merit to it, though we may still withhold a judgment of greatness or stature. Stature is secured only when a work, beyond displaying artistic excellence and affording aesthetic satisfaction, is assessed positively on the score of satisfying certain subsidiary purposes of art—persuasive, magical, devotional, didactic, and commemorative purposes. "Our evaluations in terms of stature," writes Osborne, "are related to these subsidiary functions and are in fact composite: provided that any artifact sustains aesthetic interest adequately, we ascribe stature to it in accordance both with the importance we attach to the subsidiary function which it fulfills and in accordance with the effectiveness with which it fulfills that function. Among the functions most often emphasized are those of promoting understanding, the presentation of nonverbal thought, and the expression of embodied feeling."[32]

Before proceeding, Osborne reminds us that there is no necessary connection between artistic excellence and stature; a work may be technically flawed or less than perfect and still be called great. Not so with a work's capacity to sustain aesthetic satisfaction. "We do not think of any work as great if it lacks the power to sustain some intensity of aesthetic experience. . . . Grandeur and nobility of conception are not alone enough to ensure that a work of art be great, though they are a necessary condition of artistic greatness. A corresponding power of aesthetic 'transportation' is also demanded" (pp. 9–10).

By citing the provision of understanding, the stimulation of nonverbal thought, and the embodiment of feelings as subsidiary functions of art, Osborne has admitted that great works of art, especially in the literary and dramatic arts, may enlighten us in many ways. Yet he would still consider it a gross misapprehension to suppose that the promotion of understanding is the main purpose of art or the quest for it our primary motivation for seeking out experiences of artworks.

It is in virtue of our existing understanding of human nature or whatever that we are able to recognize and assess the insight, the penetration and the truth of a work. To use it as a source of data for the sake of understanding is to misuse it as a work of art. We ascribe stature to art objects from alien cultures or the distant past without knowing or worrying about the function they once served for understanding—or influencing—life and the world within the culture and for the people among whom they originated. We admire a Benin bronze head, select one Dogon ancestral figure as great while ascribing only ethnological interest to another, without needing to know what their functions were in their own society or how effective they were believed to be for the fulfillment of those functions. We can only speculate about the meaning and purpose of Palaeolithic Cave Art. The statues around San Augustin in Colombia impress as magnificent though nobody knows the meaning they once held or the purposes they served and certainly people who are now overwhelmed by them do not pause to ask whether or how they contribute to an understanding of life and the world. We call the Elgin Marbles great, but they certainly function differently in the British Museum for the art institution of our own culture from the meaning they had when affixed to the Parthenon for the Greeks of the fifth century B.C. Greek drama no doubt still holds for us insights into human nature; but we do not maintain it in being in order that we may learn. This conception of art is too intellectualized and does not correspond with usage. Even with the art of our own time we are more interested in experiencing imaginatively what it would be like if people and the world were as they are represented to be than in learning from it how things really are. (pp. 10–11)

This passage (which does not negate what Levi said about the aesthetic wisdom of artists in chapter 3) deserves serious pondering by all those prone to overestimating the didactic, political, and social uses of art.

To repeat, Osborne's discussion of the critical evaluation of art features two aesthetic principles, artistic excellence and the satisfaction of aesthetic interest, and one nonaesthetic principle, the stature of a work of art. The last tends to be decided on the basis of three subsidiary principles: a work's contribution to understanding, exemplification of nonverbal thought, and embodiment of significant qualities and emotions. These principles may be inconsistently instantiated in given artworks and are often confused, but they yield convenient categories that let us realize more clearly what we are doing when we evaluate works of art and can help us avoid unnecessary disputes and misapprehensions. This classification of principles should prove invaluable to any teacher of art undertaking to guide the young to a better understanding and appreciation of art. Osborne's views on assessment thus provide one more example of applied aesthetics and another reason for considering the philosophy of art an important resource for teaching art.

We have reviewed analyses of the aesthetic concepts of representation, expression, aesthetic experience, and critical evaluation in order to illustrate what philosophers of art do and how they do it. It would be difficult to deny that even these brief examples of the philosopher's work contribute a number of insights crucial to the teaching of art. Most of all, what these sample analyses reveal is the human quest for reasonableness in matters of art and culture. As such, aesthetics should be part of the cognitive stock of any teacher of art.

Some Uses of Aesthetics in the Teaching of Art

Thus far in this chapter we have discussed different kinds of philosophical aesthetics (traditional philosophical speculation and contemporary conceptual analysis), the aesthetic complex (consisting of artist, object, audience, and society), and typical concerns of aesthetics (the nature, meaning, and value of art). We have also covered typical questions of aesthetics (about art objects, appreciation and interpretation, critical judgment, artistic creation, and cultural context), and analyses of four aesthetic concepts (representation, expression, aesthetic experience, and critical evaluation).

The remainder of this chapter indicates some uses of aesthetics in the teaching of art, which chapter 8 will elaborate upon. I see four uses of aesthetics for purposes of art education: a broad philosophical framework for justifying the teaching of art, subject matter in the form of specific content and skills, methods of analysis and principles of dialogue for thinking clearly about art, and aesthetic conundrums or puzzles that can stimulate problem solving and produce an understanding of aesthetic issues.

Examples of the first use of aesthetics, the construction of a philosophical framework that can justify the teaching of art, are evident in the appeal theorists of art education make to what Levi in chapter 3 called constitutive and revelatory theories of art. This is to say that we can justify the teaching of art on the basis of art's power to stimulate the imagination and expand perception, promote the integration of the human person, develop aesthetic intelligence, realize aesthetic value, and provide humanistic understanding. Chapters 7 and 8 of this volume will argue the merits of a compound justification of discipline-based art education that is drawn from the ideas of some major philosophies of art. Though philosophies of art tend to be grounded in different ideas about the nature of reality and knowing, when examined closely they often reveal a remarkable similarity in their characterization of the good to be derived from art. Thus while Beardsley's instrumental theory of aesthetic value differs fundamentally in its categories of analysis from Nelson Goodman's, it nonetheless accommodates the kind of awareness Goodman calls understanding, for ex-

ample, the perception of new worlds and the reinterpretation of worlds
in light of those perceived. And both John Dewey the pragmatist and
E. F. Kaelin the phenomenologist value the communicative function of
art. Finally, although Levi's view of art as one of the humanities encompasses such benefits as aesthetic wisdom and humanistic insight,
it certainly does not deny the pleasures of aesthetic experience, which
he regards as self-justifying.

The second use of aesthetics is as a source for subject matter. For
instance, aesthetic concepts, ideas, and theories, of which this chapter
offered a scant sampling, can become the content of teaching about
art. The third use of aesthetics is to adopt its methods of philosophical
analysis and critical reflection. In addition to clarifying concepts like
medium, form, content, subject matter, style, and so on, aesthetics has
perhaps been most helpful from a practical point of view in its extensive
scrutiny of the concept of critical judgment. We now have a much better
idea of the different sorts of judgments we can make of works of art
(e.g., cognitive, moral, and aesthetic), of the relevant types of reasons
that ground them, and of the phases of criticism (description, interpretation, and evaluation) and their interconnections.

The fourth use of aesthetics is a variant of the third and centers on
especially intriguing puzzles that occur in art. Here we are concerned
not so much with inherently ambiguous concepts as with problematic
situations. This approach reverses the traditional way of doing aesthetics, which consists of first formulating a systematic and comprehensive theory of art and then deriving from it guidelines for practice.
In the conundrum approach to aesthetic understanding, the problem
is presented first and then relevant theory is brought to bear in order
to solve it.

This approach is featured in *Puzzles about Art: An Aesthetics Casebook*
compiled by four philosophers of art.[33] In this volume contributors ask
such questions as the following: Are the paintings by Betsy the chim-
panzee works of art? Should a museum director who has invited an
artist to contribute a work to the museum's collection accept a piece
of driftwood the artist just picked off the beach? In displaying a work
that shows the erasure of another artist's drawing, is a museum exhibiting the destruction of as existing work or the creation of a new
one? Should artists who regard self-mutilation as an art form receive
exhibitions of their work? Should we honor the deathbed request of
an artist that certain of his unsold works be destroyed? Does the public
have the right to have a federally commissioned work removed when
they find it obstructive or offensive? Can an abstract painting devoid
of all representational matter in any way be said to be a portrait of a

person? And so forth. In all the applications alluded to, aesthetics has shown itself to be an important source of subject matter and critical skills for teachers of art in the schools. It helps teachers to deal more effectively with a host of questions that inevitably arise in attempts to build a well-developed sense of art in the young.

We have now concluded descriptions of the four disciplines of discipline-based art education. Without a grasp of the character of these disciplines it is impossible to know how to orchestrate their various aspects for purposes of aesthetic learning. Teachers of art in the schools and those who work in colleges of education and schools of art to prepare these teachers cannot, of course, be expected to have expert knowledge of these disciplines, just as teachers of science and mathematics and history are not expected to be scholars in these and their related disciplines. But a good general knowledge of them is possible. In truth, there is no choice in the matter. Any well-developed sense of art must be grounded in an acquaintance with art history, a feeling for the qualities of materials gained through manipulating them, a knowledge of the principles of judgment, and an ability to reflect on problematic aspects of art and cultural situations. If we were able to take it for granted that under current arrangements all teachers of art were already receiving a solid liberal or general education and passing through a truly professional curriculum of teacher education, we would also have reason to assume that they already possess a foundation on which to build a program of discipline-based art education. But of course this is not the case, and in certain respects we are still at the drawing board. But there is reason to believe that the conditions for reform are better today than they have been for some period, and now is the time to act. To further this task I turn to a description of a humanities conception of discipline-based art education that features the teaching of art as a humanity.

7

Toward a Humanities-based Conception
of Art Education

The humanities cannot be dismissed. Far from being outmoded, they are eternally relevant because they are the arts of communication, the arts of continuity, and the arts of criticism. Language remains the indispensable medium within which we move and breathe. History provides that group memory which makes the communal bond possible. Philosophic criticism is the only activity through which man's self-reflection modifies the conditions of his existence. The cup of the humanities, therefore, must be the vessel from which we drink our life.

—A. W. Levi

This chapter is transitional. It effects a bridge from material that provides a basic understanding of the role of the arts in society and of the four disciplines of discipline-based art education to an extended argument for the inclusion of discipline-based art education within a humanities framework. But first I will summarize the earlier chapters so as to ensure that as background knowledge they inform the remainder of this volume.

A Review

In an effort to explain the low status of aesthetic learning in today's schools, Levi in chapter 1 set out the historical and sociological reasons for the discrepancy between the level of appreciation of the arts and humanities common among the Founding Fathers and their contemporaries and the lamentable state of affairs described in the report *Toward Civilization*. Nurtured on the largely aristocratic cultural ideals of the Enlightenment, Washington and Jefferson unapologetically expressed an enthusiasm for art and its role in public and private life that was a blend of their own conservative aesthetic tastes and advocacy of a civic culture. These ideals were placed on the defensive during the second epoch of American civilization. As the frontier was opened up and Jacksonian democracy competed with the Jeffersonian ideal, the clash between Jacksonianism and Jeffersonianism in matters of culture gave rise to prejudices that are still with us, namely, the views that the arts are elitist and undemocratic, on the one hand, and unmasculine, on the other. Levi countered these negative attitudes by associating elitism with excellence and by upholding the right of access of every person in a democratic society to the best. He also pointed out that, beyond certain biological characteristics, the differences between men and women are hardly fixed or absolute. During the third epoch of American civilization, the current age of industrialism and commercialism, acquisitive instincts tend to prevail over moral and aesthetic commitments. The scandals of Wall Street, corruption of officials in high places, and inordinate spending on art for investment purposes rather than civic purposes all attest to the primacy of the materialistic impulse.

Since attitudes toward art and culture are a function of historical evolution and social context, Levi's brief examination of the three historical epochs of American society revealed the loss of the perception of art and art education as a critical necessity for private and public well-being. Even a revolutionary increase in cultural consumption and the current surfeit of art, which would appear to satisfy every kind of aesthetic appetite, do not invalidate the assertion that art is no longer vital to contemporary Americans. Nor need we support this perception by probing the depth of many people's involvement with art to verify our suspicion that their involvement does not spring from truly aesthetic motives. For we have a telling indicator of society's cultural values in what public school curricula require, and here basic art education hardly exists.

Levi went on to discuss the relation of art to the general welfare, understood as the effects of a socially accepted art that is directed toward improving the quality of public life. As a counterexample to the physical decay of today's urban centers he described the alliance between politics and aesthetics that was achieved in the golden age of Renaissance Florence. For all their vices and the illicit sources of their wealth, the leaders of Florence undertook the building of their city in a spirit of community pride born of a tradition of civic patronage. Buttressed by the theories and attitudes of classical humanism, this civic concern culminated in an ideal of culture that was superbly expressed in the architectural schemes of Florence. Renaissance Florence thus stands as a shining contrast to our contemporary squalor.

Yet art is much more than a public utility, and it has value beyond promoting the general welfare. Because it occasions valuable aesthetic experiences, art is also a critical necessity for personal well-being, as

Levi explained in chapter 2 and about which more was said in chapter 6. When art serves the human person directly and not via one of its public or civic manifestations it assumes a more private character and becomes a source of illumination and wisdom as well as a stimulus to inner growth. Art fulfills this more intimate function through its constitutive and revelatory capacities. In its constitutive aspect the experience of art affects the shaping of the human personality positively, and in its revelatory aspect it enriches individual awareness.

Levi pointed out that in the modern period the constitutive theory of art finds its most forceful expression in the writings of Friedrich Schiller, Herbert Read, and John Dewey. Schiller held that in the progressive perfection of human civilization an aesthetic stage lay midway between the raw state of nature and the ultimate end of human freedom; the aesthetic phase therefore is an indispensable preparation for the latter. It was the study of great works of art, moreover, that was to be the vehicle for developing in persons a sense of beauty that was strongly related to a sense of the good, and the formal impulse evident in artistic creation was to be the model for the harmonious integration of the individual personality. For Schiller, then, aesthetic education was to have a pronouncedly moral tenor; without the integration achieved during the aesthetic stage neither the good life for the person nor political and moral freedom for society would be possible.

This belief goes back to antiquity and to Plato and, in addition to being championed by Schiller, it was also expressed by Herbert Read. Read, too, was convinced that individuals must achieve inner equilibrium before being capable of moral goodness and that aesthetic education is a key not only to ethical virtue but also to truth and a freer society. The experience of art crystallizes the emotions into patterns that are in effect molds of virtue. In the United States a constitutive theory of art was propounded by John Dewey, this country's greatest philosopher. His notion of experience drew inspiration from art's generally acknowledged ability to unify disparate elements into an expressive whole that was an important locus of consummatory value.

The revelatory capacity of art was emphasized by a group of writers from Hegel onward for whom the cognition of reality and the criticism of life were crucial considerations. Art's revelatory powers were featured in Rebecca West's effort to specify the emotions she felt while responding to artistic masterpieces and in Kenneth Clark's descriptions of what he called moments of vision. Both these writers' accounts testify to the exaltation of self that results from an encounter with a great work of art. West describes the emotion as one of realized potency, while Clark speaks in terms of energized spirit, possession, self-discovery, and incandescence—all prominent in his personal experiences of van Gogh's landscape paintings and Giorgione's *The Tempest*.

Since Rebecca West spoke of the information works of art provide, Levi cautioned that we must not expect such information to be like the data supplied by science; nor is our relation to artworks similar to the one we have to scientific theories. Our commerce with works of art is more aptly described as communion or participation, and the aesthetic wisdom of artists is more properly understood as a revelation of the human truth of things, whether the subject be love, old age, religious faith, or nature. The insight achieved through works of art, Levi noted, usually carries with it a clarity—or *claritas*, as the Middle Ages preferred to call it—so extraordinary as to compel our assent. But this will not always happen; some artworks, such as Giorgione's *The Tempest*, remain irreducibly mysterious and resistant to interpretation.

With remarks about art and the general welfare and about art and the human person in mind, Levi next discussed, in chapter 3, the nature of artistic creation, the first of the four disciplines that discipline-based art education considers relevant to the teaching and appreciation of art. If the meanings of certain artworks seem destined to remain forever elusive and mysterious, so does the nature of the creative process, that capacity of artists that Dewey described as their ability "to work a vague idea and emotion over in terms of some definite medium."

Levi probed the mystery of artistic creation with the disposition and knowledge of a philosophical humanist. He provided generalizations from critical and philosophical writings, pointed to the aesthetic preferences of individual artists, consulted the words of artists themselves, and made references to cultural history. Levi regarded works of art as images of human import saturated with feeling that reflect the lived intensity of artists' lives. Among the effects of such works on viewers are enhanced perceptual power and a new ability to see. But Levi believed that we come closer to comprehending the phenomenon of artistic creation when we examine what we know about artists' beliefs and when we see creative activities under the rubrics of act and message.

Implicit in the ideal of artistic creation as act are two distinct traditions of Western philosophy. One is the Aristotelian, with its notion of the realization of an idea through the imposition of form on matter. Though the imagination of artists is exercised and their feelings are engaged, they create in an intellectual, self-conscious manner and can be relatively articulate about what they are doing. The other view of creation is the Platonic, which sees artists merely as mediums through which external and uncontrolled forces work their will. In the Platonic tradition creation is mainly emotional, and artists must necessarily remain inarticulate about intentions and meanings.

The distinction between an Aristotelian and a Platonic approach to creation is also apparent in the importance the former assigns to rehearsal through preliminary sketches and drawings and the value Plato set on emotional spontaneity. The Aristotelian tendency predominated until well into the nineteenth century, when the open-air painting of the Impressionists supplanted reliance on the studio and on preparatory work. The adjustment of sensation to changing aspects of atmosphere necessitated a recourse to feeling and immediacy that Levi interpreted as a reassertion of Platonism in artistic creation.

The Platonism of the modern period had two different strains. A highly personal and intimate attachment to nature was distinctive of the Impressionists, van Gogh, and Cézanne. The Abstract Expressionism of the mid-twentieth century, however, while still prizing spontaneity, was also more ideological. The canvas was perceived as an arena in which existential encounters of artists with materials took place—or so we have been persuaded to think by Harold Rosenberg's critical writings. Even descriptions of Abstract Expressionist works of considerably less dynamism than the energy fields of a de Kooning or Pollack tended to be phrased in terms of action and struggle. In sum, whether artistic creation follows the Aristotelian or the Platonic path depends on differences in artists' attitudes, temperaments, dispositions, commitments, and the times in which they live. Levi used Henri Matisse's painting of his *Still Life with Green Buffet* to illustrate both Aristotelian and Platonic conceptions of artistic creation. Matisse's effort may be understood as either the deliberate imposition of form and idea on matter (Aristotelian) or as inspired and possessed creation (Platonic).

It might seem that a concern with the nature of artistic creation ends with the release of a work into the public world, where it must stand on its own and provide opportunities for aesthetic enjoyment. There is a view, however, holding that creativity resides not so much in the artist's activity as in the work itself as it unfolds in the experience of a beholder.[1] Another view holds that any account of aesthetic enjoyment that does not include the percipient's awareness of the artist's creative act is incomplete. Being the product of human agency, a work of art invokes a sense of human performance, of the actions of an individual who, in the production of an art object, made certain choices and executed the work more or less skillfully, intelligently, and wisely. Percipients therefore respond not only to transfigured materials and artistic ideas but also to the agent responsible for them.[2] This also seems to have been Levi's position, for he considered any discussion of aesthetic experience defective if it did not take notice of the creative presence of the artist.

Under the rubric of "message" Levi understood artistic creation as the attempt by artists to advance philosophical ideas through their work. Painters of this persuasion tend to think that certain forms—the square, the curve, the spiral, and so on—possess an inherent power to express metaphysical values and are therefore pivotal to communicating the artists' ideas. Indeed, writing in 1941 Alfred H. Barr, Jr., the founding director of the Museum of Modern Art, said that the history of modern art since Impressionism could be written in terms of the shape of the square confronting the silhouette of the amoeba! And we may further note that for the conceptual artist of our day "idea" has become all important. Levi, without denying the possibility of judging artistic excellence, preferred to emphasize the artistic validity found in different forms and styles. He thought it was foolish to value Cézanne's attitude toward nature more highly than van Gogh's inasmuch as both artists created powerful and original images—Cézanne the painter of aesthetic vision itself and van Gogh the giver of imaginative form to intense inner urgings.

Levi concluded his observations on artistic creation as message with remarks concerning those other kinds of "messages" written by artists, their verbal statements. Although from the Renaissance to the modern period artists have reflected on their craft and occasionally published their views, they did so principally as individuals. The twentieth century, however, has become the age of affiliations among artists, with the manifesto being their typical product (which casts doubt on the rather widespread assumption that artists prefer to remain mute about their work). But the relation between the published aims of artistic programs and the works purportedly exemplifying them is often obscure.

Levi carried the theme of the imposition of order on form over to chapter 4 on art history. But he had completed just under two pages at the time of his death. Because of my own interest in T. S. Eliot's writings on culture and criticism and my understanding of Levi's works and cast of mind, I retained the theme of tradition in describing the efforts of art historians to understand and explain works of art under the aspects of time, tradition, and style. The task was to indicate how art history conveys a sense not only of art's past but also of its continuing relevance. In the process I distinguished three conceptions of art history—art history as the survey or chronology of art, art history as a series of discrete historical studies, and art history as a self-reflective discipline. After describing the nature of art history as a scholarly discipline and its characteristic aims and methods as well as the uses of art history in a general education program, I indicated how the attitudes and dispositions of art historians and the times in which they live affect the kind of art history they write. In this connection art history texts by Helen Gardner, E. H. Gombrich, H. W. Janson, and Hugh Honour and John Fleming were compared and contrasted, some typical examples of art-historical investigation were provided, and one philosophy of art history, Erwin Panofsky's, was examined in some depth.

In the course of these descriptions, comparisons, and explanations, a number of issues surfaced that are central to comprehending the nature of art history. To the question of the possibility of a value-free art history the answers are primarily negative, as reflected in the debate, for example, over the question of the relative values of autonomous, versus contextualist, revisions of art-historical understanding. A related question, often growing out of the autonomy-versus-contextualism controversy, is whether the history of art is, strictly speaking, the history of works of art *(Kunstgeschichte)* or cultural history *(Geistesgeschichte)* or, as some contemporary art historians would have it, essentially social history.

So far as Eliot's imperative to develop the historical sense is concerned—by imparting the pastness as well as the presentness of the past—I said that while the history of art reveals that works of art are indeed created at different times and with different intentions and functions in their creators' minds, they nonetheless have an extraordinary capacity to transcend their original place, time, and doctrine. They are able to do this through their aesthetic appeal and the universal or compelling messages they contain, the greatest works of art tending to combine significant human import with vitally expressive form. It is this dual capacity of art that prompted Robert Penn Warren, the first poet laureate of the United States, to say in his Jefferson Lecture that we value works of art because they are a continual source of fresh experience and constantly return us to ourselves.[3]

The discussion of chapter 5 centered on art criticism, and although overlap between the concerns of art history and art criticism was noted, three central functions of criticism were emphasized: refining perception, making reasoned assessments of aesthetic value, and raising the level of thinking and talking about art. Berenson's description of the life-enhancing values of Renaissance art, Fry's insights into Postimpressionist painting, Rosenberg's accounts of the changed political and cultural context of avant-garde art, Kramer's interpretation of modernism, and Jencks's of postmodernism illustrated these functions of criticism. In Berenson and Fry the educative function of criticism was paramount, a function they felt important in light of the narrow range of criteria people tend to use in judging artistic excellence. Both were, to recall Schapiro's characterization of Berenson, sages and teachers with a supreme message for viewers—that more than anything else, a work's form is the principal source of aesthetic enjoyment. And it must be admitted that Berenson's descriptions of the formal values of Giotto's paintings and Fry's descriptions of the work of Cézanne made the appreciation of formal qualities a standard feature in aesthetic experience for a new generation.

Interest in a work's tactile values, spatial composition, movement, representational features, and color is, of course, a constant in aesthetic appreciation, with one or more of these aspects of art being emphasized depending on artists' and beholders' preferences. The vicissitudes of modern life, however, have meant that greater attention has had to be given to the changed social, political, and cultural contexts of art. In particular the ease with which artworks can be transported and reproduced within a global system of mass communication has made it imperative to gain an understanding of the consequences of the "museum without walls" that André Malraux talked about. One of these effects was what Kramer called stylistic pluralism, and what Rosenberg called the emergence of "one-man cultures," which no longer had strong ties to tradition.

Rosenberg was especially astute in his descriptions of what was going on in the work of Jasper Johns, which parodied Abstract Expressionist painting. Kramer showed special insight into the impulses of modernism and the avant-garde when he detected two terms of a dialectic, a radical one and a more traditional one. He believed the latter deserved more attention because it valued historical continuity and creatively engaged tradition in forging new artistic values, whereas the radical term attempted to effect a sharp break with the past. He further estimated the cultural cost of vanguard art's abandonment of high seriousness in its turn toward persiflage and systematic inversion. Charles Jencks, on the other hand, while acknowledging that much that is called postmodern art exemplifies a rejection of the serious in art, saw in what he calls Free-Style Classicism a refusal to turn against the past. Rather, he takes the history of art to be an organic continuum and discerns in the current phase of postmodernism in art and architecture the reweaving of modernist ideas and materials with the tradition of humanism. Moreover, Jencks is less concerned than Kramer about postmodernism's pluralism and eclecticism, taking it to be an appropriate expression of a pluralistic society. Rosenberg, Kramer, and

Jencks, then, though they all help to increase perception about the new and make reasoned qualitative judgments of value, are principally concerned with understanding the nature of modernism and postmodernism and what these portend for the life of culture. In this respect art criticism fuses with cultural criticism. The chapter on criticism concluded with some observations about the similarities and differences in the aims of art critics and teachers.

At several points in this book Levi and I have mentioned the manner in which the disciplines of discipline-based art education overlap and intertwine, but chapter 6 illustrated one way in which aesthetics clearly differs from criticism. Whereas critics tend to say what a particular work represents or expresses or make estimates of its capacity to afford aesthetic experience, philosophers of art analyze such concepts as representation, expression, and aesthetic value, as well as a range of others, that have relevance to an understanding of art in general.

H. Gene Blocker thus examined the meaning of artistic representation and in the process unfolded the philosophical drama of how the concept of representation came to replace that of imitation. He did this mainly by pointing out the interpretive dimension of representation and its reliance on conventions of artistic creation favored at a particular time. Blocker further clarified the nature of the tension between what a work of art represents, which points to something external to the work, and the work's internal or intrinsic values, which tend to draw attention to the work itself. He termed this tension the autonomy-heteronomy problem in aesthetics.

John Hospers's analysis of the concept of artistic expression took a different tack. He began his dissection of what is probably the most troublesome and problematic concept in theorizing about art by identifying four senses of the term—artistic expression as process, properties, communication, and evocation. He then proceeded to indicate not only the principal theorists associated with each sense—Dewey, Croce, Collingwood, Tolstoy, Arnheim, and others—but also the conceptual difficulties inherent in each sense. As Hospers unraveled these complexities he showed that the problem of expression in art turns on such questions as the role of the medium and feeling in achieving expression, the character of expressive communication, the status of an art object's expressive properties, and the nature and importance of the feelings aroused by an artwork. None of these senses is without difficulties, though the properties sense of expression seems to be the one the majority of contemporary aestheticians consider most relevant and helpful in accounting for an artwork's expressive qualities—those qualities that hold a special interest for viewers during aesthetic experience.

Just what aesthetic experience consists in was the burden of Monroe Beardsley's analysis, one that took into account criticisms of his earlier efforts to clarify and sharpen this concept. Beardsley's important contribution is a complex characterization of aesthetic experience (it is both compound and disjunctive) that contains more or less five features (object directedness, detached affect, felt freedom, active discovery, and wholeness or integration). When these features, or at least some of them, are notably present, we may speak of experience having a significant aesthetic character. Whether it will ever be possible to give a wholly satisfactory account of so complex a strand of human experience as the aesthetic is doubtful; but when our experience of a work of art is unsatisfactory it is often because it lacks one or more of the features described by Beardsley. Beardsley gradually came to give greater weight to the cognitive dimension of aesthetic experience than he had done in his earlier efforts, and this change reflects his accommodation of certain aspects of the writings of E. H. Gombrich, Rudolf Arnheim, and Nelson Goodman.

What Blocker, Hospers, and Beardsley do for the concepts of representation, expression, and aesthetic experience, Harold Osborne does for critical evaluation. Instead of making aesthetic judgments of particular works, which is the usual activity of critics, Osborne identifies the different kinds of standards critics typically use when they judge the value or worth of artworks. Though the character of the criteria applied will vary according to the nature of the object under examination, Osborne thinks that critical judgment in general stresses three standards: artistic excellence, capacity to afford aesthetic satisfaction, and stature, the first two of which are based on aesthetic and the third on nonaesthetic reasons. "Artistic excellence" refers to an artist's creative finesse in manipulating materials and achieving artistic aims. "Aesthetic satisfaction" implies the special kind of pleasure or enjoyment provided by works of art, while "stature" includes a range of art's subsidiary functions—magical, doctrinal, didactic, commemorative, persuasive, and so on—among which the promotion of understanding, the expression of nonverbal thought, and the embodiment of feeling tend to be emphasized most often. Osborne cautions that some of these standards conflict with each other and that there is no necessary relation between, say, artistic excellence and stature. Perhaps most controversial in Osborne's analysis may be his refusal to regard the promotion of understanding as the preeminent function of art; this puts him at odds with, for example, Nelson Goodman's cognitive theory of art.

Relations among the Disciplines

The discussion of the disciplines of discipline-based art education—artistic creation, art history, art criticism, and aesthetics—still leaves us with questions about their incorporation into an arts program. For example, if each discipline is totally discrete and separate, then it is difficult to see how teachers can establish connections among them. If, however, they are in fact interrelated, how are teachers to understand their differences? And if it turns out that these differences are negligible, why distinguish among them in the first place?

Levi—to anticipate the discussion in a later part of this chapter—has given us a way of imagining entities that are fuzzy around the edges. His "radiation theory" of definition, as he calls it, relies neither on Aristotelian essences of classes of objects nor on Wittgensteinian family resemblances. Rather, it suggests a "physical image of a dynamic center radiating outward like the ripples from a series of stones thrown into a pond and intermingling at their periphery with no blurring of the original sources of impetus."[4] This enables us to speak of the dominant radiating intentions of the four disciplines of discipline-based art education and to describe them as follows: in artistic creation the dominant radiating intention is the making of unique objects and is born of the human need to express ideas and feelings in visual forms; in the history of art it is to understand works of art under the aspects of time, tradition, and style and is born of the human need to be reminded of roots and to recall things worth remembering and experiencing; in art criticism it is the refinement of perception and the rendering of qualitative judgments and is born of the human need to perceive clearly and to separate the meritorious from the meretricious; in aesthetics or the philosophy of art it is the clarification of key concepts and ideas and is born of the quest for reasonableness in our thinking about art and for avoidance of dubious assumptions.

The question before us now is this: if we are to regard the four disciplines of discipline-based art education as resources to help art teachers to achieve the objectives of art education, how can their concepts and procedures be brought to bear on classroom activities? How do they become integrated in the minds of teacher education specialists, art teachers in the schools, and, ultimately, the students? This is the challenge of discipline-based art education, and it taxes all of our pedagogical wisdom. We can tackle this problem by distinguishing between the ultimate or overarching objectives of discipline-based art education and certain intermediate ones.

We may say that the ultimate objective of discipline-based art education is to develop in students the capacity to understand and appreciate serious works of art.[5] On the one hand this general statement presupposes that positions have been taken on such theoretical issues as the character, meaning, value, and function of works of art (the things to be understood and appreciated) and on the nature of the good or worthwhile life (the reason for trying to understand and appreciate art); but on the other it is silent on problems of teaching, learning, and schooling, which bear on curriculum design and evaluation. If we now also say that the capacity to understand and appreciate works of art is evident when students know how to do certain things, when they know how to deploy the skills and knowledge required to experience works of art appropriately, we have an idea of performance that can serve as the intermediate objective of discipline-based art education. Further, we can conveniently break down performance into steps, stages, skills, and understandings that must be attained if it is to be judged adequate. It is at this intermediate level, that is, in developing relevant aptitudes and in teaching the items of information needed for acceptable appreciative performance that the teacher can turn to the four disciplines in question for help.

In the next chapter we will examine the skills and understandings instruction should impart and the level of accomplishment or performance it is reasonable to expect from students of different ages. For now it is enough to realize that teachers can derive much of what they need to know to teach aesthetic appreciation effectively, as well as many of the concepts they will present to students directly, from the disciplines under discussion. Pedagogical competence refers to the teachers' ability to so use the disciplines. Discipline-based art education, then, puts pedagogical competence in matters of art in the service of guiding students toward a skilled aesthetic performance (intermediate educational goal) that is evidence of students' having acquired the capacity for understanding and appreciating serious works of art (final educational aim). Once more I refer to this capacity, for convenience's sake, as aesthetic percipience.

We should realize that aesthetic percipience, the ideal outcome of discipline-based art education, is first of all a genuine attainment and, second, implies certain excellences of mind. A person percipient in matters of art possesses not only a body of knowledge about art that bears on its understanding but also a disposition to prize the experiences afforded by works of art and to seek them out for the benefits they convey. To the aesthetically percipient person art is not only a strange necessity, as Rebecca West called it, but a critical one as well. Art satisfies a distinctive human longing and is one of life's immeasurable goods, exceeded in importance only by moral and intellectual virtue. Chapter 6 had something to say about the values that art serves, namely, aesthetic gratification, expanded powers of awareness, humanistic insight, and the expression of human freedom, the very energies and potencies that justify our valuing the arts as highly as we do. Accordingly, it is a realization of art's great value potential that prompts us to place the teaching of it within the area of the humanities.

The Humanities: General Considerations

The usual procedure in defining the humanities is to contrast them to the sciences and to emphasize their axiological or value priorities, a practice we will follow here. The tone is set by Levi in his redefinition of the humanities (which will occupy the last part of this chapter) when he says that what the humanities contribute is a "unique gift to the valuational consciousness of man"[6] and that in offering this gift they embrace values "with an earnestness that is to be found nowhere in the spectrum of knowledge and education."[7]

Others have stated the case differently. We have already referred to C. P. Snow's Rede Lecture in which natural scientists and their characteristic attitudes, values, and activities constituted one culture of mind and literary intellectuals and humanists another. Snow described the dissimilarities between these two cultures in terms of the dominant ethical disposition of each and concluded that, on the whole, scientists more than humanists possess the necessary intellectual equipment and the moral resolve to tackle global problems of overpopulation, hunger, threatening nuclear war, and environmental deterioration. Yet the terms and substance of Snow's distinctions were hotly debated.

Unhappy with Snow's moralism, Roger Scruton, a British philosopher of art, has recently recalled the more traditional associations of the term culture with the arts and humanities. In contrast to Snow, Scruton believes that our contemporary situation has greater need of the humanities than ever before and that they they alone can keep us in touch with a world from which science in large has banished all traces of personal meaning.[8] Scruton consequently recommends placing greater stress on aesthetics and aesthetic education as a remedy. His attitude, moreover, is similar to that of James Ackerman, an art historian–critic who, in remarking on art's constant capacity to move, stimulate, and mystify, suggests that in contrast to our understanding of science, our relation to works of art is more akin to love and affection.[9] Israel Scheffler has likewise emphasized the essentially abstract and impersonal nature of science:

> A scientific theory is a law-like statement or set of statements, formulated in the vocabulary of a scientific discipline, which claims to give a truthful representation of the phenomena studied by the discipline. A scientific theory is judged by its contribution to the understanding of such phenomena; in practice, it is assessed by its logical coherence, its explanatory power, and its heuristic fruitfulness, as judged by the methodological canons of the discipline. Science tends toward increasing systematization of theory and progressive abstractness of vocabulary. In its drive toward ever more comprehensive explanation, its theories comprise increasingly autonomous and integrated structures, with constituent terms departing further and further from the familiar language of everyday practical experience. The organization of theoretical knowledge within a scientific discipline is, in short, dictated by the twin aims of general understanding and the further growth of such understanding.[10]

To sum up, we may say with Levi that there is a sense in which science must render unto reality what reality demands (laws of causation, for example, cannot be matters of the poetic imagination). The humanities, on the other hand, push against reality in order to make room for human value; they inject human purpose into a meaningless universe and in doing so make use of the resources of myth, religion, literature, and the arts. The sciences seek to discover the way things are and to explain them matter-of-factly, whereas the humanities express values dramatically and help us envision human possibilities.

To be sure, science is a great adventure pervaded by drama and suspense, and the theoretical edifices it builds have undeniable beauty and elegance. Furthermore, scientists instantiate in their work admirable human traits and values (for example, objectivity in observation, truthfulness in reporting, courage and self-denial in the acknowledgment of error), and in their own way they can serve as moral exemplars. Yet science as a whole has little or nothing to say about human purpose, feelings, and meaning. It cannot satisfy the emotional requirements of the majority of persons because that simply is not its principal business. But that task *is* preeminently the business of the humanities. To evoke once more Ernst Cassirer's image of the circle of humanity that includes all forms of human symbolic culture, a well-rounded education encompasses its entire circumference. Science is certainly one large and indispensable sector, but the circle cannot not be closed if the humanities are slighted or omitted.

The Humanities: Contemporary Issues

An argument for placing discipline-based art education under the aegis of the humanities has a responsibility to mention some of the difficulties currently besetting humanistic studies. It is well known that the humanities and liberal studies have generally suffered decline in recent decades. This slippage is often attributed to the ascendancy of science and technology and the eagerness of institutions of higher education to concentrate their resources in these prestigious areas. Students thus perceive the humanities as contributing little if anything to their future earning power and tend to abandon liberal studies as soon as requirements in them are loosened—as they have been at many universities. Not surprisingly these attitudes are reflected in the secondary schools. Recently, though, there have been signs of a possible turnaround as voices urge a renewed emphasis on humanistic studies. I refer to the works associated with the excellence-in-education movement of the 1980s. The argument for discipline-based art education in this volume is generally consistent with the spirit and point of view of these works.[11]

Other voices, however, while not questioning the value of studying traditional humanistic works, deemphasize the differences between the humanities and the sciences or, more specifically, between aesthetic and scientific understanding. Nelson Goodman is one. He conceives of both art and science as cognitive symbolic systems whose common aim is human understanding and the discovery of connections among things.[12] The force and persuasiveness of Goodman's writing notwithstanding, one may still ask, as Osborne did, whether understanding is the principal function that works of art perform or whether it is not the case that such understanding as they do provide is so special that it is misleading to claim the general purpose of the arts is similar to the objectives of the sciences. Ackerman, a sympathetic reader of Goodman, has expressed similar reservations. And in truth Goodman himself acknowledges that there is a world of difference between a visually expressive design and a scientific theory that exhibits abstract and logical, not dramatic, relations. Yet Goodman's interest in a general theory of understanding and the universal processes of what he calls worldmaking inclines him to underplay differences.

Yet another line of argument tends to resolve the boundaries between the humanities and the sciences by construing the works of each alike as "texts" whose distinctive feature is their pronounced tendency to undermine themselves. This tendency is revealed through a method known as deconstruction. There is not space here to elaborate on this contemporary intellectual movement except to say that it reveals no conspicuous interest in the humanistic functions of works of art. Negative and nihilistic in outlook, it has therefore no relevance for art education.[13] Though not always politically motivated, it often is, and it expresses a currently pervasive frame of mind that takes a dim view of the accomplishments of Western civilization.

Another problem for the humanities are complaints about *how* they are studied. The charge is that the humanities have abandoned the substantive—that is, the idea of a tradition or a body of works exemplifying values and human possibilities worth transmitting from generation to generation—in favor of the procedural—the methods and analytic skills of humanistic scholarship. Proceduralism has been characterized by E. D. Hirsch, Jr., as a commitment to educational formalism in American schooling, that is, the separation of the teaching of skills from the teaching of specific content, with decisive stress on the former.[14] Hirsch thinks that by overemphasizing skills the schools are seriously contributing to the erosion of the nation's capacity to maintain social cohesion and to compete economically with other advanced countries. Social unity on the other hand presupposes a set of common beliefs that make communication and intersubjective sympathy possible. Yet Hirsch asserts that we are increasingly ignorant of such shared assumptions, and he traces the situation, arguably I think, to John Dewey and the progressive movement in education. In humanities courses, which should be the bearers of the prime responsibility for conveying a cohesive value system, educational formalism has meant teaching students how to think critically without giving them much in the way of content and knowledge to think about; or how to conduct moral debates while vigorously denying the existence of absolute ethical standards by which to judge actions. Art education would be equally guilty of formalism if it were content, say, merely to teach students the skills of aesthetic criticism—vitally important though these are—without familiarizing students with works of artistic excellence that would reward the deployment of these skills.

The most vocal current criticism of the humanities concentrates on *what* they teach—or have taught until recently—that is, the traditional canon of works of literature, philosophy, and the arts. In actuality this canon has not been as resistant to change as its detractors sometimes claim; additions and deletions have always been made, but gradually, cautiously, and on the basis of aesthetic, moral, and intellectual criteria. Today, however, arguments for a rejection of the Western humanist tradition are based on the allegation that its corpus of major works is elitist, racist, imperialist, ethnocentric, and sexist (i.e., masculinist, patriarchal, phallocentric). The traditional canon, it is said, should be either replaced or considerably supplemented with works by members of hitherto unrepresented or underrepresented groups. These developments are questionable because they promote the study of a reconstituted body of works principally on the basis of political and ideological grounds, and as a way of discrediting the traditional canon and the civilization responsible for it.[15] In brief, if teachers in programs of discipline-based art education are to accept a definition of the field that places art education within the humanities, they should make certain they know what they are committing themselves to. I now turn to an understanding of the humanities that is well adapted to the conception of discipline-based art education this volume embraces.

The Humanities: Levi's Redefinition

Levi's view of the humanities will serve as a theoretical foundation of a humanities conception of discipline-based art education. In summarizing his views I am not forcing educational relevance on material framed in academic remoteness from possible practical applications. Although Levi's writings about the humanities often address the problems of liberal education in the higher educational sphere, he has also indicated the suitability of his analysis for community college humanities programs, for high school humanities studies in a program known as the International Baccalaureate, and for aesthetic education generally.

Levi first recalls the extraordinary history of the humanities, a tradition that extends back to the Platonic Academy, which placed its faith in mathematics as the source of moral and aesthetic principles. The tradition was continued by the Romans who revered certain Greek texts because of their inherent pedagogical worth. This classical culture was preserved by the monasticism of the Middle Ages and then blossomed forth once more to inspire the Renaissance. It was extended into John Locke's time, when Greek and Roman classics were used to humanize the law, and it is still being honored in the present age by those who acknowledge that this tradition serves man in ways the sciences cannot.

Writing as a philosopher of culture with a strong interest in the history of ideas, Levi elaborates a redefinition of the humanities for today's world. Only a sketch of his account can be adumbrated here, but I hope it will make it clear that Levi recognizes two emphases or phases, which are complementary rather than contradictory, and that each is necessary to our gaining adequate insight into the nature of the humanities. I also hope to establish the second of these emphases as a particularly convenient link to discipline-based art education.

As a first measure, Levi takes the customary step of differentiating between the sciences and the humanities or, to use his terms, between the scientific chain of meaning and the humanistic complex. Unlike C. P. Snow, who based his distinction between the two cultures of scientists and humanists on the ethical predispositions of the members of each culture, Levi finds their differences rooted in two divergent tendencies of the human mind, the Understanding and the Imagination, which, as they superintend the sciences and the humanities, respectively, provide each with characteristic purposes, methods, vocabularies, criteria of judgment, and products. The preeminent concerns of the scientific chain of meaning are true and false propositions, the problem of error, causality and scientific law, prediction and chance, and fact and matter of fact; whereas the humanistic complex addresses such matters as reality and appearance, the problem of illusion, destiny and human purpose, fate and fortune, drama and the dramatic event, and tragedy.[16] The common thread running through the scientific complex, as I shall henceforth call it, is a commitment to objectivity and factuality, while the one running through the humanistic complex is a commitment to human purposiveness and drama.

But as soon as Levi marks the distinction between the scientific and the humanistic complexes, he is at some pains to qualify it. Adopting a maxim of Alfred North Whitehead's, he seeks simplicity but distrusts it. The sciences and the humanities, says Levi, "need to be seen as *tendencies* rather than as pure specimens or as subject-matter disciplines, and . . . the distinction between a science and an art probably indicates more a polarity than a disjunction."[17] Both the tendency toward factuality and exactitude and the tendency toward concern for human significance should be seen as forming separate and distinct radiating centers of intention from which impulses spread outward with diminishing intensity, making themselves felt in other circles that are dominated by different central interests. We have already noted this rippling effect when pointing out how the specific aims and methods of each of the disciplines in discipline-based art education often play important if subsidiary roles in the others. The same observation can be made with respect to the humanistic and scientific impulses.

To take art historians as an example: the writings of Mark Roskill and Erwin Panofsky illustrate the alternating impulses of factuality and imaginative reconstruction, yet Panofsky, unlike Roskill, convincingly argued that art history is essentially a humanistic and not a scientific discipline. We may further suggest that when art historians regard themselves as custodians of aesthetic memory, whose intellectual and moral obligation is to describe and interpret a heritage that a people needs to remember, they exhibit a spirit germane to the humanistic complex but foreign to the scientific complex. Similarly divergent impulses occur in philosophical aesthetics (psychological and empirical aesthetics obviously fall squarely in the scientific area). It was one of the purposes of chapter 6 to show that conceptual analysis (and the detached approach it requires) can play a vital role in fostering a better appreciation of art. But when it becomes an end in itself it often produces results that, while they may be intellectually dazzling, often prove to be humanistically sterile.[18] The same pull between sciencelike exactitude and poetic imagination is experienced by practitioners of art criticism and is even evident in the creative work of some artists.

Levi concludes then that there are no inherently scientific or humanistic subject matters, only scientific or humanistic treatments of subject matters. Both art and science can take the human person, nature, and society as their subjects and submit them to alternative treatments. Thus we have Wordsworth and Newton on nature, Rembrandt and Vesalius on man, and Durkheim and Balzac on society. Yet in any given instance it is usually not difficult to tell which complex, the scientific or the humanistic, predominates. We know, for example, the humanistic attitude is being taken when talk centers on the dramatic, the moral, and the sympathetic.

We should realize, however, that to define the humanities in terms of attitudes and treatments while denying the existence of inherently humanistic subjects is in effect to define them procedurally. Casting the humanities in this light has the advantage of putting us on guard against too rigid a compartmentalization of human mental and spiritual life, against erecting boundaries that excessively constrict and exclude. At the same time we have seen that mere proceduralism poses a clear and present danger to education. Hence to teach only humanistic attitudes and strengthen humanistic impulses would leave students rudderless and prone to superficial learning. A substantive conception of the humanities must also be supplied, and this requires significant content. Here is Levi's proposal for such a counterbalance.

Levi recalls the conception of the liberal arts that reigned from the sixth century until well into the fourteenth.[19] The liberal arts were composed of the trivium (grammar, rhetoric, and dialectic) and the quadrivium (arithmetic, geometry, astronomy, and music). Although these arts were differentiated in terms of subjects or areas of study, they were essentially perceived as practical arts, as ways of doing things or organizing experience. It was the revisionism of the Renaissance that transformed these arts into subject matters. The transition was made to a substantive understanding of the liberal arts or humanities that is still dominant today. Levi, a strong believer in cultural continuity, honors the legacy of the Middle Ages as well as that of the Renaissance by retaining what he deems best in both traditions, but with a difference. As a preliminary step he divides the liberal arts (the medieval contribution) into three categories: the arts of communication, the arts of continuity, and the arts of criticism. Then he aligns these arts with subject areas (the Renaissance contribution) that are still found in the typical humanities programs or curriculums of today: he assigns the arts of communication to languages and literature; the arts of continuity to history; and the arts of criticism (by which Levi means critical reflection generally) to philosophy. In doing this Levi does not contradict his insistence that there are no inherently humanistic subject matters, if by "inherent" we understand yielding only to humanistic treatment and no other. But subjects like literature, history, and philosophy are preeminently suited to humanistic treatment; put differently, the humanistic attitude, and the three arts in which it expresses itself, finds its purest and most rewarding exercise in these subjects.

It now remains to coordinate the three arts and their corresponding subjects with three of the disciplines in discipline-based art education and to make provisions for the fourth. It should be apparent that the arts of continuity, which have history as the characteristic arena for their exercise, are associated with the discipline of art history; that the arts of criticism, which have philosophy as their typical subject area, pair nicely with philosophy of art or aesthetics. That leaves the arts of communication and the subject of languages and literature to be accommodated. Can they be assimilated to the discipline of art criticism? I think it is possible if we recall that the visual arts communicate after their own fashion. Questions about the propriety of construing art as a language notwithstanding, it is clear that works of visual art enrich awareness by conveying meanings, insights, and deeply felt human qualities. Yet, visual works of art usually communicate, that is, disclose their meanings, only after prolonged probing, careful analysis, and astute interpretation by a percipient—or, better, by a percipient under the guidance of an art critic or tutelage by an art teacher functioning as a critic. Art criticism, then, is needed to complete the act of artistic communication, to make it efficacious for the percipient, and in this it is really not very different from literature as a liberal arts subject, for there, too, much effort is spent on elucidating the meanings or messages of literary works. In short, if we grant the visual arts the power to communicate and if we assign to art criticism the mediating task of preparing percipients for apprehending this communication in its fullest and most rewarding form, then all three of Levi's liberal arts—communication, continuity, criticism—can be accounted for in a definition of discipline-based art education.[20]

What about the discipline of artistic creation? Discipline-based art education, it is clear, attaches importance to artistic creation. Levi in his original analysis did not explicitly provide for creativity, but he approved an emendation of his analysis that would. One can subsume artistic creation under the arts of communication simply by saying that because art criticism would be impossible without works to be analyzed and interpreted, creation is, in a sense, a preparatory phase for criticism. (The same could, incidentally, be said for art history and philosophy of art; neither could get off the ground without the prior creative activities that resulted in artworks.) Yet it would be misguided to consider artistic creation as merely instrumental, and we will therefore make artistic creation a fourth "c"—the arts of creation—in its own right. By granting artistic creation equal standing with the other disciplines, we acknowledge what is in fact the case: that through creative activities students learn much that will contribute to a deeper, better-informed appreciation of works of art. The four disciplines of discipline-based art education, namely, artistic creation, art history, art criticism, and aesthetics, and the corresponding four arts, namely, the arts of creation, the arts of continuity, the arts of communication, and the arts of criticism (critical reflection), have now been assembled, aligned, and placed within the framework provided by Levi. The argument for a humanities conception of discipline-based art education is essentially complete, except for a few words about the goals or objectives of the whole enterprise. And here we will notice again that what Levi says about the humanities applies in equal measure to discipline-based art education humanistically conceived.

As we have said, the humanities are concerned with human values and pursue this concern with an earnestness and concentration found in no other field of inquiry. On this there is almost universal consensus. Levi notes that laymen, politicians, educational theorists, humanists, and other interested parties all make remarkably similar claims about the humanities: "The humanities *teach* values and judgment. They *reveal* wisdom and values. They enable us *to ask and to answer* what it means to live well. From them we *derive* our notions of freedom, justice, and compassion,"[21] and they "teach appreciation for the beautiful and the permanent."[22] But just what does it mean to teach values?

A fully satisfactory answer to this question would require a more searching analysis of the very slippery concept of value than I can undertake here. But it is worth noting and keeping in mind for future reference that Levi understands values to be affective volitional meanings.[23] That is, values are, first of all, concepts or ideas, but by being "affective" they engage our sense of approval and disapproval, and by being "volitional" they make claims on our inclination to choose or to avoid. Values, then, are not taught merely by acquainting students with humanistic meanings; it is also necessary that students respond with feelings of approval or disapproval and cultivate an inclination to act accordingly.

8

Teaching Art as
a Humanity

When we perceive the arts as "humanities" it is crucial that we
interpret them as a demand that we pause, and in their light, reexamine our own realities, values, and dedications, for the arts not
only present life concretely, stimulate the imagination, and integrate
the different cultural elements of a society or of an epoch, they also
present models for our imitation or rejection, visions and aspirations
which mutely solicit our critical response.
—A. W. Levi

To understand what it means to teach art as a humanity I recall the
previously made suggestion that, broadly speaking and with appropriate reservations, art can be thought of as a form of communication.
In passages intended for this volume Levi declares: It has become
traditional to utilize the example of language as the source of our basic
metaphors of analysis. The painter's palette is an "alphabet" of colors
as the musician's is an alphabet of sounds. The painter has available
a "syntax" of forms as the musician has a syntax of scales and tonalities.
Since all communication systems, including that of the natural languages, possess "elements" combinable according to "modes of organization," and ultimately consisting of "completed structures," such
colorful analogizing makes a certain basic sense. Each of "the languages
of art" has its own medium of application: the spaces and solids of
architecture and sculpture; the timbre, loudness, range, pitch, and res-
onance of musical instruments; the canvas, pigments, and organic compounds of the painter. Organization in the visual arts compounds line,
shape, color, texture, volume, and modeling into organic constructions
like buildings, statues, paintings, etchings, and watercolors, while music uses melody and counterpoint, harmony and rhythm, dynamics
and tempo to produce its own organic constructions of song, chorale,
concerto, quartet, and symphony. And in one way or another, each of
the languages of art has its own "notation." To develop critical awareness of the ways and means of communication in the various arts can
be a humanistic enterprise of the first order.

With respect to the external usefulness of the arts in adding to our perception of former times, our "historical organ" is becoming more and more visual and sensory. Careful analysis, say, of Holbein's portrait of Jane Seymour or Shakespeare's *As You Like It* or Hardwick Hall, the countess of Shrewsbury's great country house in Derbyshire, will tell one as much about Tudor England as the magnificent historical writing of Trevelyan. But internally as well, the alternations of continuity and change are built into the materials of the history of art, music, and literature. To follow the destiny of the symphony from Haydn to Stravinsky, of the novel from Fielding to Proust, or of easel painting from Rembrandt to de Kooning is to learn to think historically, and to recognize the significance of such terms as "classic" or "romantic," "mannerist" or "baroque," in the evolution of aesthetic forms and styles is clearly to learn the role of temporality in human experience.

It used to be thought that the idea that works of art give us of a bygone age is far more serene, happy, and acceptant than that which we get from reading its chronicles, history, and literature. The plastic arts, it was believed, do not lament or accuse. Any devotee of Bosch or Bruegel, of Hogarth or Goya could have insisted otherwise. For it is clear that just as there is an art of celebration and acceptance, so there is an art of alienation and disaffection—an art that has examined the foundations of its society and found them rotten. What is important here is not the respective merits of aesthetic affirmation or negation, but the fact that we are in the presence of critical judgment and moral evaluation. It has not always been clear that in teaching the arts whether to appeal to merely formal values is enough. But when we perceive the arts as humanities, it is crucial that we interpret them as a demand that we pause and, in their light, reexamine our own realities, values, and dedications. For the arts not only present life concretely, stimulate the imagination, and integrate the different cultural elements of a society or of an epoch; they also [Levi concludes] present models for our imitation or rejection, visions and aspirations that mutely solicit our critical response.

Teaching art as a humanity, then, entails, among other things, explaining the ways in which art exhibits life concretely, stimulates the imagination, integrates the different cultural elements of a society, and presents models for imitation or rejection. These aims are also embraced by discipline-based art education. They are further compatible with the reasons for teaching art contained in the Arts Endowment report *Toward Civilization* and are congruent with T. S. Eliot's imperative that we convey not only the pastness of the past but also its current relevance. The task now is to indicate how these ends can be achieved through a curriculum of discipline-based art education. In doing this I present a programmatic definition of art education based on Levi's ideas that sets store by the value of the humanities in general and the distinctive values of the visual arts in particular. As a first step it will be helpful to explain the meaning of discipline-based art education, whose special features will be filled in as we proceed through a discussion of a humanities-based curriculum—or what, once again, I call a "percipience" curriculum—in the second part of this chapter.

Discipline-based Art Education

History. Most of the theoretical antecedents of discipline-based art education can be traced back to mid-century, when a number of writers were engaged in reconceptualizing the field of art education. These writers argued that instead of devoting itself to the development of a general creativeness or personal self-expression, the teaching of art should emphasize an educated understanding and appreciation of art itself, a perceptive awareness grounded not only in creative activities but also in the history of art, art criticism, and aesthetics.[1] This reconceptualization was strongly influenced by the climate of the early 1960s, which engendered serious discussion about the nature of disciplines and the structure of subjects, and its chief impetus was Jerome Bruner's influential *The Process of Education*.[2] Bruner argued that the high road to learning leads through the discovery of the basic ideas and concepts of important subjects. The idea was that learners should emulate the procedures of practitioners in the disciplines; and, in keeping with the interests of the time, it was primarily the physical and biological sciences and mathematics that educators explored for suitable methods. Similar ideas and images of learning were quickly adopted by many theorists of art education who claimed that the teaching of art, too, involves thinking and acting in the manner of practitioners—with art historians, art critics, and philosophers of art being added to the standard model of the artist. In addition to being influenced by Bruner, art educators were also beginning to realize that encouraging young people to express themselves creatively did not necessarily involve teaching them anything significant about art, either about its peculiar character, functions, or history. But the conception of art as a major school subject with distinctive goals, content, and methods required art-educational theorists to be knowledgeable not only about the nature, meaning, and value of art but also about the various functions art performs and the ways in which it should be created, experienced, and judged. It also called for new ideas about the design and evaluation of appropriate curriculums.

The notion of discipline-based art education builds on these prior efforts in the field of art education, and in this respect the approach is self-consciously derivative. Those responsible for its development and promotion have been quite explicit on this point. Not only that; they have made concerted efforts to cooperate with schoolteachers, educational institutions that prepare art teachers, and professional art education associations. To repeat, theorists of discipline-based art education assert not only that the content and procedures for teaching art should be derived from several key disciplines but also that an understanding and appreciation of art is more educationally significant and defensible than the development of such general objectives as creativity and self-expression. This does not mean there is no place for creative activities in discipline-based art education. Indeed, their position is quite secure. *Beyond Creating*, the publication that introduced the idea of discipline-based art education to a large audience, does not state that creative activities should be abandoned or left behind.[3] "Beyond" suggests that creative activities should be supplemented by additional kinds of study that also serve the goal of understanding and appreciating art.

Perceptions. Proposals for discipline-based art education have been before the public long enough to have elicited both assent and dissent. One criticism has been that discipline-based art education is something less than a systematic theory. By way of rebuttal one may point out that the approach has been more thoroughly conceptualized than is commonly supposed; I mention as an example the essay by Michael Day, Gilbert Clark, and W. Dwaine Greer titled "Discipline-based Art Education: Becoming Students of Art," which at the time of this writing is the most carefully researched, systematic, and comprehensive formulation of the approach in the literature.[4] The volume at hand has many points in common with the Day, Clark, and Greer position but differs from it by placing a discussion of discipline-based art education in a humanities context. It also devotes more attention to the social environment of art education in the United States, to descriptions of the disciplines in question, and to the articulation of a curriculum scheme.

But in truth, the idea of discipline-based art education is not a theory or philosophy of art education. Its advocates see it as a *challenge* to conceptualize a way of teaching art; it also bespeaks an attitude or orientation adopted by those who accept this invitation. In these terms,

this book can be regarded as a response to the challenge just mentioned—one, needless to add, that the authors think is defensible and
worthy of implementation.

Personnel. The realization of the ambitious aims of discipline-based art
education depends on professionals on two levels. On the first, and in
the pivotal role, we find teachers in the schools, without whom nothing
whatsoever could be accomplished. In the early years of schooling, the
task of art instruction will in most cases fall to the general classroom
teacher for the simple reason that in many parts of the country elementary art specialists are either unavailable or in short supply. Where
they are available, they should be instrumental in actualizing the program outlined here. It is taken for granted that in the secondary grades
art will be taught by art specialists. The approach also recommends
that the planning and implementation of programs should be district-
wide and rely whenever possible on the cooperation and support of
school administrators, parent groups, and cultural organizations. Little
is said here, however, about such problems.

On the second level, that of conceptualization and planning, discipline-based art education calls for the services of academic professionals and practitioners from the spectrum of disciplines involved,
namely, artists, art historians, art critics, and philosophers of art. But
to construct a curriculum that is sound as well as responsive to the
needs and capabilities of learners and suitable for implementation in
the schools, the help of learning theorists, developmental psychologists, curriculum specialists, and others is also necessary. It is equally
important to establish and maintain an exchange of ideas among
professionals on the two levels, that is, among educators, artists, and
academic scholars. This goal is often very hard to accomplish; yet the
need to build bridges spanning the disciplines and practice was one of
the major reasons for initiating the series of which this book is the
introductory volume. To repeat, in this series a philosopher of the
humanities, a philosopher of art, an art historian, an art critic, and an
artist collaborate with educational specialists. Whether or not these
undertakings will produce the anticipated results, the chances for progress would be far poorer without the dialogue they seek to bring about.

Variety as Well as Structure. Discipline-based art education allows considerable latitude in several respects; the approach prescribes neither
a canon of works that must be studied nor a rigid course of study. For
example, at the time of this writing several centers of discipline-based
art education are putting in place differently accented programs. Still,

it is expected that certain tenets should not be compromised, one of which is that the works of art selected for study should be of the highest quality and be outstanding exemplars of the features they embody.[5] With this proviso, the visual arts—which are the focus of discipline-based art education—may be dealt with quite liberally. Exemplars of excellence may be drawn from traditional and modern art as well as from the newer media of film and television, from design and architecture, and from the arts of non-Western civilizations.

When making decisions about content selection, it is easy for program planners to become engulfed in an ideologically charged atmosphere in which the traditional courtesies and decorum of debate are sacrificed to heated political advocacy. This is especially the case in disputes centering on the role to be played in an arts curriculum by the great works of the Western cultural heritage. The authors of this volume do not join in the current denigration of the Western cultural heritage, the tendency, as previously mentioned, to regard it in such pejorative terms as racist, sexist, and elitist. Indeed, quite the contrary. But neither do we deny the importance—already emphasized in chapter 7—of comparative cultural studies, at a proper time and in their proper place. The inclusion of such studies acknowledges the significance of entertaining alternatives, which is one of the aims of humanistic education. For example, in his *The Future of the Humanities* Walter Kaufmann gives four reasons for studying the humanities: to conserve and cultivate the greatest works of humanity, to foster a critical spirit, to teach vision, and to reflect on alternatives.[6] And Harold Osborne, certainly no denigrator of Western values, put it well when he said that "the best and perhaps the only sure way of bringing to light and revivifying . . . fossilized assumptions, and of destroying their power to cramp and confine, is by subjecting ourselves to the shock of contact with a very alien tradition."[7]

Cumulative Learning. Another tenet of discipline-based art education holds that aesthetic learning should in some meaningful sense be cumulative and progressive. In order to ensure coherence and direction, learning should proceed through carefully designed units that reflect the readiness and growing capabilities of students. This view assumes nothing other than that later accomplishments should build on earlier mastery.

Three further considerations flow from a developmental view of aesthetic learning. First, a program structured in terms of a progression through phases makes criteria available for judging when a certain phase has been mastered and students are ready to move on to the next one. Evaluation, in other words, is systematically built into teaching. Second, the extent to which, and the times at which, the four disciplines—or, as we have also called them, the arts of creation, continuity, communication, and criticism—are resorted to by teachers will be a condition of students' particular levels of aesthetic development. This means that art educators will not have uniform recourse to artistic creation, art history, art criticism, and aesthetics at all levels of teaching art from grades K–12. Third, the problem of selecting content from a seemingly bewildering array of acceptable examples—works from the visual arts in their different manifestations, cultural and ethnic origins, and degrees of sophistication—will tend to sort itself out when the appropriateness of works to the phases of aesthetic development is taken into consideration. We will go into these matters more fully in due course.

A Percipience Curriculum for Discipline-based Art Education

In what follows I present a modified restatement of ideas set forth elsewhere.[8] This may perhaps be excused when one considers that in many arts, most notably in music but also in the visual arts and literature, artists' variations on a theme are common and not inherently suspect. Not only that; reworking usually involves refining.

The curriculum to be described is one I have variously called an art world or excellence curriculum but which, as I have indicated, I will now refer to as a percipience curriculum, although the idea of an art world and a commitment to excellence are retained. The general purpose of a percipience curriculum is to help build in the young a well-developed sense of art that will enable them to confront works of art as sensitive and informed percipients—that is, as well-educated generalists—for the sake of the worthwhile experiences that works of art at their best are capable of affording. These benefits were described in chapter 6, and I recall them here: the experience of a high level of aesthetic gratification, the expansion of perceptual powers to their fullest, the provision of humanistic insights, and the extension of individual and social freedom. Once more, by "percipience" I mean a possession of mind that manifests itself in a mature and discerning awareness in matters of art and culture. The term, then, implies not just perception but the knowledge, judgment, and wisdom that informs it. The difference between a seasoned critic and a novice lies precisely in the former's vastly greater powers of percipience.

How, then, can schooling inculcate a sense of art in the young that will be adequate to the requirements of sensitive and informed perception of works of art? Before addressing particulars, we should point out that aesthetic learning is a lengthy process. Even if seriously undertaken and pursued persistently it can only be partly successful, for a person can spend a lifetime trying to become familiar with some works of art whose meaning, as in the case of Giorgione's *The Tempest*, may still remain elusive.

The stretch of time allotted to the study of art in discipline-based art education will articulate itself, as mentioned, into rather distinct phases, each building on the preceding one and feeding into the next. A view of aesthetic development, however, is made more convincing if coordinated with a suitable theory of learning that shows how a person's apperceptive mass gradually assumes greater richness and interpretive power. In this connection, I present some general observations about cognitive development.

The principal relevance of cognitive psychology for the teaching of art lies in four principles: (1) what is seen and understood is a function of one's conceptual framework, which consists of schemata for understanding the most simple and elementary as well as the most complex phenomena; (2) the ideas and concepts of one's conceptual framework are hierarchically organized, with some ideas subsuming others; (3) new ideas and information are processed most effectively when they are related to existing patterns of thought; and (4) one's cognitive structure changes as the mind assimilates new information. The presumption of the above mental structures yields an image of mind not as a passive receptacle but as an active, participating, constructive power.[9] This concept of mind also sets a twofold task for teachers of art. It is first necessary to form some idea of the conceptual frameworks learners bring to given assignments; second, it is crucial to have a clear idea of the body of knowledge and skills about art that the young should acquire. And to say this is to emphasize that teachers must be exceptionally well acquainted with both their subject and their students. Yet, as Lee Schulman has recently remarked, how difficult it is to acquire sufficient familiarity with one, let alone both.[10]

When the cultivation of a sense of art proceeds from the assumption that learning progresses through phases, learning experiences will range from the simple to the more complex and will be both sequential and cumulative. Since the description of the phases of aesthetic learning is the topic of this chapter's final section, I will say here only that instruction moves from simple exposure, familiarization, and formal perceptual training in the early years of schooling to the building of historical, appreciative, and critical awareness in the later years. Such a progression is, I think, consistent with what we know about the dynamics of human cognitive growth.

Additionally, this line of development exhibits flexibility in various ways. First, it accommodates itself to the disposition of younger learners to favor concrete activities as well as to adolescents' greater abstractive and reasoning powers. Second, it provides for different teaching methods at different times and levels; not only discovery methods but also didactic teaching, coaching, and critical dialogue may be appropriate. Third, this line of development, emphasizing as it does the acquisition of skills and concepts of increasing scope and complexity, allows latitude with respect to the activities engaged in and the works selected for examination and discussion—but without degenerating into empty educational formalism. For it was emphasized that a significant sense of art cannot evolve in the absence of repeated and sustained commerce with works of high aesthetic quality. From this combination of the formal and the substantive something resembling a canon of works to be studied will after all emerge.

Again we take note of the fact that the recommended developmental scheme is inherently amenable to evaluation inasmuch as relevant assessments can be made at any point along the way. For example, at the end of each phase it would be appropriate to determine whether learners' conceptual maps have been sufficiently elaborated. Has a degree of perceptual finesse been acquired by the end of the elementary years? Has a sense of art's history been established by grade ten? Is an appreciation of selected classics, masterworks, and exemplars evident by grade twelve? Is there reason to believe that the content, skills, and dispositions of one phase have been propaedeutic to the next such that proficiency in later stages is evidence of mastery previously attained? At the end of a percipience curriculum are there signs that all learning has been integrated meaningfully in the mind of the learner? Finally, the attainment of an appropriate degree of aesthetic percipience should be all the warrant that is needed for conferring credibility on the curriculum that presumably helped bring it about, in other words, for a positive assessment of the program as a whole.

More likely, however, evaluation will disclose only degrees of success, for factors other than program design, the competence of teachers, and the cooperation of learners often come into play. There are such things as the seriousness of the school's commitment to art education, the professionalism of its teaching and administrative staff, and the substance of its curriculum. Schools that, as a whole, commit their talents and energies to worthwhile goals may find themselves inhibited by local, district, or state constraints. Even parents, as noted earlier, are often unpersuaded of the need for formal study of the arts. Evaluation must take all such matters into account, for it would be unethical to hold teachers and schools responsible for conditions over which they have little or no control. Several recent studies, for example, have revealed how severely a school's bureaucracy often infringes on the time that teachers can devote to teaching.[11]

It may be important to mention briefly that while the phases of aesthetic learning—exposure, familiarization, perceptual training, historical study, exemplar appreciation, and critical reflection—are instrumental to building a sense of art (as all learning is always instrumental, a means), they have intrinsic values as well. There is nothing in the conception of art presented here that would deprive students of the enjoyment of working with art materials or looking at pictures.

Perhaps some of the points just made can be reinforced by recasting them as images or metaphors. Let us exploit the geographical connotations of "art world" to speak metaphorically of an art education curriculum as itinerary, as a plan for learning to traverse the art world with tact and sensitivity. The image combines a word current in talk about art—the art world—with the idea of travel, which is a common experience of many and the expectation of many more. This permits the envisioning of vicarious journeys through the world of art (not that real journeys are impossible, if we count occasional trips to museums and so forth). To bring the image into sharper focus: the travel anticipated is not casual and aimless but is undertaken specifically for enlightenment and aesthetic enjoyment. And while the art world as a significant realm of value is certainly inviting, it is also in many respects inaccessible and confusing to the untutored—hence the need for a well-structured plan to lend purpose and sequence to teaching and learning activities. To repeat, the objective of an art curriculum as itinerary is to prepare students to traverse the art world with knowledge, sensitivity, and skill. Such an image, I think, generates relevant pedagogical questions in a more interesting way than conventional curriculum jargon does.

What are the special features of the art world, its major points of interest? How long should one sojourn at particular places? What kind of preparation is necessary in order to reap the full rewards of one's travels? What might be some secondary stops, even some places to rest? Who should be the guide of the young and write the guidebooks that tell of worthwhile things to see? Are there "rules of the road" that must be obeyed? By what criteria should all of this—itinerary, guides, guidebooks, value of experiences—be assessed? And who should do the assessing?

In the real world of art we rely on knowledgeable and experienced critics to steer us toward what is worth our while and away from what would be a waste of time. Good critics help persons to think about many of the perplexities and issues works of art present. In short, as we saw in chapter 5, we understand criticism rightly when we take it to consist of the teaching of perception, the reasoned evaluation of works of art, and the improvement of the climate in which we think about art. The teacher in the role of critic is thus the guide of the young, the person who will enable the young to find their way about the art world.

Like any analogy the one between the critic and the teacher has its limits. For example, in an insightful essay titled "Teaching and Learning in the Arts," Henry Aiken points out that critics are more likely to be preoccupied with their own efforts to understand and assess works of art. And the pressures of seeing as much art as possible and of meeting publication deadlines considerably reduce the amount of time they can devote to educating their readers, although that is certainly an important aim of many of them.[12] In short, the critic's concern is narrower and more specialized than that of the teacher of art who must take into consideration students' learning readiness, the difficulties they may be experiencing, and the most appropriate manner in which gradually to increase their aesthetic skills and knowledge about art. Moreover, the art critic tends to assume an already educated audience while the teacher has the task of bringing the learner to an educated state. Both art critic and teacher celebrate the achievements of the creative life, but it is the teacher's responsibility day in and day out to indicate through talk, gestures, and reticences what is involved in apprehending the complexities and qualities of works of art and to make clear how difficult it is to develop an authentic taste.

Phases of Aesthetic Learning

The expression "phases of aesthetic learning" avoids the somewhat more loaded one "stages of aesthetic development." The latter phrase is associated with the empirical work of Michael J. Parsons and Abigail Housen, both of whom have separately conducted intensive investigations into the nature of aesthetic growth.[13] Although nothing that follows is, I think, inconsistent with the findings of these researchers— indeed, in certain respects their work nicely supports the recommendations to be made—my intention is different. The following discussion is inherently prescriptive, and its recommendations derive more from the definition of discipline-based art education presented in this volume than from anything else.

Phase One of Aesthetic Learning:
Perceiving Aesthetic Qualities (Grades K–3)

The interpretation of discipline-based art education presented here considers mature works of art to be the principal loci of aesthetic qualities. Nowhere else can these properties be found in such abundance and concentration. Youngsters in the first phase of aesthetic learning, however, obviously cannot perceive the full range of qualities works of art possess; the emphasis will therefore be on developing a child's awareness of aesthetic qualities wherever they may occur. We might say that this is the time for experiencing with heightened perceptiveness the everyday world in preparation for experiencing the world of art and also for a first, casual acquaintance with a few components of the art world. By the end of phase one students should not only have become more attentive to the aesthetic qualities of their environment but they should also have realized that aesthetic qualities are prominently featured in works of art. Youngsters will further have discovered that as objects artworks are quite out of the ordinary since they are usually found in special places set aside for their exhibition—for example, in art museums—and since they are discussed in special spaces in newspapers and magazines. In short, learners will have acquired a rudimentary concept of the art world.

Phase one of aesthetic learning poses no special difficulties for the experienced art teacher. Its objectives, moreover, can be achieved through many of the activities currently taught in art courses for the young student. Because aesthetic qualities are present in myriad phenomena, the problem of content selection at this level is not as severe as it will become during, say, phases four and five, when attention centers on the development of a sense of history and the cultivation of exemplar appreciation and critical analysis. Content selection during this initial phase is affected primarily by the teacher's sensitivity, love of art, and sympathy for young children.

Neither does the first phase of aesthetic learning make particular demands so far as teaching method is concerned. Basic perceptual habits can be acquired and the early development of a sense of art accomplished by involving youngsters in creative activities of various kinds. Learning will thus progress from awareness of the simple qualities of things to the recognition of aesthetic qualities in works of art, including the works students themselves make. Teaching would for the most part be informal and not overly abstract, for that would be would inappropriate for young learners. But although there may be a close resemblance between a phase-one art classroom in discipline-based education and one in a traditional curriculum, there is also an important underlying difference. Teachers will be more conscious of the cumulative, progressive nature of aesthetic learning, the fact that one phase builds on and leads into another. This goal, however, does not imply a lock-step sequence of activities of the sort associated with the attainment of countless behavioral objectives. Customary activities would simply be undertaken with a different end in view; in particular, young learners would be envisioned as future reflective percipients and traversers of the art world. Such commitments will allow art teachers to go about their business with a sense of direction and purposiveness that should transmit itself to the students.

If phase one aesthetic learning is preparatory for later phases, it is also true that it builds on the schemata young children bring to school. These will be variously structured for different children; they will be relatively rich or impoverished depending on a child's home and immediate environment. It is thus apparent that schools must do what they can to rectify cases of aesthetic deprivation. There must be remedial instruction for those Morris Weitz called "underperceivers."[14]

In speaking of the ubiquity of aesthetic qualities in the world, we draw attention to one of the basic categories of human experience, sheer qualitative immediacy, which has been of great interest to philosophers. For example, in his *Art as Experience* John Dewey formulated a controversial definition of art that began not with the completed work in the museum—what he referred to as the museum-pedestal conception of art that drives a wedge between art and the ongoing experiences of everyday life—but by examining the generic qualities of human experience itself. Phase one of aesthetic learning takes a page from Dewey's writings. But no one, Levi believed, described the universal categories of human experience better than another American philosopher, Charles Sanders Peirce. In an essay on Peirce and painting, Levi explains how Peirce's description of human experience enables us to understand painting, and perhaps art in general, as devoted to the illumination of perceptual quality, the expression of dynamic interaction, and the exploration of symbolic meaning, although the proportions and ratios of quality, movement, and meaning will vary from art form to art form and from work to work. Peirce gave very simple names to these three categories of experience: Firstness, Secondness, and Thirdness. In words he had intended for this volume, Levi explains them as follows.

By Firstness Peirce means the immediate qualitative aspects of all our perceptual experience: the color of magenta, the odor of attar, the sound of a railway whistle, the taste of quinine. It means all in experience that is immediate, fresh, of the absolute present, novel, spontaneous, vivid. What the world was to Adam on the day he opened his eyes to it, before he had drawn any distinctions, or had become conscious of his own experience—that is *first*, present, immediate, fresh, original, spontaneous, free, vivid, conscious, evanescent.

If in Firstness is to be found the "feeling" character of the universe, in Secondness is to be found its "activity." Whenever we have the experience of tension, the sense of things confronting one another, of pushing against one another or causing one another, Secondness is the focus of our perception. It is the sense of the action and reaction of bodies, of movement in all its infinite variety, of dynamism in the world and the sense of strain and muscular effort in our own bodies. Naturally it is impossible to isolate Secondness except through an artificial direction of attention or by metaphor. But perhaps one comes closest to its essence by calling it the oppositional element in experience. For wherever there is antagonistic juxtaposition, shock, surprise, sudden movement, gesticulation, and violence, our senses are in the presence of Secondness.

If Firstness lies in the qualities of things, and if Secondness lies in their oppositions, then Thirdness lies in their meaning. All items in experience have qualitative immediacy and interactive force. They also point to something beyond themselves, stand for something beyond their immediate presence, have the capacity to symbolize ideas or meanings that transcend their own local particularity. Thus whenever there is generality, whenever individual elements in experience symbolize classes, or permit generalizations, Thirdness is present.

Of course, Firstness, Secondness, and Thirdness, as Peirce presents them, are not really separable in actual fact. They are genuine *aspects* of a whole (as quality, movement, and meaning are genuine aspects of a painting), and they can be separated only by acts of exclusive attention or abstraction. They are a map of experience; an account of what to look for. Here, for example, is a dark storm cloud in a summer sky. When we see it simply as a dense black eclipse before our eyes, we are attending to its Firstness. When we sense that it is really out there (as opposed to the region in which we are)—as blotting out the sun, as pressing forcefully against the atmosphere, or as moving swiftly driven by the wind—then we are attending to its Secondness. And when we look upon it as a sign of what is to come and mutter "So it's going to rain!," then its meaning is foremost in our consciousness, and we are attending [concludes Levi] to its Thirdness.[15]

Phase one of aesthetic learning is the time for discovering the qualitative immediacy of things. To be sure, the qualities that immediately present themselves to the young are not always those that lift the spirit. Blight, decay, and deterioration are also aesthetic qualities. But surely the purpose of art education is to cultivate habits of perception that hold potential for making the human habitat more attractive and liveable. The early years of schooling are not the time for stressing the dark side of life; they are a time for expanding and freshening vision, for discovering those properties of things that foster interest and delight.

To sum up this part. During the first phase of aesthetic learning the task of discipline-based art education begins. The conceptual frameworks young children bring to school undergo modification, aesthetic dispositions start to form, and elementary aesthetic mapping occurs. The young are in effect informally initiated into the mysteries of art and the art world. They intuitively discover what is involved in composing material into a work of art (albeit a child's work of art), and they accordingly learn something about how a work of art communicates. They also intuitively realize that although some aesthetic qualities—for example, those of nature—are simply there for the perceiving, other qualities are added to the world by human beings. In all of this they are becoming aware of one of the essential features of aesthetic experience, a sense of object directedness, which was discussed in chapter 6.

Phase Two of Aesthetic Learning:
Developing Perceptual Acumen (Grades 4–6)

During the second phase of aesthetic learning—and, of course, I am merely suggesting the points at which one phase evolves into another, exactitude is not required here—instruction becomes more formal, although not inordinately so. Ideally, everything acquired during phase one is utilized. Creative activities are continued for their intrinsic, as well as for their instrumental, values, but interest in making works gradually diminishes and attention shifts to the object and its various aspects. Now not only the qualitative immediacy of things is noted but also their relations and meanings, what Peirce called Secondness and Thirdness, or at least those relations and meanings young learners can perceive and grasp. Attention is increasingly centered on the work of art. This is the time for intensive perceptual training, for learning what to look for and talk about. The students' own products may still serve as objects of perception, but there is now an unmistakable movement toward greater awareness of the character of mature works of art and a more developed idea of the art world. It is crucial at this point that the teacher have sound knowledge not only of the ways aesthetic materials can be deployed but also of the aesthetic structure of works of art—that is, stratified objects saturated with feeling and human import that have the capacity to afford aesthetic experiences of high magnitude. Nowhere is the teacher's familiarity with the principles of art more essential, for without it there is no prospect of offering intelligent guidance to the students' aesthetic noticing. What is more, teachers must now be more thoughtful about method than they needed to be with phase-one students.

At the time of this writing, several discipline-based art education programs are using a method called "aesthetic scanning." As Harry S. Broudy and Ronald Silverman describe it, aesthetic scanning involves the perception of the vividness and intensity of the affective and emotional qualities conveyed by an object's colors, gestures, shapes, and textures (sensory properties); the design, composition, or arrangement of elements that provide unity through balance, repetition, rhythm, and context (formal qualities); the skill with which objects have been created (technical merits); and the import or message of objects as aesthetically expressed (expressive significance).[16] This method enables persons to make contact with works of art and is therefore quite suitable for promoting the aims of the second phase of aesthetic learning. Aesthetic scanning, however, has its detractors. Some have likened it to superficial speed reading; others have said that it sleights the synoptic character of aesthetic vision (of which Osborne makes so much in his account of aesthetic percipience); still others, that it neglects contextual understanding. But these objections would point to true liabilities only if aesthetic scanning constituted the whole of art teaching, a claim Broudy and Silverman do not make. The method will, I think, work quite well when understood as one phase of the complete act of response to art. For a persuasive model of the complete act I refer to Kenneth Clark's discussion of his own pattern of reacting to artworks, a pattern that consists of moments of impact, scrutiny, recollection, and renewal.[17]

The first stage of response—that is, impact—consists of initial general impressions, which are usually of a painting's relationships of tone, shape, and color. These impressions are then followed by a period of careful inspection, or scrutiny, for first impressions can often be misleading. During this stage of aesthetic response perception centers on such things as a work's color harmonies, the quality of drawing, technical considerations, and representational elements. With further scrutiny, there are attempts to detect a dominant motive or root idea from which a work derives its overall effect. Yet Clark realizes that concentrated attention on a work's various aspects is difficult and can be sustained for only relatively short periods of time. And so to let the faculties gather strength for completing the task of responding, beholders must momentarily abandon scrutiny in favor of recollecting various kinds of information relevant to perceiving the full significance of a work. Such recollection, as Clark puts it, permits the senses to get their second wind and is preparatory to his fourth phase of aesthetic response, the resumption of aesthetic experience and the renewed energizing of the spirit. Renewal saturates the self with a work's complex of values and leads to a freshening of vision. As Goodman might say, actual worlds get refigured in light of the worlds of works. (Elsewhere I have used Clark's discussion of Vermeer's *The Artist in His Studio* to illustrate this sequence of response.)[18]

What keeps the stage of scrutiny from being at its most exacting and fruitful in the early years of aesthetic learning is, of course, the relatively impoverished cognitive stock of young learners. This limits their capacity for recollection, for calling up those nips of art-historical and other kinds of information that nurture and renew aesthetic experience. Yet within the limits of their knowledge and skill during phase two the young can learn to give accounts of their impressions of works (impact), engage in rudimentary analysis (scrutiny), and apply what knowledge they do possess (recollection), which enables them to enjoy the first intimations of heightened perception (renewal).

Whatever the preferred terminology, developing perceptual awareness is central to phase two of aesthetic learning. Students elaborate and refine their aesthetic maps and gain a better understanding of the sorts of things they will encounter when traversing the art world. They will, in short, acquire some of the fundamental skills and attitudes required for knowing, appreciating, and judging works of art. Most of all, they will have become aware that works of art must be addressed in a certain way if they are to yield such benefits as they are capable of providing. The realization that aesthetic experiencing demands a special kind of attention if justice is to be done to a work's unique features is perhaps as important a result of phase two as improved aesthetic perceptiveness itself. Students learn, for example, that aesthetic attending involves object directedness, which, as we have seen, implies that percipients not only have to concentrate their perceptual powers on the artwork itself but must also submit to the work and permit it to direct their responses. In doing this, learners may further experience a sense of active discovery, of new things seen and felt. And perhaps they might even manage to distance in an aesthetically appropriate way their idiosyncratic feelings and inclinations as their attention ranges attentively over the whole spectrum of a work's properties; they may, in short, master the skill of detached affect required of experienced aesthetic respondents.

Phase Three of Aesthetic Learning: Developing a Sense of Art History (Grades 7–9)

During the first two phases of aesthetic learning the young discover that in one of its major guises the world appears as a world of qualities; they begin to appreciate the sheer qualitative immediacy of life. Following close upon this is the realization that works of art are human artifacts designed to be interesting to perception and that when we experience works of art properly we move from first impressions to the scrutiny of a constellation of aesthetic properties to recollection of what we know about art and human experience. I think that, with the qualifications mentioned, learners must experience the first two phases of aesthetic learning before they can undertake the study of art history and begin to think of art in terms of time, tradition, and style. Having learned how the world presents itself qualitatively and how works of art embody aesthetic properties and meanings in special ways, students in the middle years of schooling are ready to discover how different ages have expressed their beliefs and values in objects that are enriched and embellished by aesthetic form.

Phase three seeks to achieve a twofold objective, or perhaps two slightly different aims that will not be completely separable in teaching or appear distinct in the learners' experience. The first aim derives directly from the overall purpose of discipline-based art education: to learn to understand and appreciate works of art for the sake of the benefits they are capable of providing. It follows that these benefits become available in all their satisfying richness and profundity only in the most sophisticated aesthetic experiences. But since it is generally agreed that the mature perception of artworks can unfold only against a background of information about art which functions tacitly during aesthetic experience, and since much of this pervasive and indispensable knowledge derives from the history of art, any program of art education that withholds such knowledge retards the cultivation of aesthetic percipience. The first purpose of stage three of aesthetic learning, then, is to enlarge the cognitive framework of the young through the study of art history, to stock their minds with images, concepts, and a vocabulary that will let them experience and talk about works of art in the informed manner of reflective beholders.

The second aim of stage three derives from the inflection a humanities interpretation imparts to the teaching of art. What, we may ask, does art history communicate, what understandings does it convey to learners? It is impossible to survey art historically, beginning with cave paintings and ending with contemporary creations, without concomitantly developing an appreciation of the evolution of civilization. Students thus realize, to borrow imagery from Friedrich Schiller, how humankind has literally risen from the state of raw nature and enslavement by brutal necessity to a state of human freedom and leisure (at least in many parts of the world) in which the rule of reason and opportunities for cultural expression have become paramount values. Works of art vividly and poignantly reveal this process; they are visual records of heroic efforts to achieve culture and civilization. Periods during which that process has been stalled or tragically set back have also left their imprint on the art-historical record, nowhere more ominously perhaps than in Goya's *Disasters of War* and in the images of death created by the contemporary German painter Anselm Kiefer. For a celebration of art's glorious accomplishments, on the other hand, we need only turn to Kenneth Clark's *Civilisation,* both the television series and the text that accompanies it. By presenting a unique account of humankind's continuous struggle for civilization and its intermittent triumphs, art history bears witness to the existence of a common human bond that transcends different beliefs.

Another humanistic insight afforded by the study of art history concerns the role and value of tradition. To see art under the aspects of time, tradition, and style is to discover an order in human artistic production. This order is also constantly being consolidated and added to as new works are located within it. We recall Janson's remark in chapter 4 that "whether we are aware of it or not, tradition is the framework within which we inevitably form our opinions of works of art and assess their degree of originality." And although there have been eras that have rejected the conventions and values of preceding periods, the evidence of continuity is far more compelling. One instance of such continuity is classicism, which, as we saw in our discussion of postmodernism in art and architecture, is enjoying yet another revival (recall that Jencks described nine streams of contemporary classicism).

Phase three of aesthetic learning is, of course, instrumental. It is a means to the acquisition of art-historical knowledge necessary for cultivated aesthetic appreciation, for an improved sense of the art world, and for grasping an artwork's aesthetic qualities and humanistic insights. But it possesses intrinsic value as well. The reading of art-historical accounts affords pleasures not unlike those of reading literature, although it is augmented by the enjoyment of viewing reproductions. Moreover, it is difficult to believe that art history, taught in accordance with the educational purposes discussed in this section and with the use of the excellent textual and audiovisual materials available today, could be anything but a rewarding activity for both learners and teachers. We are, after all, talking about introducing young persons to some of the finest creative achievements of the human spirit. Certainly it is not the case that young people are indifferent to excellence. They value outstanding performances by athletes and entertainers, and there are signs that they increasingly appreciate intellectual and artistic excellence. Indeed, Hirsch reminds us that the young hunger for facts and information about that which interests them and may even develop an insatiable curiosity that it is difficult to satisfy. If this seems too optimistic a projection, it remains true that phase-three aesthetic learning, while accomplishing the objectives just mentioned, need not be dull or unengaging.

The study of art history may have another extrinsic value in a preventive or remedial sense. Television, the movies, and popular music are currently the single most potent force shaping the tastes of youth. Young people embrace them uncritically and are under their impact for more hours of the day than adults consider wholesome. Art history cannot compete on an equal footing with the mass media for the attention of the young, but it can at least present students with alternatives of taste and style and open their eyes to their own often crude preferences.

The teaching method appropriate to phase three should reflect the greater maturity and seriousness of this level. Although aesthetic learning during the first two phases should be substantive and instill the concepts and skills of both artistic creation and perception, teaching should not be excessively formal. Since the objectives of the initial stages can be achieved somewhat informally, teachers can to some extent rely on learners' acquiring the necessary understandings as much from what they are encouraged to do as from what they are deliberately taught. During the third phase of aesthetic learning, however, grades 7–9, instruction necessarily becomes more structured. A measure of discipline not previously exacted is now in order, for a sense of art history and its traditions can be acquired only through systematic study over time.

Although the study of the history of art centers on the major works of the cultural tradition, this does not mean that historical units cannot contain practical exercises that lend a further degree of concreteness to the enterprise. (I say "further degree of concreteness" because there is nothing abstract or theoretical about perceiving artworks in their particularity or historical context.) Students could, for example, explore their immediate environment for traces of its cultural past. Museum visits, when possible, are certainly in order. The maintenance of art-historical portfolios suggests itself; for example, a collection of reproductions, catalogues, clippings, and the like could serve as reminders of things seen and discussed or of things one day to be seen in the original. Some modest experimentation with the materials and techniques of a given period and style could prove effective. Experienced teachers will think of still more possibilities. Certainly the volume on art history in this series will have much to say on the subject. Teachers should be wary, however, of reversing the figure and ground of art-historical study, for it is the sense of art history that it is important to develop during phase three. Everything else is instrumental to this.

There is no need here to prescribe content for instruction in phase three of aesthetic learning; resourceful art teachers should have no trouble finding suitable material. Since the study of art history recommended for the middle years is essentially that of art's chronology and genealogy as it is typically presented in survey courses, there will be a surfeit of content. The survey nature of this phase will not allow students to linger long over any particular period or work of art; but, to return to our travel metaphor, they will nonetheless garner passing glimpses of a few of the mansions that grace the cultural landscape. In some of them they will sojourn for longer periods of time during the fourth phase of aesthetic learning when exemplar appreciation becomes the primary objective.

Despite a certain latitude permitted in selecting texts and materials for phase three of aesthetic learning, it must be insisted that once the chronological survey has reached Greek antiquity instruction should proceed with a heavy stress on Western art. To anticipate objections that will immediately be raised to such a recommendation, I should point out that the study of non-Western art will be expressly provided for in stage four, which accommodates a global dimension through cross-cultural studies and multicultural comparisons. But acquaintance with examples from the treasure house of Western culture, arranged in historical sequence, is indispensable for the third stage of aesthetic learning. It is now, in the middle years of schooling, that students acquire a historical sense as part of the intellectual wherewithal they will need for becoming knowledgeable travelers in the art world, for developing into reflective percipients instead of remaining mere onlookers. And to help young persons effect this transition we must let them see how the world they know relates to the world of art. And as for the world they know, it is undeniable that students today are living in a society that is still solidly situated within Western civilization. This country's political and cultural institutions make sense only when seen in that framework; major works of contemporary art still take the Western tradition for granted even when they assault it. The visual environment in which the young find themselves—the appearance of everything from architecture to product design to advertising—derives predominantly from forms and styles in the Western mode. Even the popular arts, whether reverently or mockingly, allude to or incorporate well-known artworks from the Western tradition. In short, regardless of their ethnic origins, students growing up in this country need a grounding in the visual arts of the Western tradition, if only to make sense of the realities of the visual world they experience daily.

Second, the young should be familiar with the artistic heritage of their own society and know something about the continuity and change of artistic conventions of Western art before engaging examples of non-Western art. Just as it is believed that a well-established self-concept is a precondition for the full appreciation of other persons, so the artistic expressions of foreign cultures are most fruitfully approached from a foundation in one's own that permits discoveries of similarities as well as of the irreducibly alien.

Third, a preparation in the Western cultural tradition, many of the concepts of which are provided by art history, is further prerequisite to assuming a truly reflective and critical attitude toward that tradition. The aim is to convey a sense of that tradition while avoiding either a mindless acceptance of its values or their doctrinaire rejection, which is so much a part of contemporary intellectual discourse. This is not an isolated or eccentric stance. I invoke in support the opinion of Richard Rorty, the distinguished philosopher who is often referred to approvingly in the writings of revisionist critics. Rorty too emphasizes the importance of being well acquainted with one's cultural heritage before undertaking to criticize it. He thinks the years of secondary education should be the period for familiarizing the young with the received tradition, while analyzing and criticizing it should be reserved for higher education.[19] So much for the defense of what used to be conventional wisdom.

Phase Four of Aesthetic Learning:
Exemplar Appreciation (Grades 10–11)

Phases four and five of aesthetic learning divide into exemplar appreciation in grades 10 and 11 and critical analysis in grade 12. Having been equipped with perceptual skills and a sense of art history and the art world in the earlier grades, students now spend extended periods (vicariously) visiting selected mansions in the cultural landscape. It is time, in other words, to study in depth some outstanding works of art, classics, masterpieces. Grades 10 and 11 develop a respectful and admiring appreciation of art in the best sense of the term.

Exemplar appreciation, in other words, is the major emphasis of phase four of aesthetic learning. Among other things this phase also offers an opportunity to examine and apply the distinction between synchronic and diachronic studies of art. It will be recalled that diachronic study is vertical, serial, and sequential and has temporal progression and continuity as its essence. Synchronic study, by contrast, is cross-sectional research that examines how in a particular cultural period the arts interact with one another and how they affect and are affected by intellectual, economic, social, and political forces. In such circumstances, as Levi pointed out, art history merges with cultural history.

Combining teaching for the appreciation of artistic excellence with an appropriate degree of synchronic study merits consideration because a full and rich understanding of a masterwork entails not only close scrutiny of its aesthetic qualities and meanings but also attention to the work's embeddedness in its cultural context. This approach might be called contextualism par excellence, for it does justice not only to the conditions surrounding the creation of a work of art, but also to its aesthetic character and to an estimate of its capacity to afford aesthetic experience. It does, however, stand in contrast to theories of art-historical interpretation that stress studying works of art solely as events in social history.

I present no list of outstanding works of art that all students should learn to appreciate in grades 10 and 11. The standard histories of art, Gardner's *Art through the Ages,* Janson's *History of Art,* Honour and Fleming's *The Visual Arts,* all discussed in chapter 4, as well as Janson's *Key Monuments of the History of Art,* provide more than a sufficient selection of works from the great ages of architecture, sculpture, and painting. F. David Martin and Lee Jacobus's *The Humanities through the Arts* is useful for its discussion of major artworks from a perceptual vantage point.[20] Large composite works or groupings of works also come to mind as particularly suitable; for example, an architectural complex such as the Acropolis in Athens, Giotto's frescoes in the Arena Chapel in Padua, the wall and ceiling paintings of the Sistine Chapel, a cathedral in the High Gothic style, Michelangelo's sculptures in the Medici Chapel, St. Peter's Cathedral, the Impressionist and Postimpressionist masters considered as a school, Cubism as exemplified in the works of Braque and Picasso, Frank Lloyd Wright's architectural legacy, and so on.[21] Other possibilities will occur to teachers. But it must be remembered that the emphasis in phase four is on appreciation, not on historical coverage; by the end of phase three students will presumably have attained fairly secure notions of where to place exemplars in the tradition.

If the suggestions for exemplar appreciation in this volume are taken largely from the cultural achievements of Western civilization and mainly, though not exclusively, from European civilization, it is not only because of the unquestionable excellence of these works but also because that is the area the authors know best. But since the aim of exemplar study is the appreciation of artistic excellence generally, cross-cultural comparisons are now appropriate and desirable. Ideas for such comparisons may be found in Benjamin Rowland's *Art in East and West*, which pairs for comparison a Greek Apollo or Kouros and an Indian Jain Tirthankara, Claude Lorrain's *Landscape of the Campagana* and Kuo Hsi's *Spring Landscape*, and Matisse's *Flowers* and Shên Chou's *Still Life*.[22] *East-West in Art*, which contains a number of essays by Theodore Bowie and other contributors, contains essays on styles in East and West and on cultural and artistic interchanges between East and West over a period of three thousand years, including, of course, contacts made during the modern period.[23] Thomas Munro's *Oriental Aesthetics* makes a strong plea for more comparative studies and provides numerous examples of Western and Eastern aesthetic theories.[24] In *The Aesthetic Experience: An Anthropologist Looks at the Arts*, Jacques Maquet discusses a wide range of work, Western, Eastern, and African.[25] Maquet's writing is especially interesting for his use of Western aesthetic theory (namely Harold Osborne's) to help explain the aesthetic character of non-Western art. I mention this because it is often assumed that Western aesthetic theory is inadequate for this purpose. But whereas phase four of aesthetic learning acknowledges the humanistic value of studying alternatives, it guards against the common abuses of multicultural education. These abuses occur when the aesthetic and cultural values of non-Western societies are uncritically presumed superior to those of the Western tradition (dogmatic multiculturalism), regarded as merely aesthetically interesting (multicultural aestheticism), or used principally as opportunities to advance political interests (ideological multiculturalism). The only form of multicultural study that is intellectually responsible is one that proceeds from what Walter Kaufmann calls a dialectical attitude toward its subject, that is, a critical stance that presumes neither the inherent superiority nor inferiority of a given culture but rather attempts to assess as objectively as possible what in it is worthwhile.[26] Only such an approach is consistent with the principles of a genuinely liberal education.

One matter needs underlining lest some of the preceding remarks be misunderstood or seem not sufficiently accented. The interpretation of discipline-based art education presented in this volume has an emphatic multicultural dimension. Throughout the curriculum (K–12), the works of various cultures, ethnic groups, and women should be shown to and studied by young people. Those more knowledgeable about cultural diversity than the present authors can be counted on to provide suggestions and available resources. Moreover, the sponsor of this series, the Getty Center for Education in the Arts, currently has projects underway in the area of multiculturalism. For the authors of this volume to feign expertise in this area would be presumptuous, although we would note that there are references in our discussions to the important contributions of non-Western cultures and women. Indeed, the title of the volume itself, *Art Education: A Critical Necessity* is a twist on the title of Rebecca West's book *The Strange Necessity*, and Levi made West's description of the potencies of art central to his discussion of art and the human person in chapter 2.

Once again, what this book is about is the development of percipience in matters of art and of an appreciation of artistic excellence. This can be accomplished through the study of works from a range of cultures and by studying artists of various ethnic origins and of both genders. Only during phase three, when the aim of discipline-based art education is to engender a sense of historical awareness, is vision confined principally to the history of Western art, for the reasons given. But in phases one, two, four, and five of aesthetic learning ample opportunity exists for addressing multicultural concerns. Other volumes in the series of which this is the introductory volume will also contain references to multiculturalism in art education.

Phase Five of Aesthetic Learning: Critical Analysis (Grade 12)

Phase five of aesthetic learning incorporates and deploys all the knowledge, skills, and dispositions acquired during the preceding phases. Students now synthesize what they have learned as they go about building their own personal philosophy of art. Such synthesizing is most appropriately carried out in seminar settings in which some of the problems and puzzles that arise in encountering and discussing works of art are dealt with in an atmosphere that encourages a free flow and exchange of ideas.

Since students cannot develop a well-considered stance toward art without some sense of critical standards, phase five pays particular attention to the concepts, skills, and traditions of art criticism. True, something will have been said along the way about criteria of artistic merit, and teachers will have been required to address some perplexing issues in art prior to this time. But now the point has been reached when criteria of aesthetic judgment will be systematically discussed and applied. The best method, I think, is to have students read and analyze samples of art criticism and to do critiques of their own. Ideas are available from the writings of critics themselves as well as from the literature of philosophical aesthetics. Another resource is the literature of art education; in recent years it has produced a considerable volume of writings that probe the problems of art criticism and analyze its concepts. The volume in this series devoted to art criticism will also provide suggestions.

With the knowledge and skills previously acquired now honed more finely and augmented by art-critical acumen, students are ready to tackle some of the thorny issues in art and the art world, such questions, for example, as those of censorship, the relations of aesthetic and moral values, the justifiability of public support for the arts, and the relation of art to the environment, to mention but a few contemporary issues.[27] If this kind of inquiry is modestly effective, then students entering the art world will have been forewarned about controversial events, of which of late there has been a steady stream. They will know how to take what they see and read and hear about and will proceed on their way with greater perspective.

To summarize: The rationale for discipline-based art education presented in this volume has made use of the image of curriculum as itinerary and proposed that art be taught as a humanity. Based on a suggested redefinition of the humanities, the teaching of the visual arts would bring to bear on diverse objectives the arts of creation, communication, continuity, and criticism. The mastery of these forms of thought and action prepares learners to be travelers and sojourners in the art world, persons who possess the interpretive capacities of the well-educated nonspecialist and who know how to confront a work of art intelligently and understand and appreciate it. The generalist's experience of an artwork constitutes the basic situation around which everything in the art curriculum is organized. The student reaches this state through a series of aesthetic learning phases: a phase of exploration and familiarization; a phase of perceptual training; a phase of

A Percipience Curriculum (Grades K–12)

General Goal: Cultivating Percipience in Matters of Art
by Teaching the Concepts and Skills of Art Conceived
as a Humanity

Arts of Creation (artistic creation)	*Arts of Communication* (art as language)	*Arts of Continuity* (art history)	*Arts of Criticism* (aesthetics)
Materials	Artistic statement	Time	Critical analysis
Techniques	Expression	Tradition	Problem solving
Artistic decision making	Interpretation	Style	Conceptualizing

Familiarization, exposure, and perceptual training (Phases 1 and 2, K–6)	⟶ Historical awareness (Phase 3, grades 7–9) ⟶	Exemplar appreciation and critical analysis (Phases 4 and 5, grades 10–12)

Teaching and learning proceed along a continuum from exposure, familiarization, and perceptual training to historical awareness, exemplar appreciation, and critical analysis, stressing discovery and reception learning, didactic coaching, and dialogic teaching methods. Evaluation of aesthetic learning centers on the development of aesthetic conceptual maps and the conditions conducive for doing so.

historical awareness; a phase of exemplar appreciation; and a phase of critical analysis.

Such a curriculum is of course an ideal, a prototype, but one that is not unrealistic provided existing ways of teaching art at the elementary and secondary levels are redefined. Major changes would have to be made at the secondary level, and, needless to say, teacher education would have to undergo considerable reform. Much more attention would have to be paid to the humanities as defined in this volume. But the detailing of such reforms is a topic for another book. The authors' principal purpose here has been to provide a rationale or justification for discipline-based art education. Central to our argument is the recognition of a fundamental human right treasured by all democratic societies—the right of all persons to have opportunities to actualize worthwhile human capacities. Included among these capacities are those associated with the experience of works of art at their best, an experience that we have described as affording aesthetic gratification, the expansion of perceptual powers, and the apprehension of an artwork's humanistic meanings. These individual satisfactions and fulfillments also make a difference collectively: a culture is more likely to enjoy robust health when persons traverse its art world with sensitivity, intelligence, and discernment. Hence an educational effort somewhat along the lines suggested here is required. We owe it to our young, to our culture, and to our country. Art education is a critical necessity.

Notes

Chapter 1. The Arts in the United States Today

1. *Toward Civilization: A Report on Arts Education* (Washington, D.C.: National Endowment for the Arts, 1988), p. 13.

2. R. A. Smith, *Excellence in Art Education: Ideas and Initiatives*, updated version (Reston, Va.: National Art Education Association, 1987), p. 68.

3. Edith Hamilton, *The Greek Way* (New York: W. W. Norton, 1942), pp. 104–5.

4. Ibid., p 57.

5. R. H. Tawney, *The Acquisitive Society* (New York: Harcourt, Brace and World, 1958), pp. 30–31.

6. Jacques Barzun, *The Use and Abuse of Art* (Princeton, N.J.: Princeton University Press, 1975), p. 127.

7. For a discussion of the aesthetic welfare, see Monroe C. Beardsley, "Aesthetic Welfare, Aesthetic Justice, and Educational Policy," *Journal of Aesthetic Education* 7, no. 4 (October 1973): 49–61; reprinted in Monroe C. Beardsley, *The Aesthetic Point of View: Selected Essays*, ed. Michael S. Wreen and Donald M. Callen (Ithaca, N.Y.: Cornell University Press, 1982), pp. 111–24.

8. Leonardo Bruni, "Panegyric to the City of Florence," in *The Early Republic: Italian Humanists on Government and Society*, ed. Benjamin G. Kohl and Ronald G. Witt, with Elizabeth B. Wells (Philadelphia: University of Pennsylvania Press, 1978), pp. 68–69. I was unable to find the translation used by Levi, and so provide the preceding reference in its place. See also Gene Adam Bruckner, *Florence: The Golden Age, 1138–1737* (New York: Abberville Press, 1983).

9. The reference is to Jacob Burckhardt's *The Civilization of the Renaissance* (1860; reprint, New York: Phaidon, 1951), part I, "The State as a Work of Art."

10. Kenneth Clark, *Civilisation* (New York: Harper and Row, 1969), chap. 13, "Heroic Materialism."

11. Jane Jacobs, *The Death and Life of Great American Cities* (New York: Random House, 1961).

12. Hannah Arendt, *The Human Condition* (Chicago: University of Chicago Press, 1958), p. 167.

Chapter 2. The Arts and the Human Person

1. Friedrich Wilhelm Nietzsche, *The Birth of Tragedy* and *The Genealogy of Morals*, trans. F. Golffing (New York: Doubleday, 1956), pp. 9, 17.

2. Fritz Jonas, ed., *Schiller's Briefe* (Stuttgart, 1892), vol. 3, p. 336. See also A. W. Levi, *Humanism and Politics* (Bloomington: Indiana University Press, 1969), p. 151.

3. References to Schiller are from Friedrich von Schiller, *On the Aesthetic Education of Man in a Series of Letters*, English and German on facing pages, ed. and trans. Elizabeth M. Wilkinson and L. A. Willoughby (New York: Oxford University Press, 1967).

4. Herbert Read, *The Redemption of the Robot: My Encounter with Education through Art* (New York: Simon and Schuster, 1966), p. xxv.

5. John Dewey, *Art as Experience* (New York: Minton Balch and Co., 1934), p. 248. See also *John Dewey: The Later Works, 1925–1953*, vol. 10, *1934*, ed. Jo Ann Boydston (Carbondale: Southern Illinois University Press, 1987), pp. 252–53.

6. Georg Wilhelm Friedrich Hegel, *The Philosophy of Fine Art*, 4 vols., trans. F. P. B. Osmaston (London: G. Bell and Sons, 1920), vol. 1, pp. 109, 117–18.

7. Rebecca West, *The Strange Necessity* (London: Jonathan Cape, 1928), p. 57.

8. Kenneth Clark, *Moments of Vision* (New York: Harper and Row, 1981), p. 7.

9. George Santayana, *The Sense of Beauty* (New York: Dover, 1955), pp. 78, 77, 78. First published Charles Scribner's Sons, 1896.

10. H. D. Thoreau, *Walden*, ed. J. Lyndon Shanley (Princeton, N.J.: Princeton University Press, 1971), p. 18.

11. Thoreau, *A Writer's Journal*, ed. Lauren Stapleton (New York: Dover, 1960), p. 188.

12. Washington Allston, quoted in Barbara Novak, *American Painting of the Nineteenth Century* (New York: Praeger, 1969), p. 48.

13. Quoted in Kenneth Clark, *Looking at Pictures* (New York: Holt, Rinehart and Winston, 1960), p. 114.

Chapter 3. The Creation of Art

1. John Dewey, *Art as Experience* (New York: Minton Balch, 1934), p.11.

2. Ibid., p. 74.

3. Henri Bergson, "The Perception of Change," in his *The Creative Mind* (New York: Philosophical Library, 1946), p. 159.

4. Germain Bazin, *French Impressionists in the Louvre* (New York: Harry N. Abrams, 1958), p. 42.

5. Quoted in Sidney Janis, *Abstract and Surrealist Art in America* (New York: Reynal and Hitchcock, 1944), p. 42.

6. Jacques Maritain, *Art and Scholasticism*, trans. Joseph W. Evans (New York: Charles Scribner's Sons, 1962), p. 9.

7. Ibid., pp. 8–9.

8. I was unable to find the translation used by Levi, but similar words can be found in *The Complete Letters of Van Gogh* (Boston: New York Graphic Society, 1978), vol. 2, p. 564.

9. Harold Rosenberg, "The American Action Painters," in his *The Tradition of the New* (New York: Horizon Press, 1959), pp. 25–26.

10. Jacques Barzun, *The Use and Abuse of Art*, p. 90.

11. Quoted in Herschel B. Chipp, ed., *Theories of Modern Art* (Berkeley: University of California Press, 1968), p. 316.

12. Ibid., p. 332.

13. Once again I have been unable to locate the source used by Levi, but similar remarks are contained in a catalogue titled *Austria Presents Hundertwasser to the Continents*, 2d ed. (Glarus, Switzerland: Janura Ag., 1976), pp. 441, 490.

14. Lin Yutang, *My Country and My People* (New York: Reynal and Hitchcock, 1935), p. 318.

15. Ibid., p. 316.

16. Quoted in Chipp, ed., *Theories of Modern Art*, p. 16.

17. Guillaume Apollinaire, *The Cubist Painters* (New York: Wittenborn, 1944).

18. André Breton, *What Is Surrealism?* (London: Faber and Faber, 1936).

Chapter 4. The Tradition of Art: Art History

1. H. W. Janson, *History of Art*, 3d ed., revised and expanded by Anthony F. Janson (Englewood Cliffs, N.J.: Prentice-Hall, 1986), p. 8.

2. W. Eugene Kleinbauer and Thomas P. Slavens, *Research Guide to the History of Western Art* (Chicago: American Library Association, 1982), chap. 2. For examples of critical art history, see Michael Podro, *The Critical Historians of Art* (New Haven, Conn.: Yale University Press, 1982).

3. Ernst Cassirer, *An Essay on Man* (New Haven, Conn.: Yale University Press, 1944), chap. 6.

4. G. Stephen Vickers, "Art and the Text that Accompanies It," in *Improving the Teaching of Art*, ed. David W. Ecker (Columbus: School of Art, The Ohio State University, 1966), pp. 179–224. This is the final report of a project devoted to the improvement of teaching art appreciation in the secondary schools. Office of Education, Bureau of Research, Cooperative Research Project No. V006, Contract No. OE–10–308.

5. Helen Gardner, *Art through the Ages*, 8th ed., 2 vols., revised by H. de la Croix and Richard G. Tansey (Chicago: Harcourt Brace Jovanovich, 1986).

6. Ibid., *Art through the Ages*, 3d ed. (New York: Harcourt, Brace and Co., 1948), p. 611.

7. Ibid.

8. E. H. Gombrich, *The Story of Art*, 13th ed. (New York: E. P. Dutton, 1978; first published 1950).

9. Ibid., pp. 372–73.

10. Vickers, "Art and the Text that Accompanies It," p. 188.

11. Ibid., p.189.

12. H. W. Janson, *Key Monuments in the History of Art: A Visual Survey* (New York: Abram's, 1964).

13. Janson, *History of Art*, 3d ed., p. 557.

14. Ibid., pp. 14–15.

15. Marcel Franciscono, "History, Textbooks, and Art: Reflections on a Half Century of Helen Gardner's *Art through the Ages*," *Critical Inquiry* 4, no. 2 (Winter 1977).

16. Ibid., p. 290.

17. Gombrich, *The Story of Art*, 13th ed., p. 318.

18. Cf. Lionel Trilling, "Why We Read Jane Austen," *The Times Literary Supplement* 75 (5 March 1976): 251; reprinted in Lionel Trilling, *The Last Decade*, ed. Diana Trilling (New York: Harcourt Brace Jovanovich, 1979).

19. Hugh Honour and John Fleming, *The Visual Arts: A History*, 2d ed. (Englewood Cliffs, N.J.: Prentice-Hall, 1986).

20. *Object, Image, Inquiry: The Art Historian at Work* (Los Angeles: J. Paul Getty Trust, 1988).

21. W. Eugene Kleinbauer, ed., *Modern Perspectives in Western Art History* (New York: Holt, Rinehart, and Winston, 1971), parts 2 and 3. Also Kleinbauer's "Art History in Discipline-based Art Education," in *Discipline-based Art Education: Origins, Meaning, Development*, ed. Ralph A. Smith (Urbana: University of Illinois Press, 1989).

22. Mark Roskill, *What Is Art History?* (New York: Harper & Row, 1976).

23. Walter Abell, *The Collective Dream in Art* (Cambridge, Mass.: Harvard University Press, 1957), esp. chap. 17.

24. James Ackerman, "Style," in *Art and Archaeology*, ed. James S. Ackerman and Rhys Carpenter (Englewood Cliffs, N.J.: Prentice-Hall, 1963).

25. Michael Ann Holly, *Panofsky and the Foundations of Art History* (Ithaca, N.Y.: Cornell University Press, 1984).

26. Kleinbauer and Slavens, *Research Guide to the History of Western Art*, chaps. 4–6.

27. Nor is it clear that if art history does adopt some of these new approaches, it will be able to maintain itself as a humanistic discipline, for often "the new art history" betrays little or no interest in the aesthetic and human values of art. Consider, for example, two reviews of widely used art history survey texts (including the Gardner, Janson, and Gombrich texts) published in the Spring 1989 and Summer 1989 issues of the *Art Journal*. The reviewer, Bradford R. Collins, is particularly dismissive of Janson's, Gombrich's, and Gardner's concern with quality, masterpieces, aesthetic enjoyment, and the refinement of judgment. Accordingly, their texts "are a matter of embarrassment" to the field. The volume at hand takes a different view of such matters, especially with regard to the uses of art history in a program of general education. It is instructive to compare Collins's beliefs with those of Franciscono discussed in this chapter.

28. C. P. Snow, *The Two Cultures and the Scientific Revolution* (New York: Cambridge University Press, 1959). This little essay generated more than a decade of debate, which is summarized, from Snow's point of view, in his *Public Affairs* (New York: Scribner's, 1971). See also R. A. Smith, *The Sense of Art* (New York: Routledge, 1989), pp. 146–56.

29. Erwin Panofsky, *Gothic Architecture and Scholasticism* (New York: Meridian Books, 1957). This volume consists of an inquiry into the common elements of the art, philosophy, and religion of the Middle Ages.

30. John White, *Art History and Education* (Hull, England: University of Hull Publications, 1962), p. 12.

31. Luigi Salerno, "Historiography," *Encyclopedia of World Art*, vol. 7 (New York: McGraw Hill, 1963), p. 512.

32. John Canaday, *The Lives of the Painters*, 4 vols. (New York: W. W. Norton, 1969).

33. Theodore Bowie, "Preface," and "Cultural and Artistic Interchanges in Modern Times," in Theodore Bowie et al., *East-West in Art* (Bloomington: Indiana University Press, 1966), a highly informative collection of essays.

Chapter 5. The Critique of Art: Art Criticism

1. For remarks along these lines, see F. E. Sparshott, "Basic Film Aesthetics," *Journal of Aesthetic Education* 5, no. 2 (April 1971): 34. Reprinted in *Film Theory and Criticism*, 2d ed, ed. Gerald Mast and Marshall Cohen (New York: Oxford University Press, 1979).

2. Meyer Schapiro, "Mr. Berenson's Values," *Encounter* 16 (1961): 57–65.

3. Ibid., p. 64

4. Kenneth Clark, "The Work of Bernard Berenson," in Clark's *Moments of Vision* (London: John Murray, 1981), pp. 108–29. That Clark felt a kinship with Berenson is evident in Clark's dedication of his major work, *The Nude*, to Berenson

5. Ibid., p. 112.

6. Clark, on the other hand, did not consider Berenson a narrow specialist. Rather he regarded him as "a true aesthete, who would compare the Renaissance painters with the best of his own contemporaries—Degas, Monet, Cézanne," names that appear in Berenson's writings at a time when they were unknown in England. Ibid.

7. S. J. Freedburg, "Berenson and Connoisseurship," *The New Criterion* 7, no. 6 (February 1989): 7–16.

8. Bernard Berenson, *The Italian Painters of the Renaissance*, rev. ed. (New York: Oxford University Press, 1930).

9. Clark, *Moments of Vision*, p. 125.

10. Jacob Rosenberg, *On Quality in Art: Criteria of Excellence, Past and Present* (Princeton, N.J.: Princeton University Press, 1967).

11. Fry, *Last Lectures* (1939; reprint, Boston: Beacon Press, 1962), p. 48. Quoted by Rosenberg in *On Quality in Art*, p. 115.

12. See, for example, the discussion of aesthetic qualities in Monroe C. Beardsley, *Aesthetics: Problems in the Philosophy of Criticism*, 2d ed. (Indianapolis: Hackett, 1981), pp. 462–64.

13. Morris Weitz, "The Role of Theory in Aesthetics," in *Philosophy Looks at the Arts*, 3d ed., ed. Joseph Margolis (Philadelphia: Temple University Press, 1987). For Weitz's further reflections on the problem of defining art, see his

The Opening Mind (Chicago: University of Chicago Press, 1977). Also see the excerpt from this volume in George Dickie, Richard Sclafani, and Ronald Roblin, eds., *Aesthetics: A Critical Anthology*, 2d ed. (New York: St. Martin's Press, 1989).

14. Roger Fry, *Cézanne: A Study of His Development* (New York: Macmillan, 1927), pp. 72–73. Quoted by Rosenberg in *On Quality in Art*, p. 110.

15. Fry, *Cézanne*, pp. 73–74.

16. Jacques Barzun, "Art and Educational Inflation," *Journal of Aesthetic Education* 12, no. 4 (October 1978): 20.

17. Harold Rosenberg, "The Premises of Criticism," in his *Art on the Edge* (New York: Macmillan, 1975), pp. 135–52.

18. Leo Steinberg, *Other Criteria* (New York: Oxford University Press, 1972), esp. chap. 2, "Jasper Johns: The First Seven Years of His Art."

19. Quoted by Rosenberg in an interview with Melvin M. Tumin, published in Rosenberg's *The Case of the Baffled Radical* (Chicago: University of Chicago Press, 1985), p. 235.

20. Rosenberg, "Twenty Years of Jasper Johns," in his *Art and Other Serious Matters* (Chicago: University of Chicago Press, 1985), p. 134.

21. Quoted by Rosenberg in *The Case of the Baffled Radical*, p. 233.

22. See Rosenberg's essay "Art and Work" in his *Discovering the Present* (Chicago: University of Chicago Press, 1973), pp. 61–68.

23. Rosenberg, "Twenty Years of Jasper Johns," p. 137.

24. Hilton Kramer, *The Age of the Avant-Garde* (New York: Farrar, Straus and Giroux, 1973).

25. Barzun, *The Use and Abuse of Art*, pp. 58–67.

26. A. W. Levi, "Psychedelic Science," *Journal of Aesthetic Education* 6, nos. 1–2: 80.

27. Kramer, *The Age of the Avant-Garde*, p. 7.

28. Hilton Kramer, *The Revenge of the Philistines* (New York: Free Press, 1985).

29. Charles Jencks, *Post-Modernism: The New Classicism in Art and Architecture* (New York: Rizzoli, 1987).

Chapter 6. The Philosophy of Art: Aesthetics

1. Monroe C. Beardsley, *Aesthetics from Classical Greece to the Present* (New York: Macmilan, 1966; University: University of Alabama Press, 1975).

2. Francis Sparshott, *The Theory of the Arts* (Princeton, N.J.: Princeton University Press, 1982).

3. Morris Weitz, "The Role of Theory in Aesthetics," in *Philosophy Looks at the Arts*, 3d ed., ed. Joseph Margolis (Philadelphia: Temple University Press, 1987), p. 153. First printed in the *Journal of Aesthetics and Art Criticism* 25 (1956): 27–35.

4. Israel Scheffler, *The Language of Education* (Springfield, Ill.: Charles C. Thomas, 1960), chap. 1.

5. See the essays by George Dickie, Robert Stecker, and Arthur Danto in *Aesthetics: A Critical Anthology*, 2d ed., ed. George Dickie, Richard Sclafani, and Ronald Roblin (New York: St. Martin's Press, 1989). Cf. Dickie, *The Art Circle: A Theory of Art* (New York: Haven, 1984).

6. Ellen C. Oppel, *Picasso's Guernica* (New York: W. W. Norton, 1988), p. 47.

7. Alexander Sesonske, ed., *What Is Art?* (New York: Oxford University Press, 1965), p. xii.

8. Donald W. Crawford, "Aesthetics in Discipline-based Art Education," in *Discipline-based Art Education*, ed. R. A. Smith, pp. 231–36.

9. Monroe C. Beardsley, "Art and Its Cultural Context," in his *The Aesthetic Point of View*, p. 352.

10. H. Gene Blocker, *Philosophy of Art* (New York: Charles Scribner's, 1979).

11. Virgil C. Aldrich, *Philosophy of Art* (Englewood Cliffs, N.J.: Prentice-Hall, 1963), chap. 2.

12. Blocker, *Philosophy of Art*, pp. 92–93.

13. John Hospers, *Understanding the Arts* (Englewood Cliffs, N.J: Prentice-Hall,1982).

14. John Dewey, *Art as Experience*, pp. 61–62. Quoted by Hospers, p. 193.

15. Quoted by Hospers, p. 195.

16. Benedetto Croce, *Aesthetics*, 2d ed., trans. Douglas Ainslie (New York: Farrar, Straus, and Co., 1922), p. 10. Quoted by Hospers in *Understanding the Arts*, p. 196.

17. Hospers, *Understanding the Arts*, p. 199.

18. R. G. Collingwood, *Principles of Art* (Oxford: The Clarendon Press, 1983), pp. 109–10. Quoted by Hospers, p. 200.

19. Hospers, *Understanding the Arts*, p. 201.

20. Ibid., p. 205. The reference is to Leo Tolstoy, *What Is Art?*, trans. Aylmer Maude (London: Oxford University Press, 1928), p. 37.

21. Hospers, *Understanding the Arts*, p. 206.

22. Ibid., p. 202. The reference is to Richard Strauss, *Autobiography* (1926). Also quoted in Harold Osborne, *Aesthetics and Criticism* (London: Routledge and Kegan Paul, 1955), p. 162.

23. Hospers, *Understanding the Arts*, p. 209.

24. Rudolf Arnheim, *Art and Visual Perception*, rev. ed. (Berkeley: University of California Press, 1974), chap. 10.

25. Monroe C. Beardsley, *The Aesthetic Point of View: Selected Essays*.

26. Guy Sircello, *A New Theory of Beauty* (Princeton, N.J.: Princeton University Press, 1975), pp. 19–20. See also R. A. Smith, *The Sense of Art* (New York: Routledge, 1989), appendix I, "Aesthetic Experience."

27. Beardsley, "Aesthetic Experience," in *The Aesthetic Point of View*, p. 293.

28. Beardsley, "Aesthetic Experience Regained," in his *The Aesthetic Point of View*, p. 90. John Fisher, a former editor of the *Journal of Aesthetics and Art Criticism*, considered this essay a model of philosophical analysis.

29. Harold Osborne, *The Art of Appreciation* (New York: Oxford University Press, 1970). An excellent volume that discusses appreciation in terms of skill, percipience, and enjoyment.

30. Harold Osborne, "Assessment and Stature," *British Journal of Aesthetics* 24, no. 1 (Winter 1984).

31. Jacques Maquet, *The Aesthetic Experience* (New Haven, Conn: Yale University Press, 1986), esp. part 1.

32. Osborne, *The Art of Appreciation*, p. 9.

33. Margaret P. Battin, John Fisher, Ronald Moore, and Anita Silvers, *Puzzles about Art: An Aesthetics Casebook* (New York: St. Martin's Press, 1989).

Chapter 7. Toward a Humanities-based Conception of Art Education

1. See Monroe C. Beardsley, "The Creation of Art," in his *The Aesthetic Point of View*, pp. 259–62.

2. This notion of performance is central to Francis Sparshott's *The Theory of the Arts*.

3. Robert Penn Warren, *Democracy and Poetry* (Cambridge, Mass.: Harvard University Press, 1975), p. 72.

4. A. W. Levi, *The Humanities Today* (Bloomington: Indiana University Press, 1970), p. 26.

5. The failure to indicate the basic purpose around which the teaching of art is organized is behind much of the confusion and lack of direction in writing about art education.

6. Levi, *The Humanities Today*, p. 46.

7. Ibid., p. 10.

8. Roger Scruton, "Modern Philosophy and the Neglect of Aesthetics," *Times Literary Supplement*, 5 June 1987, 604, 616–17. Reprinted in Peter Abbs, ed., *The Symbolic Order* (New York: Falmer Press, 1989).

9. James S. Ackerman, "Worldmaking and Practical Criticism," *Journal of Aesthetics and Art Criticism* 39, no. 3 (Spring 1981): 258.

10. Israel Scheffler, *Of Human Potential* (Boston: Routledge and Kegan Paul, 1985), p. 5.

11. I refer to Ernest L. Boyer's *High School* (New York: Harper and Row, 1983); Mortimer J. Adler's *The Paedeia Program* (New York: Macmillan, 1984); Theodore Sizer, *Horace's Compromise* (Boston: Houghton Mifflin, 1984); and John Goodlad's *A Place Called School* (New York: McGraw-Hill, 1984), among others. I have discussed these volumes in my *Excellence in Art Education*, updated version (Reston, Va.: National Art Education Association, 1987), chap. 5.

12. See Nelson Goodman, *Languages of Art*, 2d ed. (Indianapolis: Hackett, 1976), *Ways of Worldmaking* (Indianapolis: Hackett, 1978), and *Of Mind and Other Matters* (Cambridge, Mass.: Harvard University Press, 1984). Goodman's philosophy of human understanding has significantly influenced the work of members of Harvard Project Zero, a basic and applied research unit in arts education founded by Goodman and currently codirected by Howard Gardner and D. N. Perkins. A previous codirector was Vernon A. Howard.

13. I have criticized this tendency in my *The Sense of Art* (New York: Routledge, 1989), chap. 8.

14. E. D. Hirsch, Jr., *Cultural Literacy*, updated and expanded version (New York: Random House Vintage Books, 1988), chap. 5.

15. A sampling of such views may be found in Vincent B. Leitch, *American Literary Criticism from the Thirties to the Eighties* (New York: Columbia University Press, 1988), esp. chaps. 7–13.

16. A. W. Levi, *Literature, Philosophy, and the Imagination*, (Bloomington: Indiana University Press, 1962), pp. 44–49; and *The Humanities Today*, pp. 59–63.

17. Levi, *The Humanities Today*, p. 44

18. It is when aesthetic analysis exhibits this penchant for scholastic analysis that it incurs harsh criticism. But not all philosophic analysis has this feature.

19. Ibid., chap. 1.

20. I perhaps invite confusion by associating Levi's arts of criticism with philosophy or aesthetics and his arts of communication with art criticism, but I hope my reasons for making these associations are clear enough. In any event, it is the general line of thinking that is important. I have treated this matter slightly differently in my *The Sense of Art*.

21. Levi, *The Humanities Today*, p. 35.

22. U.S. Congressman, Frank Thompson, *Congressional Record: House Proceedings*, February 27, 1968. Quoted by Levi, ibid., p. 34.

Chapter 8. Teaching Art as a Humanity

1. For a discussion of these antecedents, see R. A. Smith, ed., *Discipline-based Art Education: Origins, Meaning, Development* (Urbana: University of Illinois Press, 1989).

2. Jerome Bruner, *The Process of Education* (Cambridge, Mass.: Harvard University Press, 1960). Reprinted in 1977 with a new preface.

3. *Beyond Creating: The Place for Art in American Schools* (Los Angeles: Getty Center for Education in the Arts, 1985).

4. Michael Day, Gilbert Clark, and W. Dwaine Greer, "Discipline-based Art Education: Becoming Students of Art," in *Discipline-based Art Education*, ed. R. A. Smith, pp. 129–93. For a sense of the time spent on writing this essay and of the extensive reviewing and criticism to which it was subjected, see p. 183.

5. Stephen M. Dobbs, "Perceptions of Discipline-based Art Education," (Los Angeles, 1988), a position paper published by the Getty Center.

6. Walter Kaufmann, *The Future of the Humanities* (New York: Thomas Y. Crowell, 1977), pp. xvii–xxi.

7. Harold Osborne, *Aesthetics and Art Theory: An Historical Introduction* (New York: E. P. Dutton, 1970), p. 13. Accordingly, chapter 4 of Osborne's history is devoted to the aesthetics of Chinese pictorial art.

8. See, for example, R. A. Smith, *Excellence in Art Education*, 1987, chap. 3; and *The Sense of Art*, chap. 6.

9. For a discussion of these principles, see Joseph D. Novak, *A Theory of Education* (Ithaca, N.Y.: Cornell University Press, 1987), and David Ausubel, Joseph D. Novak, and Helen Hanesian, *Educational Psychology: A Cognitive View*, 2d ed. (New York: Holt, Rinehart, and Winston, 1978). See also R. L. Travers, *Essentials of Learning*, 5th ed. (New York: Macmillan, 1982), and Howard Gardner, *The Mind's New Science* (New York: Basic Books, 1987).

10. Lee Schulman, "Toward a Pedagogy of Substance," *AAHE Bulletin* 41, no. 10 (June 1989).

11. Ernest L. Boyer's *High School* (New York: Harper and Row, 1983) is representative of a clutch of studies that appeared in the 1980s.

12. Henry Aiken, "Teaching and Learning in the Arts," *Journal of Aesthetic Education* 5, no. 4 (October 1971); reprinted in Aiken's *Predicament of the University* (Bloomington: Indiana University Press, 1971). See also Smith, *The Sense of Art*, pp. 106–7.

13. Michael J. Parsons, *How We Understand Art* (New York: Cambridge University Press, 1987); and Abigail Housen, *The Eye of the Beholder* (Ann Arbor, Mich.: U.M.I. Dissertation Information Service, 1989). See also her "Museums in an Age of Pluralism," in *Art Education Here* (Boston: Massachusetts College of Art, 1987).

14. To borrow a term from Morris Weitz in his "Art: Who Needs It?" *Journal of Aesthetic Education* 10, no. 1 (January 1976): 25.

15. A. W. Levi, "Peirce and Painting," *Philosophy and Phenomenological Research* 23, no. 1 (September 1962): 34. See also Levi's *Literature, Philosophy, and the Imagination* (Bloomington: Indiana University Press, 1962), pp. 140–44.

16. See Harry S. Broudy, *The Role of Imagery in Learning* (Los Angeles: Getty Center for Education in the Arts, 1987), pp. 52–53.

17. Kenneth Clark, *Looking at Pictures* (New York: Holt, Rinehart and Winston, 1960), pp. 15–18.

18. Smith, *The Sense of Art*, pp. 71–75.

19. Richard Rorty, "The Dangers of Over-Philosophication—Reply to Arcilla and Nicholson," *Educational Theory* 40, no. 1 (Winter 1990): 41–44.

20. F. David Martin and Lee Jacobus, *The Humanities through the Arts*, 3d ed. (New York: McGraw-Hill, 1983).

21. A number of volumes in the Norton Critical Studies in Art History series are relevant here (New York: W. W. Norton, 1969-   ): Robert Branner, ed., *Chartres Cathedral* (1969); James H. Stubblebine, ed., *Giotto: The Arena Chapel Frescoes* (1969); John Rupert Martin, ed., *Rubens: The Antwerp Altarpieces* (1969); Charles Seymour, Jr., ed., *Michelangelo: The Sistine Chapel Ceiling* (1972); and Ellen C. Oppler, ed., *Picasso's Guernica* (1988).

22. Benjamin Rowland, *Art in East and West* (Cambridge, Mass.: Harvard University Press, 1954).

23. Theodore Bowie et al., *East-West in Art: Patterns of Cultural and Aesthetic Relationships* (Bloomington: Indiana University Press, 1966).

24. Thomas Munro, *Oriental Aesthetics* (Cleveland: Press of Western Reserve University, 1965).

25. Jacques Maquet, *The Aesthetic Experience* (New Haven, Conn.: Yale University Press, 1986).

26. Walter Kaufmann, "The Art of Reading," in his *The Future of the Humanities* (New York: Thomas Y. Crowell, 1977), pp. 59–80.

27. A number of such issues are discussed in Margaret P. Battin, John Fisher, Ronald Moore, and Anita Silvers, *Puzzles about Art* (New York: St. Martin's Press, 1989).

Suggested Reading

Chapter 1. The Arts in the United States Today

All references begin with Alexis de Tocqueville's *Democracy in America*, edited by J. P. Mayer (1835; reprint, New York, 1969), especially chapter 11, titled "In What Spirit the Americans Cultivate the Arts." De Tocqueville observed that in the new American democracy the mixing of classes was resulting in a taste for usefulness over beauty, a preference for shoddiness over excellence, a decline in quality in favor of quantity, and the worship of the commonplace over greatness and the ideal (pp. 469–70). Next in order of importance is Max Lerner's *America as a Civilization*, 2d ed. (1957; reprint, New York, 1987), especially chapter 11, "The Arts and Popular Culture," in which Lerner discusses three themes: the distinction between the fine arts and popular culture, the possibility of high standards of creativity, taste, and achievement in a democratic society, and the question of a democratic aesthetic. See also Max Lerner, "Myth America," *The New Republic* (September 7, 1987), in which he writes that American civilization today "is not lacking in vitality, but in judgment and prudence. Its high arts as well as its popular culture revel in obsessions and excesses" (p. 12). Richard Hofstadter's *Anti-intellectualism in American Life* (New York, 1963) is excellent for explaining how attitudes toward the arts and culture in America have been influenced by religious evangelism, the commercial impulses of business, and the primitivism and sentimentality of educationists. Though not restricted to American life, the forces affecting modern attitudes toward the arts and culture are well discussed by Jacques Barzun in *The House of Intellect* (New York, 1959), especially chapters 1 and 2, and *The Use and Abuse of Art* (Princeton, N.J., 1975). R. H. Tawney's belief about the dominance of the acquisitive instinct, quoted by Levi in chapter 1 of this volume, is expressed in different terms by John Dewey in *Liberalism and Social Action* (New York, 1963), and John Kenneth Galbraith in *Economics and the Public Purpose* (Boston, 1973), chapter 7. "Economics," says Galbraith, "has never had a serious view of the arts" (p. 61).

For perspective on the debate regarding the relative merits of high and popular culture, *Mass Culture: The Popular Arts in America,* edited by Bernard Rosenberg and David M. White (Glencoe, Ill., 1957), is a good place to begin, especially the essays by the editors and Dwight Macdonald and Clement Greenberg. The collection also contains excerpts from de Tocqueville's *Democracy in America* and Walt Whitman's *Democratic Vistas.* See also Macdonald's *Against the American Grain* (New York, 1962), which contains his much-discussed essay "Masscult and Midcult," chapter 1. Greenberg's influential essay "Avant-Garde and Kitsch," first published in *Partisan Review* (Fall 1939), is reprinted in his *Art and Culture* (Boston, 1961) and in his *Perceptions and Judgments: 1939–1944* (Chicago, 1988), which is volume 1 of his collected writings, edited by John O'Brian. The terms and character of the debate are said to have changed with the publication of Susan Sontag's essay "Notes on Camp," first published in the *Partisan Review* (Fall, 1964) and later in her *Against Interpretation* (New York, 1966). The Camp sensibility is discussed by Hilton Kramer in chapter 5 of this volume, and the defense of high culture is carried on, as it must be, in the pages of *The American Scholar, Commentary,* and *The New Criterion.* See, for example, Samuel Lipman, "Redefining Culture and Democracy," *The New Criterion* (December 1989). For a defense of popular culture from a sociological point of view, see Herbert J. Gans, *Popular Culture and High Culture* (New York, 1974). Gans presents an analysis, not altogether convincing, of a number of taste cultures. See also his "American Popular Culture and High Culture in a Changing Class Structure" in Judith H. Balfe and Margaret J. Wyszomirski, eds., *Art, Ideology, and Politics* (New York, 1985). Two modern classics that have argued the case for high culture are Matthew Arnold, *Culture and Anarchy* (1869; reprint, New York, 1969) and José Ortega y Gasset, *The Revolt of the Masses* (1929; reprint, Notre Dame, Ind., 1983). An eloquent defense of the Arnoldian ideal of culture is Robert Penn Warren's *Democracy and Poetry* (Cambridge, Mass., 1975), the 1974 Jefferson Lecture in the Humanities by America's first poet laureate. By "poetry" Warren implies art in general. For a collection of writings that in effect dismisses the importance of high culture and the standards it implies, see Dennis A. Mann, ed., *The Arts in a Democratic Society* (Bowling Green, Ohio, 1977). For changes in attitudes toward culture and cultural consumption, see Joseph Benson and Arthur J. Vidich, *The New American Society* (Chicago, 1971). Modern society, write the authors, "makes possible the life of the sophisticated consumer of the arts," which is to say "consumption of the arts in their old classic and ultramodern forms has become a basic way of life in suburbia, in middle-class urban developments, and in Iowa, where farmers' wives can now purchase 'original' oil paintings directly from Sears, Roebuck" (p. 125). For a personal history of taste in America, see Russell Lynes's *The Taste-Makers* (New York, 1955), a lively text, which has a useful bibliography on the subject. Also informative is Aline B. Saarinen's *The Proud Possessors* (New York, 1958), about the tastes of American art collectors, and Lillian B. Miller's *Patrons and Patriotism* (Chicago, 1966), which traces efforts to encourage the fine arts in the United States from 1770 to 1860.

For works on American art and art history, one might begin with John W. McCoubrey, ed., *American Art, 1700–1960: Sources and Documents* (Englewood Cliffs, N.J., 1965), which extends from Samuel Willard's sermons in 1689 to Harold Rosenberg's essay on action painting in 1952. A good companion volume is Barbara Rose, ed., *Readings in American Art Since 1900: A Documentary Survey* (New York, 1968). See also Oliver Larkin, *Art and Life in America*, rev. ed. (New York, 1964); John A. Kouwenhoven, *The Arts in Modern American Civilization* (New York, 1967, first published in 1948 under the title *Made in America*); David M. Mendelowitz, *A History of American Art* (New York, 1960); Lloyd Goodrich, *Three Centuries of American Art* (New York, 1966); Samuel M. Green, *American Art: A Historical Survey* (New York, 1966); Wendell G. Garrett et al., *The Arts in America* (New York, 1969); Louis Kronenberger, ed., *Quality: Its Image in the Arts* (New York, 1966); John Wilmerding, *American Art* (Harmondsworth, New York, 1976); Milton Brown et al., *American Art* (New Jersey, 1979); John I. H. Baur, *Revolution and Tradition in Modern Art* (New York, 1967); Milton W. Brown, *American Art to 1900* (New York, 1977); D. C. Driskell, *Two Centuries of Black American Art* (New York, 1976); R. Doby, ed., *Contemporary Black Artists in America* (New York, 1971); Sam Hunter and John Jacobus, *American Art of the Twentieth Century* (New York, 1974); Milton Brown, Sam Hunter, Naomi Rosenblum, and David Sokol, *American Art* (Englewood Cliffs, N.J., 1979).

For works on the early history of American art, see John Thomas Flexner, *First Flowers of Our Wilderness* (New York, 1947) and *The Light of the Distant Skies* (New York, 1954); Louis B. Wright, *Culture on the Moving Frontier* (Bloomington, Ind., 1955); Louis B. Wright et al., *The Arts in America: The Colonial Period* (New York, 1966); Russell B. Nye, *The Cultural Life of the New Nations: 1776–1830* (New York, 1960); F. O. Mathiessen, *The American Renaissance* (New York, 1941); Van Wyck Brooks, *The Flowering of New England* (New York, 1936); Eleanor B. Berman, *Jefferson among the Arts* (New York, 1947); and Neil Harris,

The Artist in American Society: The Frontier Years, 1790–1860 (New York, 1966).

Chapter 2. The Arts and the Human Person

Levi's discussion of the arts and the human person centers on constitutive and revelatory theories of art. His explanation of constitutive theory features the writings of Friedrich Schiller, Herbert Read, and John Dewey.

There are now two standard English translations of Schiller's *On the Aesthetic Education of Man in a Series of Letters:* one by Reginald Snell (New York, 1965) and another, much more ambitious, undertaking by Elizabeth Wilkinson and L. A. Willoughby (New York, 1967), which has English and German on facing pages, a book-long introduction, commentary, glossary, appendices, and bibliography. For the placement of Schiller in historical perspective, see the standard history of aesthetics by Monroe C. Beardsley, *Aesthetics from Classical Greece to the Present* (New York, 1966), pp. 225–30. "No greater claim for the aesthetic education of man," writes Beardsley, "has ever been staked out" (p. 230). See also two articles on Schiller in the *Journal of Aesthetic Education:* Walter Grossman, "Schiller's Aesthetic Education" (January 1968), and Vernon A. Howard, "Schiller: A Letter on Aesthetic Education to a Later Age" (Winter 1986), an imaginary letter composed by Howard. Grossman's article is reprinted in R. A. Smith, ed., *Aesthetics and Problems of Education* (Urbana, Ill., 1971). Herbert Read's *The Redemption of the Robot* (New York, 1966), which contains his reflections on art education over a long career, recalls Plato and Schiller in setting out his own ideas. His major treatise on art education is *Education through Art* (New York, 1956). For perspectives on Read's educational thinking, see the three articles by John Keel, Richard Wasson, and Michael Parsons in the *Journal of Aesthetic Education* (October 1969). For a study of Read's aesthetics, see David Thistlewood, *Herbert Read: Formlessness and Form* (Boston, 1984). Hilton Kramer has some interesting observations on Read's career in "The Contradictions of Herbert Read," in his *The Age of the Avant-Garde* (New York, 1973). John Dewey's *Art as Experience* (New York, 1934) is, of course, a modern classic on the constitutive powers of aesthetic experience. Yet Dewey's aesthetics is not well understood and is more complex than sometimes assumed. For interpretive studies, see D. W. Gotshalk, "On Dewey's Aesthetics," *Journal of Aesthetics and Art Criticism* (Fall 1964), reprinted in R. A. Smith, ed., *Aesthetics and Criticism in Art Education* (Chicago, 1966); C. M. Smith, "The Aesthetics of John Dewey and

Aesthetic Education," *Educational Theory* (Spring 1971), reprinted in
R. A. Smith, ed., *Aesthetics and Problems of Education* (Urbana, Ill.,
1971). Smith suggests that there may be two theories, not one, of
aesthetic experience in Dewey's aesthetics. On the occasion of the reis-
suance of Dewey's *Art as Experience* (1934) in his collected works,
which is being published by Southern Illinois University Press, the
Journal of Aesthetic Education (Fall 1989) published a symposium containing contributions by Joe R. Burnett, John Fisher, and Richard Shus-
terman. A recent study of Dewey's aesthetics is Thomas M. Alexander,
*John Dewey's Theory of Art, Experience, and Nature: The Horizons of
Feeling* (Albany, N.Y., 1987). In *Philosophy and the Modern World*
(Bloomington, Ind., 1959), Levi devotes a major chapter to Dewey's
philosophy. For Plato's views on art, beauty, and education, it is helpful
to read first the chapter on Plato in Beardsley's *From Classical Greece
to the Present* (New York, 1966), after which the various dialogues,
including, of course, the *Republic*, can be examined. For interpretive
studies, see Eric A. Havelock, *Preface to Plato* (Cambridge, Mass., 1963),
especially chapter 1, "Plato on Poetry"; excerpts reprinted in R. A.
Smith, ed., *Aesthetics and Problems of Education* (Urbana, Ill., 1971). For
a recent interpretive essay, see Iris Murdoch, *The Fire and the Sun: Why
Plato Banished the Artists* (New York, 1977). Murdoch's own ideas about
the educative function of the arts are set out on pp. 85–89. For similar
views, see William Arrowsmith, "Art and Education," in James E.
Miller, Jr., and Paul D. Herring, eds., *The Arts and the Public* (Chicago,
1967). The standard translation of Plato's *Republic* remains that of F.
M. Cornford, numerous editions.

Before turning to revelatory theories of art, one must confront the
monumental figure of German Idealism, Immanuel Kant, and especially his *Critique of Judgment*, translated by J. H. Bernard, 2d ed. (London, 1914). It is advisable to go to secondary sources before tackling
the *Critique*. Beardsley's discussion of Kant is helpful (chapter 9), but
more readable is Harold Osborne's *Aesthetics and Art Theory: An Historical Introduction* (New York, 1970), chapter 7. See also Donald W.
Crawford, *Kant's Aesthetic Theory* (Madison, Wis., 1974). Practically all
standard anthologies in aesthetics reprint something from Kant's *Critique of Judgment*. See, for example, George Dickie, Richard Sclafani,
and Ronald Roblin, *Aesthetics: A Critical Anthology*, 2d ed. (New York,
1989). Hegel's revelatory theory of art is found in his major work on
aesthetics, *Philosophy of Fine Art*, 4 vols., trans. F. P. B. Osmaston (London, 1920). For interpretive studies, see Jack Kaminsky, *Hegel on Art*
(Albany, N.Y., 1970), an effort to preserve what is most valuable in
Hegel's thinking. Chapter 6 discusses Hegel's views on painting. See

also Israel Knox, *The Aesthetic Theories of Kant, Hegel, and Schopenhauer* (New Jersey, 1978), and Warren E. Steinkraus and Kenneth I. Schmitz, eds., *Art and Logic in Hegel's Philosophy* (Atlantic Highlands, N.J., 1980). In additon to Rebecca West's *The Strange Necessity* (London, 1928), quoted by Levi, see her *Black Lamb and Grey Falcon* (New York, 1941) and *The Court and the Castle* (New Haven, Conn., 1957). See also J. Marcus, ed., *The Young Rebecca: Selected Essays, 1911–1917* (London, 1981); P. Wolfe, *Rebecca West: Artist and Thinker* (Carbondale, Ill., 1971); Wolfe, *Rebecca West: A Celebration* (New York, 1977); and Victoria Glendenning, *Rebecca West: A Life* (New York, 1987), the latter being the occasion for an article about West by Terry Teachout, "A Liberated Woman," *The New Criterion* (January 1988), in which we read: "Wherein lay her salvation?" It lay in "'the strange necessity' of artistic expression. This necessity never left her, never diminished in intensity" (p. 21). In addition to Kenneth Clark's *Moments of Vision* (New York, 1981) quoted by Levi, see his *The Nude* (Garden City, N.Y., 1956), *Leonardo da Vinci* (Baltimore, 1958), *Looking at Pictures* (New York, 1960), *Landscape into Art* (Boston, 1961), *What Is a Masterpiece?* (New York, 1981), and *Civilisation* (New York, 1969).

Chapter 3. The Creation of Art

Levi's philosophical discussion of artistic creation drew heavily on biographical information, theoretical reflection, and the analysis of artworks. The following references are grouped under three headings: comments by artists about their work, philosophical analyses of the concepts of creativity and artistic expression, and psychological and scientific accounts of creative and artistic work. A good introduction to the topic is Albert Rothenberg and Carl R. Hausman, eds., *The Creativity Question* (Durham, N.C., 1976). The collection contains excerpts from standard philosophical and scientific works.

Art and Artists

The literature on artists' lives and artists' comments about their work is now quite large. The modern classic, of course, is *Vasari's Lives of the Artists: A Selection* (New York, 1957), which discusses Renaissance artists from Cimabue and Giotto to Michelangelo. In the same vein is John Canaday, *Lives of the Painters*, 4 vols. (New York, 1969); it begins with the late Gothic period and carries through Postimpressionism. Indispensable for the modern period is Herschel B. Chipp, ed., *Theories of Modern Art* (Berkeley, Calif., 1968). Long a standard reference in the literature is Robert J. Goldwater and Marco Treves, eds., *Artists on Art from the XIV to the XX Century*, 3d ed. (New York, 1974). See also Robert Motherwell and Bernard Karpel, series editors, *Documents of Modern Art*, 13 vols. (New York, 1955); and Robert Motherwell, senior editor, *Documents of Twentieth-Century Art* (New York, 1971–); H. E. Janson, series editor, *Prentice-Hall Sources and Documents in the History of Art Series* (Englewood Cliffs, N.J., 1965–); Elizabeth G. Holt, ed., *Literary Sources of Art History: An Anthology of Texts from Theophilus to Goethe* (New York, 1947); Elizabeth G. Holt, ed., *A Documentary History of Art*, 2 vols., 2d ed. (New York, 1957); Elizabeth G. Holt, ed., *From the Classicists to the Impressionists: A Documentary History of Art and Architecture in the Nineteenth Century* (New York, 1966). Other works and collections that provide insight into the nature of artistic creation are Brewster Ghiselin, ed., *The Creative Process* (New York, 1955), which contains selections by artists, writers, composers, philosophers, and psychologists; Robert L. Herbert, ed., *Modern Artists on Art* (Englewood Cliffs, N.J., 1964); Seldon Rodman, ed., *Conversations with Artists* (New York, 1961), with, that is, painters, architects, and sculptors; and Barbara Rose, ed., *Readings in American Art since 1900* (New York, 1968). Matisse's remarks on art and painting are collected in Jack D. Flan, ed., *Matisse on Art* (New York, 1978). Other works by artists that are uncommonly percipient about art and their own work are *Paul Klee: Pedagogical Sketchbook*, trans. Sibyl Moholy-Nagy (New York, 1953); *The Journal of Eugène Delacroix*, trans. Walter Pach (New York, 1961); and *The Complete Letters of Vincent van Gogh*, 3 vols. (Greenwich, Conn., 1958). A little-known work, but one rich in quotations by artists about their work, is Harold Osborne, *Abstraction and Artifice in Twentieth-Century Art* (New York, 1979). Two further works about artists are Rudolf and Margot Wittkower, *Born under Saturn* (New York, 1969), which discusses the character and conduct of artists from antiquity to the French Revolution, and Edmund B. Feldman, *The Artist* (New Jersey, 1982), which consists of personal reflections for the general reader.

Philosophical Discussions

Once more, begin with the Rothenberg amd Hausman collection, *The Creativity Question*, especially the classical references to Plato and Aristotle, and later Kant, as well as Blanshard, Maritain, Peirce, Bergson, Beardsley, Croce, Collingwood, and Hausman. See also Vincent Tomas, ed., *Creativity in the Arts* (Englewood Cliffs, N.J., 1964); Jacques Maritain, *Creative Intuition in Art and Poetry* (New York, 1954); Henri Bergson, *The Creative Mind* (New York, 1946); Monroe C. Beardsley, "On the Creation of Art," *Journal of Aesthetics and Art Criticism* (Spring 1965), which has been frequently reprinted, for example, in Beardsley's own *The Aesthetic Point of View*, edited by Michael J. Wreen and Donald M. Callen (Ithaca, N.Y., 1982), and in *Aesthetics and Criticism in Art Education*, ed. R. A. Smith (Chicago, 1966); D. W. Gotshalk, "Creativity," in *Aesthetic Concepts and Education*, ed. R. A. Smith (Urbana, Ill., 1970); R. K. Elliott, "Versions of Creativity," *Proceedings of the Philosophy of Education Society of Great Britain* (1971), reprinted in *Aesthetics and Arts Education*, ed. R. A. Smith and Alan Simpson (Urbana, Ill., 1991); J. P. White, "Creativity and Education: A Philosophical Analysis," in *Education and the Development of Reason*, ed. R. F. Dearden, P. H. Hirst, and R. S. Peters (Boston, 1972); Jack Glickman, "Creativity in the Arts," in *Culture and Art*, ed. Lars Aagaard-Morgensen (Atlantic Highlands, N.J., 1976), reprinted in *Philosophy Looks at the Arts*, 3d ed., ed. Joseph Margolis (Philadelphia, 1987); W. E. Kennick, "Creative Arts," in *Perspectives in Education, Religion, and the Arts*, ed. Howard E. Kiefer and Milton K. Mauritz (Albany, N.Y., 1970); Virgil C. Aldrich, *Philosophy of Art* (Englewood Cliffs, N.J., 1963), especially chapter 1, "The Work of Art"; Milton C. Nahm, *The Artist as Creator* (Baltimore, Md., 1956); and F. E. Sparshott, "Philosophy and the Creative Process," *West Coast Review* (1966). Finally, the American Society for Aesthetics has published two indexes of articles and reviews to the *Journal of Aesthetics and Art Criticism*, several of which are devoted to creativity and artistic creation. See John Fisher, ed., *Cumulative Index, Volumes I-XXXV, 1941-1977* and Supplement to the *Cumulative Index, Volumes XXXVI-XL, 1977-1982* (Philadelphia, 1979 and 1982). The *British Journal of Aesthetics* also publishes articles on the topics in question, as does the *Journal of Aesthetic Education*. Scan the indexes for each journal. See also *The Philosopher's Index* for a comprehesive listing of philosophical discussion on all topics, including creativity and artistic creation. In general, philosophers express less interest in creativity today than previously, in part because the question of creativity is essentially a psychological rather than a philosophical problem. Philosophical analysis for the most part attempts to clear up the conceptual issues posed by an inherently ambiguous concept. There has been a similar decline of interest in recent years in creativity as the principal goal of art education and hence a decline of interest in the concept. Educators now generally regard the making of works of art as contributing to the understanding and appreciation of art, a basic assumption, for example, of discipline-based art education.

Psychological Studies

As might be expected, the psychological literature on creativity and artistic creation is vast, amounting to a major industry, and thus only a few representative sources can be mentioned here. Once more, begin with Rothenberg and Hausman's *The Question of Creativity* for the relevance of psychological studies by Freud, Maslow, Kubie, Getzels, Mackinnon, Barron, Guilford, Torrance, and Rogers, among others. For a collection of original essays that provide contemporary perspectives, see Robert J. Sternberg, ed., *The Nature of Creativity* (New York, 1988), although the essays are not restricted to accounts of artistic creation. See also H. H. Anderson, ed., *Creativity and Its Cultivation* (New York, 1959); D. W. Mackinnon, ed., *The Creative Process* (Berkeley, Calif., 1961); J. W. Getzels and P. W. Jackson, *Creativity and Intelligence* (New York, 1962); Rudolf Arnheim, *Picasso's Guernica: The Genesis of a Painting* (Berkeley, 1962); H. E. Gruber, G. Terrell, and M. Wertheimer, eds., *Contemporary Approaches to Creative Thinking* (New York, 1962); Arthur Koestler, *The Act of Creation* (New York, 1964); George F. Kneller, *The Art and Science of Creativity* (New York, 1965), and *Creativity and Personal Freedom* (New York, 1968); Frank Barron, *Creative Person and Creative Process* (New York, 1969) and *Artists in the Making* (New York, 1972); John D. Roslausky, ed., *Creativity* (New York, 1970); P. E. Vernon, ed., *Creativity* (London, 1970); Abraham Maslow, *The Farther Reaches of Human Nature* (New York, 1972); Mihaly Csikszentmihalyi, *Beyond Boredom and Anxiety* (San Francisco, 1975); and J. W. Getzels and M. Csikszentmihalyi, *The Creative Vision: A Longitudinal Study of Problem-Finding in Art* (New York, 1976); Jacob Bronowski, *The Visionary Eye* (Cambridge, Mass., 1978); D. N. Perkins, *The Mind's Best Work* (Cambridge, Mass., 1981); Ellen Winner, *Invented Worlds* (Cambridge, Mass., 1982); and Howard Gardner, *Frames of Mind* (New York, 1983).

Chapter 4. The Tradition of Art: Art History

Basic reference works on the nature of art history are W. Eugene Kleinbauer, ed., *Modern Perspectives in Western Art History* (New York, 1971), which has a lengthy bibliographic essay and contains a number of essays on the nature of art history and its intrinsic and extrinsic perspectives; Etta Arntzen and Robert Rainwater, *Guide to the Literature of Art History* (Chicago, 1980), a compendious volume (616 pages) that includes references not only to the nature of art history but also to each of the visual arts and to the arts of Western and non-Western societies; W. Eugene Kleinbauer and Thomas B. Slavens, *Research Guide to the History of Western Art* (Chicago, 1982), perhaps the most useful introduction to the field for the nonspecialist; Lois Swan Jones, *Art Research: Methods and Resources: A Guide to Finding Art Information*, 2d ed. (Dubuque, Ia., 1984); W. McAllister Johnson, *Art History: Its Use and Abuse* (Toronto, 1988), a more discursive and often witty discussion by a Canadian scholar; Paul Brazier, *Art History in Education: An Annotated Bibliography and History* (London, 1985), interesting not only for its references to British, American, and some Canadian literature but also for a sense of how thinking about the importance of teaching art history in the schools evolved in this century; and Marcia Pointon, *History of Art: A Student's Handbook,* 2d ed. (Winchester, Mass., 1986), written primarily for a British audience and featuring both traditional and revisionist references.

For other works that contain discussions of art history as a discipline and examples of art-historical criticism, see Erwin Panofsky, "The History of Art as a Humanistic Discipline," in his *Meaning in the Visual Arts* (Garden City, N.Y., 1955) and *Studies in Iconology* (New York, 1962); Heinrich Wölfflin, *The Principles of Art History,* trans. M. D. Hottinger (New York, 1932); Jan Białostocki, "Iconography and Iconology" and Luigi Salerno, "Historiography," in the *Encyclopedia of World Art,* vol. 7 (New York, 1963); James S. Ackerman and Rhys Carpenter, eds., *Art and Archaeology* (Englewood Cliffs, N.J., 1963); Wylie Sypher, ed., *Art History: An Anthology of Modern Criticism* (New York, 1963); Max Dvořák, *The History of Art as the History of Ideas,* trans. John Hardy (London, 1984); Michael Podro, *The Critical Historians of Art* (New Haven, Conn., 1982); Arnold Hauser, *The Philosophy of Art History* (New York, 1959); Thomas Munro, *Evolution in the Arts and Other Theories of Culture History* (Cleveland, n.d.); W. Eugene Kleinbauer, "Geistesgeschichte and Art History," *Art Journal* (Winter 1970/71) and "Art History in Discipline-based Art Education," in *Discipline-based Art Education: Origins, Meaning, and Development,* ed. R. A. Smith (Urbana, Ill., 1989); E. H. Gombrich, *Meditations on a Hobby Horse* (London, 1971), *Ideals and Idols* (New York, 1979), and *Reflections on the History of Art,* edited by Richard Woodfield (Berkeley, Calif., 1987); Michael Ann Holly, *Panofsky and the Foundations of Art History* (Ithaca, N.Y., 1984); and for two reviews of Holly's book, A. W. Levi, "*Kunstgeschichte als Geistesgeschichte:* The Lesson of Panofsky," *Journal of Aesthetic Education* (Winter 1986) and R. A. Smith, "What Is Art History?" *Studies in Art Education* (Spring 1987); Mark Roskill, "Iconography," in his *The Interpretation of Pictures* (Amherst, Mass., 1989). See also four articles in the *Art Journal:* H. W. Janson, "Art Critics, Art Historians, and Art Teaching" (Summer 1973) and "Artists and Art Historians" (Summer 1974); James Johnson Sweeny, "Art History and the Artist" (Spring 1961); and Alfred Neumeyer, "Four Art Historians Remembered: Wölfflin, Goldschmidt, Warburg, Berenson" (Fall 1971).

Some recent writings that revise traditional assumptions about the nature and methods of art history, are James S. Ackerman, "Toward a New Social Theory of Art," *New Literary Theory* (Winter 1973); Svetlana Alpers, "Is Art History?" *Daedalus* (Summer 1977); Svetlana Alpers and Paul Alpers, "Ut Pictura Noesis? Criticism in Literary Studies and Art History," in *New Directions in Literary History*, ed. Ralph Cohen (Baltimore, 1974); Hans Belting, *The End of the History of Art?*, trans. Christopher S. Wood (Chicago, 1987); A. L. Rees and F. Borzello, eds., *The New Art History* (Atlantic Highlands, N.J., 1988); Donald Preziosi, *Rethinking Art History* (New Haven, Conn., 1989); Norma Broude and Mary D. Garrar, eds., *Feminism and Art History: Questioning the Litany* (New York, 1982); Mary D. Garrard, *Artemisia Gentileschi: The Image of the Female Hero in Italian Baroque Art* (Princeton, N.J., 1989); James Elkins, "Art History without Theory," *Critical Inquiry* (Winter 1988); and Mark Roskill, "Revisionist Interpretations and Art History Today," in his *The Interpretation of Pictures* (Amherst, Mass., 1989). In mentioning these works the impression should not be gained that art-historical revisionist thinking constitutes a revolution in art-historical inquiry and teaching. Svetlana Alpers acknowledges that much excellent work in traditional research modes is still being done. And in the introduction to the second edition of his *What Is Art?* (Amherst, Mass., 1989), Mark Roskill notes that despite efforts to move art history in fresh new directions, "there has not been great change in the structure of the discipline as a whole. There are more and newer specializations, but most art historians are required from student days to know something of European art from the Renaissance on, and many are at work teaching it in one form or another or referring to its history—as literary scholars, critics and cultural historians also do" (p. 5). The Getty study *Object, Image, Inquiry* (Los Angeles, 1988) further suggests that much art-historical research continues to be done in traditional modes. It would be unwise, moreover, to derive ideas for curriculum design and teaching strategies for the schools from debates currently raging on the frontiers of scholarship. Teaching and curriculum design should take their leads from the conventional wisdom and canon of the field. This is simply sound pedagogical sense. It should be noted, however, that in his *The Interpretation of Pictures*, which I came across only after the chapter on art history in this book had been written, Roskill does accommodate certain assumptions of revisionist thinking. What is more, he says that a more descriptive title for his earlier volume would be *Art History as a Discipline: Some Classic Cases*. Though he qualifies his earlier characterization of art history as a science, he disdains neither the importance of ascertaining matters of fact where possible nor the value of rational disagreement. In *The Interpretation of Pictures* he also provides an excellent example of self-corrective scholarship and how progress is achieved in art-historical understanding. He acknowledges that in light of new microscopic documentation his earlier interpretation of Vermeer's *Woman Weighing Pearls*, now titled *Woman Holding a Balance*, must be revised.

For representative references on the idea of style, perhaps the core concept of art-historical scholarship, see Paul Zucker, *Styles in Painting* (New York, 1950); Meyer Schapiro, "Style," in *Anthropology Today*, ed. A. L. Kroeber (Chicago, 1953), reprinted in Morris Philipson, ed., *Aesthetics Today* (New York, 1961); and J. V. Cunningham, ed., *The Problem of Style* (Greenwich, Conn., 1966), although this collection is devoted primarily to analyses of style in literature; Thomas Munro, "Style in the Arts: A Method of Stylistic Analysis," in his *Toward Science in Aesthetics* (New York, 1956); Carl J. Friedrich, "Style as the Principle of Historical Interpretation," *Journal or Aesthetics and Art Criticism* (December 1955); James S. Ackerman, "Style," in *Art and Archaeology*, ed. Ackerman and Rhys Carpenter (Englewood Cliffs, N.J., 1963), reprinted in R. A. Smith, ed., *Aesthetics and Criticism in Art Education* (Chicago, 1966); Margaret Finch, *Style in Art History* (London, 1974); Peter Gay, *Style in Art History* (New York, 1974); Nelson Goodman, "The Status of Style," *Cultural Inquiry* (June 1975); Berel Long, ed., *The Concept of Style* (Philadelphia, 1979); Irving Zupnick, "The Iconology of Style," *Journal of Aesthetics and Art Criticism* (Spring 1981); Rudolf Arnheim, "Style as a Gestalt Problem," and Anita Silvers, "The Secret of Style," *Journal of Aesthetics and Art Criticism* (Spring 1981); Mark Roskill, "Style as a Tool of Interpretation," in his *The Interpretation of Pictures* (Amherst, Mass., 1989). A continuing multivolume series edited by John Fleming and Hugh Honour is titled *Style and Civilization*.

The following references provide an excellent introduction to the work of Erwin Panofsky: William S. Heckscher, "Erwin Panofsky: A Curriculum Vitae," *Record of the Art Museum, Princeton University* (Princeton, N.J., 1969); Erwin Panofsky, *Meaning in the Visual Arts* (Garden City, N.Y., 1955), *The Life and Art of Albrecht Dürer*, 4th ed. (Princeton, N.J., 1955), *Gothic Architecture and Scholasticism* (New York, 1957), *Studies in Iconology* (New York, 1962), *Netherlandish Painting*, 2 vols. (New York, 1971); and Michael Ann Holly's *Panofsky and the Foundations of Art History* (Ithaca, N.Y., 1988).

As this volume was going to press the third edition of Frederick Hartt's *Art: A History of Painting, Sculpture, and Architecture* (New York, 1989) appeared. Although not included in the discussion of art history survey texts in chapter 4, it may be noted that Hartt's remarks about Chardin stress less the formal features of his paintings and emphasize instead the quality of noble dignity that Chardin conferred on Parisian lower-middle-class life, mostly on its humble objects, which he typically portrayed in still lifes, but also on domestic life. The third edition combines two volumes in one.

Chapter 5. *The Critique of Art: Art Criticism*

Currently there is nothing in the reference literature on art criticism comparable to the systematic guides that are available to those seeking information about creativity, art history, and aesthetics. References to art criticism are scattered through writings on art history, aesthetics, special studies, and monographs. This "state of the art" raises a question about the status of art criticism as a discipline. Yet despite overlap with other disciplines, art criticism is a recognizably distinct activity, and it is possible to identify a literature that is neither art history nor aesthetics. The following literature encompasses the practice of criticism, and the next section refers to the philosophical literature on the concept of criticism. To begin to gain a sense of the relevant literature, one might start with the section on art criticism as a related discipline in Kleinbauer and Slavens, *Research Guide to the History of Western Art* (Chicago, 1982), which discusses historical and re-creative criticism and judicial or evaluative criticism. Leaving aside here historical criticism, the authors give as examples of re-creative criticism Walter Pater's *Studies in the History of the Renaissance* (London 1873); André Malraux's *The Voices of Silence,* translated by Stuart Gilbert (Princeton, N.J., 1978); and Vincent Scully's *The Earth, the Temple, and the Gods: Greek Sacred Architecture* (New Haven, Conn., 1962). Characteristic of such writing is its high literary quality that draws attention to itself. This tendency is evident in much of Bernard Berenson's criticism as well, which was influenced by Walter Pater's *Studies in the History of the Renaissance.* The authors also mention Heinrich Wölfflin's *Classic Art: An Introduction to the Italian Renaissance* (New York, 1952); Rensselaer W. Lee's *Ut Pictora Poesis: The Humanistic Theory of Painting* (New York, 1967); and E. H. Gombrich's *Art and Illusion: A Study in the Psychology of Pictorial Representation* (New York, 1960). All these writers possess exceptional re-creative powers.

Yet it is under the rubric of judicial criticism that we recognize what is more commonly accepted as art criticism. For a type of judicial criticism concerned with excellence, the authors mention Roger Fry's *Vision and Design* (New York, 1981) and his *Cézanne: A Study of His*

Development (New York, 1927), discussed in the chapter on criticism in this volume; and for criticism reflecting the values of truth, sincerity, and honesty, they refer to John Ruskin's *Seven Lamps of Architecture* (London, 1849) and *The Stones of Venice*, 3 vols. (New York, 1851–53). Kenneth Clark, on the other hand, provides highly evaluative criticism in such works as his lecture *What Is a Masterpiece?* (London, 1979). In connection with this lecture it is worth reading Eugène Fromentin, *The Old Masters of Belgium and Holland*, which has an introductory essay by Meyer Schapiro (New York, 1963), and Walter Cahn's *Masterpieces: Chapters in the History of an Idea* (Princeton, N.J., 1979). Yet Kleinbauer and Slavens acknowledge that associating critics with only one kind of criticism is often difficult and misleading. They give as examples of critics who use a variety of methods in assessing artistic value Hilton Kramer, *The Age of the Avant-Garde: An Art Chronicle of 1956–1972* (New York, 1973), and, we may add, *The Revenge of the Philistines: Art and Culture, 1972–1984* (New York, 1985), both of which are discussed in the chapter on criticism in this volume; Irving Sandler, *The Triumph of American Painting: A History of Abstract Expressionism* (New York, 1970); Meyer Schapiro, *Modern Art: 19th and 20th Centuries* (New York, 1978); and Leo Steinberg, *Other Criteria: Confrontations with Twentieth-Century Art* (New York, 1972). Dore Ashton likewise remarks the pluralism of her methods in her *Out of the Whirlwind* (Ann Arbor, Mich., 1987), a volume in the continuing series edited by Donald Kuspit titled Studies in the Fine Arts: Criticism. Terry Barrett in "A Consideration of Criticism," *Journal of Aesthetic Education* (Winter 1989), discusses the different aims and assumptions of a number of contemporary art and photography critics.

Without implying too much order or system, the following references exemplify or bear on the practice of art criticism. Charles Baudelaire, *The Mirror of Art*, translated by Jonathan Mayne (Garden City, N.Y., 1956); Lionello Venturi, *History of Art Criticism*, translated by C. Marriott and edited by Gregory Battock (New York, 1964); Herbert Read, *The Meaning of Art* (New York, 1972), and *The Philosophy of Modern Art* (New York, 1955); Gregory Battock, *The New Art: A Critical Anthology* (New York, 1966); Brian O'Doherty, *Object and Idea: An Art Critic's Journal, 1961–1967* (New York, 1967); John Canaday, *Culture Gulch: Notes on Art and Its Public in the 1960s* (New York, 1969); Barbara Rose, *American Art Since 1900*, rev. ed. (New York, 1975); Richard Kostelantz, ed., *Younger Critics of North America* (Fairwater, Wis., 1976); Rackstraw Downes, ed., *Fairfield Porter: Art in Its Own Terms, Selected Criticism, 1935–1975* (New York, 1979); John W. English, *Criticizing the Art Critics* (New York, 1979); Sanford Schwartz, *The Art Presence* (New

York, 1982); Peter Plagens, *Moonlight Blues: An Artist's Art Criticism* (Ann Arbor, Mich., 1986); Stephen C. Foster, *The Critics of Abstract Expressionism* (Ann Arbor, Mich., 1980); Barbaralee Diamonstein, ed., *The Art World: A Seventy-Five Year Treasurey of ARTnews* (New York, 1977); Amy B. Sandback, *Looking Critically: 21 Years of Artforum Magazine* (Ann Arbor, Mich., 1984); Arlene R. Olson, *Art Critics and the Avant-Garde* (New York, 1980); Robert Hughes, *The Shock of the New* (New York, 1981); Peninah Petruck, *American Art Criticism: 1910–1939* (New York, 1981); Elizabeth G. Holt, ed., *The Emerging Role of Exhibitions and Critics* (Washington, D.C., 1980); David Carrier, *Artwriting* (Amherst, Mass., 1987); Annette Kahn, *J.-K. Huysmans: Novelist, Poet, and Art Critic* (Ann Arbor, Mich., 1987); Theodore F. Wolff, *The Many Masks of Modern Art* (Boston, 1989). Clement Greenberg deserves special mention for his *Art and Culture* (Boston, 1961) and two volumes of collected critical writings edited by John O'Brian, *Perceptions and Judgments: 1939–1944*, vol. 1 (Chicago, 1988), and *Arrogant Purpose: 1945–1949*, vol. 2 (Chicago, 1988). Another expression of contemporary formalist criticism is Michael Fried's *Three American Painters: Kenneth Noland, Jules Olitski, Frank Stella* (Cambridge, Mass., 1965).

The following references supplement the works of Berenson, Fry, Rosenberg, Kramer, and Jencks discussed in chapter 5. For additional readings by Berenson, see his *Rudiments of Connoisseurship* (New York, 1962), *Aesthetics and History* (New York, 1948), and *Seeing and Knowing* (Greenwich, Conn., 1953). For insight into Berenson's life and career, see Ernest Samuels, *Bernard Berenson: The Making of a Connoisseur* (Cambridge, Mass., 1979), and *Bernard Berenson: The Making of a Legend* (Cambridge, Mass., 1987). See also Colin Simpson, *Artful Partners: Bernard Berenson and Joseph Durien* (New York, 1986). Additional works by Roger Fry not discussed in chapter 5 are *Vision and Design* (New York, 1981) and *Transformations* (Garden City, N.Y., 1956). See also Jacqueline V. Falkenheim, *Roger Fry and the Beginning of Formalist Art Criticism* (Ann Arbor, Mich., 1980); and Frances Spalding, *Roger Fry: Art and Life* (Berkeley, Calif., 1980). Additional writings of Harold Rosenberg are *The Tradition of the New* (New York, 1959), *The Anxious Object* (New York, 1964), *The De-definition of Art* (New York, 1972), *Arshile Gorky* (New York, 1962), *Artworks and Packages* (New York, 1969), and *Barnett Newman: Broken Obelisk and Other Sculptures* (Seattle, 1971). Hilton Kramer's critical writings to 1985 are collected in the two volumes previously mentioned. He continues to write criticism for *The New Criterion*, of which he is editor. For a sampling, see "David Smith in Washington" (January 1983), "At the Picasso Museum" (January 1986), "Modernism and Its Enemies" (March 1986), and "The

Anselm Kiefer Retrospective" (February 1988). Some representative works of Charles Jencks are *Post-Modern Classicism* (London, 1980), *Current Architecture* (New York, 1982), *The Language of Post-Modern Architecture*, 4th ed. (London, 1984), *Modern Movements in Architecture*, 2d ed. (Harmondsworth, Eng., 1985), and *What Is Post-Modernism?* (New York, 1986).

Chapter 6. The Philosophy of Art: Aesthetics

As in most disciplines, there is some disagreement in philosophy of art about the basic purposes, topics, and concepts of the field. What is less subject to debate is a reliance on the methods of philosophical analysis to clarify concepts and resolve disputes. To gain a sense of the sources and topics of aesthetics, one may begin with the cumulative indexes of the *Journal of Aesthetics and Art Criticism*, ed. John Fisher, *Cumulative Index: Volumes I-XXXV, 1941-1977* (1979), and *Supplement to the Cumulative Index, Volumes XXXVI-XL, 1977-1982* (1982). The British counterpart of the American journal is the *British Journal of Aesthetics*. The *Journal of Aesthetic Education* (1966–) was started with the intention of bridging the gap between scholarship in the philosophy of art and other disciplines and educational theory and practice. Philosophical discussions of art and other related topics occur in a number of other philosophical journals as well, which are abstracted in *The Philosopher's Index*. The standard history of aesthetics is Monroe C. Beardsley's *Aesthetics from Classical Greece to the Present: A Short History* (New York, 1966; reprint, University, Ala., 1975). A short version of Beardsley's history may be found in the *Encyclopedia of Philosophy*, vol. 1, editor-in-chief Paul Edwards (New York, 1967). See also chapter 1, "An Historical Introduction to Aesthetics," in George Dickie's *Aesthetics: An Introduction* (New York, 1971). A major scholarly accomplishment is Władisław Tatarkiewicz's *History of Aesthetics*, 3 vols., translated by J. Harvell (vol. 1), C. Barnett (vol. 2), and D. Petsch (vol. 3) (The Hague, 1970-74). See also his *History of Six Ideas*, trans. C. Kasparek (Boston, 1980). Roger Scruton discusses recent aesthetics in Britain and America in his *The Aesthetic Understanding* (New York, 1983).

Excellent for both substance and continuous reading is Harold Osborne's *Aesthetics and Art Theory: An Historical Introduction* (New York, 1970). John Hospers has helpful discussions of aesthetics in his "Problems of Aesthetics," *Encyclopedia of Philosophy*, vol. 1 (New York, 1967) and *Understanding the Arts* (Englewood Cliffs, N.J., 1982), perhaps at the time of its publication the best introduction to the conventional wisdom of aesthetics. The major anthologies in the field convey a sense of its historically important works and topics from antiquity to the present, its central concepts, and contemporary issues. Among the more interesting and useful are Alexander Sesonske, ed., *What Is Art? Aesthetic Theory from Plato to Tolstoy* (New York, 1965); Monroe C. Beardsley and Herbert M. Schneller, eds., *Aesthetic Inquiry: Essays in Art Criticism and the Philosophy of Art* (Belmont, Calif., 1967), a collection of essays from the *Journal of Aesthetics and Art Criticism;* Lee A. Jacobus, ed., *Aesthetics and the Arts* (New York, 1968); John Hospers, ed., *Introductory Readings in Aesthetics* (New York, 1969); Harold Osborne, ed., *Aesthetics* (Oxford, 1972); Morris Weitz, ed., *Problems in Aesthetics,* 2d ed. (New York, 1970); W. E. Kennick, ed., *Art and Philosophy,* 2d ed. (New York, 1979); Patricia H. Werhane, ed., *Philosophical Issues in Art* (Englewood Cliffs, N.J., 1984); Joseph Margolis, ed., *Philosophy Looks at the Arts,* 3d ed. (Philadelphia, 1987); and George Dickie, Richard Sclafani, and Ronald Roblin, eds., *Aesthetics: A Critical Anthology,* 2d ed. (New York, 1989).

Some noteworthy works of aesthetics since mid-century are Monroe C. Beardsley, *Aesthetics: Problems in the Philosophy of Criticism,* 2d ed. (Indianapolis, 1981), which contains an update of the literature since 1958 that bears on the volume's topics; Virgil C. Aldrich, *Philosophy of Art* (Englewood Cliffs, N.J., 1963); Melvin Rader and Bertram Jessup, *Art and Human Values* (Englewood Cliffs, N.J., 1976); Nelson Goodman, *Languages of Art* (Indianapolis, 1968); George Dickie, *Art and the Aesthetic: An Institutional Analysis* (Ithaca, N.Y., 1974); Roger Scruton, *Art and Imagination* (London, 1974); Mary Warnock, *Imagination* (Berkeley, Calif., 1976); Richard Wollheim, *Art and Its Objects,* 2d ed. (New York, 1980); Joseph Margolis, *Art and Philosophy* (Atlantic Highlands, N.J., 1980); Arthur Danto, *The Transfiguration of the Commonplace* (Cambridge, Mass., 1981); Francis Sparshott, *The Theory of the Arts* (Princeton, N.J., 1982); David Best, *Feeling and Reason in the Arts* (Winchester, Mass., 1985); and Marcia M. Muelder, *Aesthetics and the Good Life* (Cranbury, N.J., 1989). I have omitted works that address primarily problems of understanding music and literature. Some earlier works that are still worth reading are John Dewey, *Art as Experience* (New York, 1934); D. W. Gotshalk, *Art and the Social Order* (Chicago, 1947); Stephen C. Pepper, *The Principles of Appreciation* (New York, 1949); Harold Osborne, *Aesthetics and Criticism* (London, 1955); Iredell Jenkins, *Art and the Human Enterprise* (Cambridge, Mass., 1958); Jerome Stolnitz, *Aesthetics and Philosophy of Art Criticism: A Critical Introduction* (Boston, 1960); and Thomas Munro, *The Arts and Their Interrelations,* rev. ed. (Cleveland, 1967).

For additional reading on the concepts discussed in chapter 6 (representation, expression, aesthetic experience, and critical evaluation), see for the concept of representation, Richard Bernheimer, *The Nature of Representation* (New York, 1961); E. H. Gombrich, *Art and Illusion*, 2d ed. (New York, 1961), *The Image and the Eye* (Oxford, 1982) and, with Julian Hochberg and Max Black, *Art, Perception and Reality* (Baltimore, 1972); Göran Hermeren, *Representation and Meaning in the Visual Arts* (Stockholm, 1969); Rudolf Arnheim, *Art and Visual Perception*, new version (Berkeley, Calif., 1974); and Nelson Goodman, *Languages of Art* (Indianapolis, 1968). For further reading on the concept of artistic expression, see John Hospers, ed., *Artistic Expression* (New York, 1971); Alan Tormey, *The Concept of Expression* (Princeton, N.J., 1971); Guy Sircello, *Mind and Art* (Princeton, N.J., 1972); and Francis Sparshott, *The Theory of the Arts* (Princeton, N.J., 1982). Though some aestheticians question whether there is such a thing as aesthetic experience, the concept refuses to go away. In addition to Beardsley's formulation discussed in chapter 6, see Jerome Stolnitz, *Aesthetics and the Philosophy of Art Criticism* (New York, 1960); Harold Osborne, *The Art of Appreciation* (New York, 1970); Michael H. Mitias, ed., *Possibility of the Aesthetic Experience* (Dordrecht, 1986), and *What Makes Experience Aesthetic?* (Amsterdam, 1988); Roger Scruton, *The Aesthetic Understanding* (New York, 1983); Earle J. Coleman, ed., *Varieties of Aesthetic Experience* (Lanham, Md., 1983); Jerry A. Farber, *A Field Guide to the Aesthetic Experience* (North Hollywood, Calif., 1982); Jacques Maquet, *The Aesthetic Experience: An Anthropologist Looks at the Visual Arts* (New Haven, Conn., 1986), which draws heavily on Osborne's characterization of aesthetic experience; and, perhaps portending a revival of interest in aesthetic experience by contemporary philosophers, Marcia M. Eaton's *Aesthetics and the Good Life* (Cranbury, N.J., 1989). Eaton opens her volume with these words: "I believe that having aesthetic experiences is a very important part of life. . . . What I hope to do is to produce a characterization of the aesthetic that will enable us to understand what it means to view something aesthetically, or to assess something from an aesthetic point of view, or to know what we must do to help make the lives of others as aesthetically full as possible" (p. 9). The literature on critical evaluation is quite large, and I mention merely some of the representative works, for example, Monroe C. Beardsley, *Aesthetics: Problems in the Philosophy of Criticism*, 2d ed. (Indianapolis, 1981), *The Possibility of Criticism* (Detroit, 1970), and *The Aesthetic Point of View: Selected Essays*, edited by Michael S. Wreen and Donald M. Callen (Ithaca, N.Y., 1982); Joseph Margolis, *The Language of Art and Art Criticism* (Detroit, 1965); Karl Aschenbrenner, *The Concepts of Criticism*

(Dordrecht, 1974); F. E. Sparshott, *The Concept of Criticism* (New York, 1967); and George Dickie, *Evaluating Art* (Philadelphia, 1988). Some earlier works still worth reading are Theodore Meyer Greene, *The Arts and the Art of Criticism* (Princeton, N.J., 1940); George Boas, *Wingless Pegasus: A Handbook for Critics* (Baltimore, 1950); and Stephen C. Pepper, *The Basis of Criticism in the Arts* (Cambridge, Mass., 1965). Three works that indicate a continuing interest in the idea of beauty are Guy Sircello, *A New Theory of Beauty* (Princeton, N.J., 1975); Mary Mothersill, *Beauty Restored* (Oxford, 1984); and Yrjö Sepämas, *The Beauty of the Environment* (Helsinki, 1986), which contains a wealth of references on aesthetics and the environment.

Chapter 7. Toward a Humanities-based Conception of Art Education

What constitutes the meaning of the humanities and its representative works is currently the subject of considerable intellectual debate. Some time will have to pass before the consequences of this debate are apparent for the teaching of the humanities in precollegiate schooling. Accordingly, it is mainly the traditional and conventional wisdom about the humanities that is at this time most relevant to thinking about art as one of the humanities. Levi's interpretation is largely traditional in that it perpetuates the legacy of the Middle Ages and the Renaissance, but is revisionist in the sense that it takes into account the expansion of the humanities in the modern world, which forces us to be more aware of non-Western as well as the Western humanities. But this latter awareness does not imply that Levi turns his back on the values of the Western cultural heritage and the contributions of bourgeois culture. In this latter connection, see a number of articles by Levi in the *Journal of Aesthetic Education*. "Psychedelic Science" (January–April 1972), especially page 80, "Homage to the Square" (April 1973), and "The Poverty of the Avant-Garde" (October 1974) all defend the values of bourgeois culture against the pop, countercultural philosophy of the 1960s. He has also published a number of articles on the humanities in the same journal that supplement the discussion in chapter 7. In addition to *The Humanities Today* and *Literature, Philosophy, and the Imagination*, see the following works in the *Journal of Aesthetic Education*: "The Uses of the Humanities in Personal Life" (January 1976), "Literature as a Humanity" (July–October 1976), and "The Humanities: Their Essence, Nature, Future" (Summer 1983). See also "Teaching Literature as a Humanity," *Journal of General Education* (Winter 1977). For his efforts to comprehend the concept of culture, see "In Search of Culture," *Journal of Aesthetic Education* (October 1977) and "Culture: A Guess at the Riddle," *Critical Inquiry* (Winter 1977).

The humanities, of course, have long been associated with the great philosophical and literary works of classical antiquity but have undergone redefinition over the centuries. Perspective on these changes may be gained from R. S. Crane, *The Idea of the Humanities*, 2 vols. (Chicago, 1967). The first volume is principally about the shifting definition and assessments of the humanities from the Renaissance to the present, while the second is devoted to essays on literary criticism and history. A study that examines the ways in which the humanities have been at the center of cultural conflicts from antiquity to the present is Otto Bird's *Cultures in Conflict: An Essay in the Philosophy of the Humanities* (Notre Dame, Ind., 1976). For discussions of various aspects of the humanities, see Ernst Cassirer, *The Logic of the Humanities*, translated by C. S. Howe (New Haven, Conn., 1961); Theodore Meyer Greene, ed., *The Meaning of the Humanities* (Princeton, N.J., 1966), a rich collection of essays; Arthur A. Cohen, ed., *Humanistic Education and Western Civilization* (New York, 1964); Howard Mumford Jones, *The Great Society: Humane Learning in the United States* (New York, 1959); Henry B. Veatch, *Two Logics: The Conflict between Classical and Analytic Philosophy* (Evanston, 1969); Wolfgang Stechow, "The Fine Arts as a Humanistic Study," in *The Humanities: An Appraisal*, ed. Julian Harris (Madison, 1962); Richard McKeon, "Character and the Arts and Disciplines," *Ethics* (January 1968), and "Culture and the Humanities," in *Changing Perspectives on Man*, ed. Ben Rosenblatt (Chicago, 1968); Thomas B. Stroup, ed., *The Humanities and the Understanding of Reality* (Lexington, Ky., 1966); J. H. Plumb, *The Crisis in the Humanities* (Baltimore, 1964); Isaiah Berlin, *The Divorce between the Sciences and the Humanities* (Urbana, Ill., 1974); Leonard B. Meyer, "Concerning the Sciences, the Arts AND the Humanities," *Critical Inquiry* (September 1974); Walter Kaufmann, *The Future of the Humanities* (New York, 1977); David L. Wagner, "The Seven Liberal Arts," in *The Seven Liberal Arts in the Middle Ages*, ed. David L. Wagner (Bloomington, Ind., 1983); Anthony Grafton and Lisa Jardine, *From Humanism to the Humanities: Education and the Liberal Arts in Fifteenth- and Sixteenth-Century Europe* (Cambridge, Mass., 1986); and Allan Bullock, *The Humanist Tradition in the West* (New York, 1985). *Daedalus* magazine has devoted two special issues to the humanities: "The Future of the Humanities" (Summer 1969) and "Theory in Humanistic Studies" (Spring 1970). Its Summer 1983 issue, "The Arts and Humanities in American Schools," is unfortunately a disappointment. Further writings on the humanities are presented in the references for chapter 8.

Chapter 8. Teaching Art as a Humanity

The following references are grouped under two headings: the literature pertaining to discipline-based art education and the teaching of art as a humanity.

Discipline-based Art Education

Since roughly the mid-eighties the idea of discipline-based art education has been the principal topic of discussion in the field. Yet for all that has been said and written there is still not a good understanding of its aims and purposes. One of the reasons is that writers often feel little or no obligation to consult an easily accessible literature on the topic. Accordingly, the following references provide an introduction to the standard literature. So far as I know the first article to feature the expression "discipline-based art education" in its title and discussion is W. Dwaine Greer's "A Discipline-based View of Art Education: Approaching Art as a Subject of Study," *Studies in Art Education* (Spring 1984). Greer was the director of the Getty Center for Education in the Arts Institute for Education on the Visual Arts from 1983 to 1989 and is currently director of its national diffusion efforts. Greer acknowledges, however, that in using the term "discipline-based art education" he was merely drawing attention to developments that can be traced back over the previous two decades. In this respect a number of writers can be said to have anticipated the central themes of the idea in question. What is more, officials of the Getty Center for Education in the Arts, the private agency that has been advocating the implementation of discipline-based art education programs in the schools since the early eighties, clearly state that they have deliberately taken their leads from the major writers in the field of art education.

The antecedents of discipline-based art education are conveniently traced in two volumes, the first, Ralph A Smith, ed., *Discipline-based Art Education: Origins, Meanings, and Development* (Urbana, Ill., 1988), a collection of essays that were first published as a special issue of the *Journal of Aesthetic Education* (Summer 1987). In additon to comprehensively researched articles on the theoretical and curriculum antecedents of the idea, this volume also contains a lengthy essay by Gilbert A. Clark, Michael D. Day, and W. Dwaine Greer, "Discipline-based Art Education: Becoming Students of Art," which at the time of this writing is the most carefully reasoned statement of the idea. The volume further contains brief descriptions by specialists of artistic creation, art history, art criticism, and aesthetics, and one on developmental psychology. By virtue of the wealth of its background information alone, this volume must be regarded as one of the basic documents of discipline-based art education.

Another important volume organized around the topics of antecedents, the four disciplines, models, and future prospects is Stephen M. Dobbs, ed., *Research Readings for Discipline-based Art Education: A Journey Beyond Creating* (Reston, Va., 1988). Though less comprehensive in its tracing of antecedents, this volume clearly reveals that some of the more active theorists of art education had been addressing for quite some time what were to become the themes of discipline-based art education. Also noteworthy are a number of publications by the Getty Center: Elliot W Eisner, *The Role of Discipline-based Art Education in America's Schools* (Los Angeles, n.d.), reprinted in *Art Education* (September 1987); Harry S. Broudy, *The Role of Imagery in Learning* (Los Angeles, 1987); Howard Gardner, *Art Education and Human Development* (Los Angeles, 1990); and Rudolf Arnheim, *Thoughts on Art Education* (Los Angeles, 1990). Eisner has been a major advisor to the Getty Center since its inception and a vocal advocate of discipline-based art education, and Broudy has been the center's philosopher-guide. His writings on aesthetic education had a major impact on the center's institute for teachers and principals, especially his notion of the uses of learning and the method of aesthetic scanning, a description of which, with the assistance of Ronald Silverman, is schematically presented in Broudy's *The Role of Imagery in Learning* (pp. 52–53). Because of Eisner's vigorous promotion of the idea of discipline-based art education and his highly visible association with the Getty Center, his writings have received considerable attention. Eisner has responded to criticisms in the *Educational Researcher* (December 1987) and *Art Education* (November 1988). The publications by Gardner and Arnheim represent an acknowledgment that even though psychology is not one of the four disciplines in which discipline-based art education is grounded, it is important for thinking about curriculum planning and the ways young people learn and develop through the study of art. For a discussion of some misconceptions about discipline-based art education, see Stephen M. Dobbs, "Perceptions of Discipline-based Art Education and The Getty Center for Education in the Arts," an internal paper (Los Angeles, 1988). Other thoughtful reflections on the discipline-based approach to art education are Ronald M. McGregor, "An Outside View of Discipline-based Art Education," *Studies in Art Education* (Summer 1985); Margaret K. DiBlasio, "Reflections on the Theory of Discipline-based Art Education," *Studies in Art Education* (Summer 1987), and Michael D. Day, "Evaluating Student Achievement in Discipline-based Art Programs," *Studies in Art Education* (Summer

1985), to mention but a few representative articles. Some of the criticism of discipline-based art education is quite direct and polemical, but other criticism is more indirect and consists of suggesting alternative ways of achieving the objectives of art education. In the former category, I would place Judith Burton et al., eds., *Beyond DBAE: The Case for Multiple Visions of Art Education* (New York, 1988), and in the latter category some of the writings of members of Harvard Project Zero, for example, Dennie Wolff, "The Growth of Three Aesthetic Studies: What Developmental Psychology Suggests about Discipline-based Art Education," in *Issues in Discipline-based Art Education: Strengthening the Stance, Extending the Horizons* (Los Angeles, 1988), the proceedings of one of several seminars conducted by the Getty Center; and Howard Gardner, "Zero-Based Arts Education: An Introduction to ARTS PROPEL," *Studies in Art Education* (Winter 1989). The seminars conducted by the Getty Center are evidence that center officials invite critical discussion of the center's policies and programs. See, for example, the range of opinion expressed in *Discipline-based Art Education: What Forms Will It Take?* (Los Angeles, n.d.); *Issues in Discipline-based Art Education*, cited above; *The Pre-Service Challenge: Discipline-based Art Education and Recent Reports on Higher Education* (Los Angeles, 1988); and *Inheriting the Theory: New Voices and Multiple Perspectives on DBAE* (Los Angeles, 1990).

Teaching Art as a Humanity

There is, of course, a voluminous literature on the nature of teaching. Just about everything that can be said has been said. Yet so far as the teaching of art as a humanity is concerned, which certainly implies teaching art humanistically as well, the standard pedagogical literature is less relevant than a thin canon of works that continue to serve as inspiration for all those who reflect on the nature of what Gilbert Highet called the immortal profession. Accordingly, I would begin with Gilbert Highet's *The Immortal Profession* (New York, 1976) and *The Art of Teaching* (New York, 1950). Highet was a classical scholar of great distinction who, in addition to authoring a number of scholarly works himself, was the translator of Werner Jaeger's *Paideia: The Ideals of Greek Culture*, 3 vols. (New York, 1943–45). Then move on to Jacques Barzun, *Teacher in America* (Indianapolis, 1981); William James, *Talks to Teachers* (New York, 1958); Alfred North Whitehead, *The Aims of Education* (New York, 1949); and Mark Van Doren, *Liberal Education* (Boston, 1959).

Perhaps no contemporary writer has spoken and written more eloquently on the humanistic aspects of teaching than William Arrowsmith; see his "The Calling of Teaching," in *Dialogue: Plymouth Series in Contemporary Thought* (Plymouth, N.H., 1979). For historical perspective, a classic is Robert Ulich's *Three Thousand Years of Educational Wisdom*, 2d ed. (Cambridge, Mass., 1954). More specific descriptions of historic teaching models are set out in Harry S. Broudy and John Palmer's *Exemplars of Teaching Method* (Chicago, 1965). A number of conceptual and practical selections on teaching the humanities can be found in Sheila Schwartz et al., *Teaching the Humanities* (New York, 1970); and James L. Jarrett has some excellent suggestions in his *The Humanities and Humanistic Education* (Reading, Mass., 1973), a work that draws on humanistic psychology as well as classical conceptions of the humanities in its discussion of teaching. A number of practical suggestions, called perception keys, can be found in F. David Martin and Lee A. Jacobus's *The Humanities through the Arts*, 3d ed. (New York, 1983).

Two recent publications of the National Society for the Study of Education are also worth looking into; see Benjamin Ladner, ed., *The Humanities in Precollegiate Education*, 83d NSSE Yearbook, part 2 (Chicago, 1984) and Elliot W. Eisner, ed., *Learning and Teaching the Ways of Knowing*, 84th NSSE Yearbook (Chicago, 1985). Also useful is Walter Kaufmann's *The Future of the Humanities* (New York, 1977), especially his analysis of four ways of reading a classical text (exegetical, dogmatic, agnostic, and dialectical), which is also relevant to "reading" a masterpiece of art. In "Forms of Multicultural Education," *Journal of Multi-cultural and Cross-cultural Research in Art Education* (Fall, 1963), R. A. Smith uses Kaufmann's analysis to discuss the uses and abuses of multicultural education.

For some doubts about the possibility of the schools' entertaining a humanistic interpretation of teaching, see Lionel Trilling, "The Uncertain Future of the Humanistic Educational Ideal," in his *The Last Decade: Essays and Reviews*, edited by Diana Trilling (New York, 1982). Yet Trilling acknowledges that educational thinking is subject to sharp swings of opinion, and so the current neglect of this traditonal ideal, discussed by Lynne V. Cheney in *American Memory: A Report on the Humanities in the Nation's Schools* (Washington, D.C., c. 1988), need not be considered a permanent state of affairs, nor, for that matter, the attack on the traditional conception of the humanities which is currently the subject of debate in higher education. See also William Bennett, *To Reclaim a Legacy* (Washington, D.C., 1984); R. Thomas Simone and Richard F. Sugarman, *Reclaiming the Humanities: The Roots of Self-knowledge in the Greek and Biblical Worlds* (New York, 1986); and Robert E. Proctor, *Education's Great Amnesia* (Bloomington, Ind., 1988).

The notion of educational amnesia is discussed by George Steiner in "Future Literacies" in his *George Steiner: A Reader* (New York, 1984). Steiner remarks on "the organized amnesia of present primary and secondary education" (pp. 428–30). This is followed nicely by E. D. Hirsch, Jr., *Cultural Literacy: What Every American Needs to Know*, updated and expanded version (New York: Vintage Books, 1988) and Diane Ravitch and Chester Finn, Jr., *What Do Our 17-Year-Olds Know?* (New York, 1987). For a number of observations about the humanities in the *Journal of Aesthetic Education*, see Harry S. Broudy, "The Role of the Humanities in the Curriculum" (Autumn 1966) and "The Humanities and Their Uses: Proper Claims and Expectations" (Winter 1983), a special issue devoted to distinguished humanities lectures of the School of Humanities of the University of Illinois at Urbana-Champaign; Richard Kuhns, "Humanities as a Subject" (Autumn 1966); Jerome Ashmore, "The Humanities and the Life-World" (April 1969); Cyril Burt, "Personal Knowledge, Art, and the Humanities" (April 1969); Haig Khatchadourian, "Humanistic Functions of the Arts Today" (April 1980); and Henry D. Aiken, "Learning and Teaching in the Arts" (October 1971), with responses by John Fisher and Monroe C. Beardsley. See also Robert L. Belknap and Richard Kuhns, *Tradition and Innovation: General Education and the Reintegration of the University: A Columbia Report* (New York, 1977); and Mortimer J. Adler, ed., *The Paideia Program: An Educational Syllabus* (New York, 1984).

A few references that will help any teacher, including teachers of art, to understand the nature of teaching are Israel Scheffler, *The Language of Education* (Springfield, Ill., 1960), especially chapters 4 and 5; Bertram Bandman and Robert S. Guttchen, eds., *Philosophical Essays on Teaching* (New York, 1969); Donald Vandenberg, ed., *Teaching and Learning* (Urbana, Ill., 1969); Ronald T. Hyman, ed., *Teaching: Vantage Points for Study* (New York, 1968); John Wilson, *Thinking with Concepts* (New York, 1963); B. Othanel Smith et al., *Teachers for the Real World* (Washington, D.C., 1969); Young Pai, *Teaching, Learning, and the Mind* (Boston, 1973); Robert Dreeben, *The Nature of Teaching* (Glenview, Ill., 1970); Maxine Greene, *Teacher as a Stranger* (Belmont, Calif., 1973); Bruce Joyce and Marsha Weil, *Models of Teaching* (Englewood Cliffs, N.J., 1972); R. S. Peters, ed., *Education and the Education of Teachers* (Boston, 1977); Jopseph D. Novak, *A Theory of Education* (Ithaca, N.Y., 1977), reprinted as a paperback in 1986; N. L. Gage, *The Scientific Basis of the Art of Teaching* (New York, 1978); Gary D. Fenstermacher and Jonas F. Soltis, *Approaches to Teaching* (New York, 1986); D. Bob Gowin, *Educating* (Ithaca, N.Y. 1981); Joseph D. Novak and D. Bob Gowin, *Learning How to Learn* (New York, 1984), which is usefully read in connection with Novak's *A Theory of Education;* Philip W. Jackson, *The Practice of Teaching* (New York, 1986), which has a chapter on learning from William James and contains references to the key literature on the topic; Jonas Soltis, ed., *Reforming Teacher Education: The Impact of the Holmes Group Report* (New York, 1987); and Vernon A. Howard, *Artistry: The Work of Artists* (Indianapolis, 1982).

Note: I have not included research and publications by art educators and others on the teaching of the various disciplines in which discipline-based art education grounds itself. Subsequent authors in this series—H. Gene Blocker and Michael J. Parsons on aesthetics, Stephen Addiss and Mary Erickson on art history, Theodore F. Wolff and George Geahigan on art criticism, and Maurice Brown and Diana Korzenik on artistic creation—will contain such references.

Index

Note on the Authors

ALBERT WILLIAM LEVI (1911–88) was for many years David May Distinguished University Professor of the Humanities and a member of the philosophy department at Washington University in St. Louis. His monumental work, *Philosophy in the Modern World*, received the first Ralph Waldo Emerson Award from Phi Beta Kappa. His other major works include *Literature, Philosophy, and the Imagination, Humanism and Politics, The Humanities Today*, and *Philosophy as Social Expression*. He possessed an avid interest in education and served for three years as rector of Black Mountain College. He was also an early member of the National Council of the Humanities. His redefinition of the humanities as the arts of communication, continuity, and criticism provides an illuminating perspective on the meaning of discipline-based art education. He had just completed a manuscript on moral philosophy and was working on this volume at the time of his death.

RALPH A. SMITH is Professor of Cultural and Educational Policy in the Department of Educational Policy Studies at the University of Illinois at Urbana-Champaign. He is a distinguished fellow of the National Art Education Association and recipient of two of its prestigious awards. Among his publications are *The Sense of Art: A Study in Aesthetic Education, Excellence in Art Education*, and a monograph, *Aesthetic Education in Modern Perspective*. He has also edited *Discipline-based Art Education: Origins, Meaning, and Development; Cultural Literacy and Arts Education; Aesthetics and Arts Education*, with Alan Simpson; and *Public Policy and the Aesthetic Interest*, with Ronald Berman. He is also the founding editor of the *Journal of Aesthetic Education* (1966–) and served for seven years as the executive secretary of the Council for Policy Studies in Art Education. His interest in teaching the arts is congruent with both Levi's redefinition of the humanities and the premises of discipline-based art education.